The Art of Classroom Management

Effective Practices for Building Equitable Learning Communities

The Art of Classroom Management

Effective Practices for Building Equitable Learning Communities

Barbara McEwan
University of Redlands

Merrill

an imprint of Prentice Hall

Upper Saddle River, New Jersey   Columbus, Ohio

Library of Congress Cataloging-in-Publication Data

McEwan, Barbara
    The art of classroom management: effective practices for building equitable learning communities /
Barbara McEwan.
        p.   cm.
    Includes bibliographical references and indexes.
    ISBN 0-13-079975-0
    1. Classroom management—Social aspects—United States.
2. Multicultural education—United States.   3. Educational
equalization—United States.   I. Title.
LB3013.M383   2000
371.102′4—dc21   99-12027
                                                        CIP

Editor: Debra A. Stollenwerk
Production Editor: Mary Harlan
Design Coordinator: Diane C. Lorenzo
Cover Designer: Mark Shumaker
Cover art: © Superstock
Production Manager: Pamela D. Bennett
Text Design and Production Coordination: Carlisle Publishers Services
Director of Marketing: Kevin Flanagan
Marketing Manager: Meghan McCauley
Marketing Coordinator: Krista Groshong

This book was set in Palatino by Carlisle Communications, Ltd. and was printed and bound
by R. R. Donnelley & Sons Company. The cover was printed by Phoenix Color Corp.

©2000 by Prentice-Hall, Inc.
Pearson Education
Upper Saddle River, New Jersey 07458

Photo credits: p. 2, Barbara Schwartz/Merrill; pp. 24, 96, 120, and 144, Anne Vega/Merrill; pp. 48
and 222, Barbara McEwan; pp. 72 and 166, Anthony Magnacca/Merrill; and p. 190, Tom Watson/Merrill.

Printed in the United States of America

10 9 8 7 6 5 4 3 2 1

ISBN: 0-13-079975-0

Prentice-Hall International (UK) Limited, *London*
Prentice-Hall of Australia Pty. Limited, *Sydney*
Prentice-Hall of Canada, Inc., *Toronto*
Prentice-Hall Hispanoamericana, S. A., *Mexico*
Prentice-Hall of India Private Limited, *New Delhi*
Prentice-Hall of Japan, Inc., *Tokyo*
Prentice-Hall (Singapore) Pte. Ltd., *Singapore*
Editora Prentice-Hall do Brasil, Ltda., *Rio de Janeiro*

෧෨

To my immediate family and to Anna, my extended family member,
in gratitude for their continual support.

To Matthew, my son, who has inspired me and challenged every idea I ever had.

And to David, who has enriched my life beyond measure.

෧෨

Preface

I wrote *The Art of Classroom Management* to provide teacher educators, teachers, administrators, and those enrolled in preservice teacher preparation programs with a comprehensive overview of legal, ethical, and cultural issues associated with classroom management. Public school educators are addressing an increasingly diverse student population that brings with it a broad range of personal needs and interests. A one-size-fits-all approach to management cannot adequately serve teachers who seek to create calm and safe learning environments for all their students. It is time to expand our shared professional vision of what is meant by the term *classroom management.*

I base my vision of appropriate management practices on a conceptual framework of democratic practices. The ideas shared within these pages take their initial inspiration from the law that governs public schools. Some of the legal concepts discussed include the following:

1. **The impact of compulsory education.** The fact that students are compelled by law into our public school classrooms heightens the professional responsibility of all educators to ensure equity in their practices.
2. **Fourteenth Amendment concepts of due process and equal protection under the law.** Equal protection ensures each student's right to the range of opportunities available in our public schools, and due process helps to protect students while they are in the classroom.

Our increasingly diverse student population also affects the choices and decisions educators must consider in terms of management and curricular practices. Interwoven throughout this book are discussions of two particular issues:

1. **Our increasingly diverse population and how educators can understand its similarities, differences, and our need for mutual dependence.** A broad range of issues related to cultural and social diversity is discussed.
2. **The dynamic elements of our social interactions and how they play themselves out every day within our public schools.**

Inclusive and welcoming management and curricular practices are a necessity. They are the most powerful means by which to ensure that all students have an equal opportunity to be successful regardless of the languages they speak, the beliefs they hold, the disabilities that challenge them, their gender, or the color of their skin.

Organization of This Book

The first chapters of this book establish an understanding of the basic rights and responsibilities shared by all members of the public school community. The early chapters focus on strategies for establishing rules and assessment procedures. Integrated throughout the strategies is a framework of law and multicultural issues and how the two can be used when determining what constitutes effective democratic management. The balance of the book is devoted to a number of supporting topics that are closely associated with how educators might effectively manage all students. The book's underlying theme is that effective management is not a simple matter of using one trick or another but rather is a thoughtful and deliberate construct for supporting every learner who enters a pubic school classroom.

Some books on classroom management are based on multicultural perspectives. Others are based on a legal perspective. Still others provide an overview of management topics and include separate chapters on multicultural issues or legal issues. This book is the first to approach management, law, and multicultural issues from an integrated perspective.

Features

Some of the special features of this text are the following:

1. **An examination of how an educator's interactions with parents directly influence the classroom climate and management options.** The chapter that addresses parental issues includes the legal and multicultural perspectives of student, teacher, and parent relations.
2. **A chapter devoted to how some students become highly visible or invisible.** Both situations are problematic in terms of student rights, and both can have their etiology in multicultural issues.
3. **A careful examination of the issues surrounding power in the classroom.** Who has it? Who wants it? How is it obtained or lost?

Every chapter begins with a scenario that frames the discussion to follow. The scenario is immediately followed by some **initial discussion questions** designed to stimulate classroom conversations about each chapter's topic or to prompt writing for a dialogic journal. Each chapter concludes with some follow-up questions or suggested classroom activities.

Each chapter also includes specific ideas for helping preservice and inservice teachers effectively address the problems and issues raised. The purpose of this book is to provide educators with practical strategies for working with all students, and, accordingly, every chapter provides ideas for addressing a variety of management issues.

Many of the ideas and strategies shared in each chapter come from my own research and personal interactions with teachers in a variety of settings around the country. All strategies have been tested in real public school situations. I hope that these good ideas will continue to support the fine work that educators do every day.

Acknowledgments

This book could never have been written without the help of the extraordinary educators who have welcomed me into their classrooms and shared their good ideas with me. I would invite anyone who thinks teaching is an easy career to follow any of these fine people for one working day. Their patience, creativity, and resourcefulness have been and remain a constant source of inspiration to me. Specifically, I would like to acknowledge the fine teaching of Anne Marie Strangio, Marina Donohue, Nancy Tolin, Lori Greenfield, Betty Powers, and Suzanne Alexander-Novak.

I want to further acknowledge the educators with whom I work who are filling the roles of administrators and specialists in our schools. Ginny Nimmo, Nancy Busse, Margie Abbot, and Bob O'Neil, among others, have been very helpful to me in the creation of this book.

I would also like to thank my university colleagues who have shared their insights and strategies with me and continually added to my understanding of what makes an effective educator. Ron Butchart, Paul Gathercoal, and Forrest Gathercoal have all helped me to understand how comprehensive the topic of classroom management really is. My colleagues at Oregon State University have also provided me with new and challenging ideas. Eileen Waldschmidt, Warren Suzuk, and Younghee Kim have taught me a great deal about issues of diversity and special needs. Karen Higgins has expanded my ideas on how to fairly and effectively assess students' work, Nora Cohen and Jean Moule have helped me to understand how learning theory and learning styles relate to student success, and Ken Winograd has provided me with an understanding of how important it is that all of us who aspire to be called educators are continually engaged in a critical examination of our teaching practices.

I want to acknowledge the fine work of the graduate students with whom I work, each bringing with them their own insights into the educational process. In particular I thank Joy Delgado, Margaret Mazzotta, and Marti O'Dell for their shared commitment to serving the special needs of children.

I would like to thank the following reviewers for their thoughtful comments during the review process: Barbara Illig-Aviles, Duquesne University; Shirley Jacob, Southeastern Louisiana University; Suzanne MacDonald, University of Akron; Bruce Mitchell, Eastern Washington University; John A. Moore, Western Kentucky University; and Will Roy, University of Wisconsin, Milwaukee.

Finally, I want to acknowledge the preservice teachers with whom I have worked for more than a decade. I have learned from each and every one of them. I am fortunate because every time I teach I am challenged by students whose ages range from 21 to 55; whose backgrounds represent a broad range of diverse needs, abilities, and interests; and whose energy and dedication to their chosen career serve as a continual inspiration to me.

Brief Contents

CHAPTER 1

The Mix of Culture, Law, and Classroom Management   2

CHAPTER 2

Why We Need Classroom Rules   24

CHAPTER 3

Revisiting Classroom Rules   48

CHAPTER 4

The Art of Equitable Assessment   72

CHAPTER 5

Democratic Consequences   96

CHAPTER 6

The Nature of and Struggle for Power   120

CHAPTER 7

Those We See and Those We Do Not See: Understanding the Issues of Highly Visible Students and Invisible Students   144

CHAPTER 8

Creating a Welcoming Climate for Parents   166

CHAPTER 9

Creating the Democratic Classroom: A Holistic Perspective   190

Conclusion   222

Contents

CHAPTER 1

The Mix of Culture, Law, and Classroom Management　　　2

Diversity and Law: Two Complex Influences That Guide Management Decisions　5

Compulsory Education　7

Student Rights: A Matter of Freedom, Justice, and Equality　9

　Freedom　10

　Justice　10

　Equality　12

Using Student Rights and Responsibilities to Create a Common School Culture　14

Educational Practices That Address Equity and Diversity　15

Building a Democratic Learning Community　16

Using Democratic Management to Teach Decision-Making Skills　19

Reflections on Teacher Education　21

CHAPTER 2

Why We Need Classroom Rules　　　24

The Need for Rules in Elementary Classrooms　26

The Importance of Rules at the Secondary Level　28

The Legal Rationale for Rules　29

The Importance of Notice　30

Clear Rules Are Not the Same as Inflexible Rules　32

Substantive Due Process　35

Legal Rules Are Equitable Rules　36

Establishing and Supporting a Democratic Classroom　38

The Relation of Rules to the Developmental Levels of Students　40

The Language of Rules　40

Using Compelling State Interests as a Framework for Rule Making　41

The Process of Developing Rules　42

Defining Rules Using Time, Place, and Manner　43

A Few Words about Consequences　45

CHAPTER 3

Revisiting Classroom Rules   48

Protecting the Health and Safety of Students   50
Developing a Reasonable Standard of Care   53
   Step One: Make a Plan   53
   Step Two: Share the Plan   54
   Step Three: Stick to the Plan   56
Any Management System Must Include Frequent Reminders   57
Revisiting Rules through a Variety of Strategies   58
One-on-One Problem Solving   59
Revisiting Rules to Reinforce Health and Safety   60
Preventing Serious Disruptions   60
Revisiting Rules through Lesson Plans   61
Revisiting Rules to Support a Moral Climate   62
Learning to Watch Students   63
Begin with a Question   64
Using Class Meetings to Revisit Rules   64
   Class Meetings and Flexibility   67
   Some Ideas for Organizing Class Meetings   68

CHAPTER 4

The Art of Equitable Assessment   72

Basics of Assessment   74
Controversies of Assessment   74
Legal Implications of Grading   76
Grades as Issues of Liberty   76
Substantive Due Process and Assessment   77
Ethical Aspects of Assessment   78
What Does a Grade Mean?   79
Teachers Are Not Employers, and Grades Are Not Employee Evaluations   80
When Family Issues Are Not Compatible with Schoolwork   81
   An Alternative Perspective on Due Dates   81
Helping Students Learn Responsibility   83
The Perils of Grade Inflation   84
Mixing Messages: Schoolwork as Punishment   85
Documenting Behavioral Issues   86

Concerns about Time   86
How to Handle Late Papers   88
The Role of Cultural Perspectives   88
Grading Homework   90
Working to Keep It Confidential   91
Alternative Assessment Practices   92

CHAPTER 5

Democratic Consequences   96
The Nature of Consequences   98
Attending to Rather than Ignoring Behaviors   100
Some Legal Considerations   100
Fair Treatment Does Not Mean the Same Treatment   102
Consistent Consequences Can Result in Tattling   103
Some Behaviors Are Not Choices   104
What Are Democratic Consequences?   106
   Consequences as a Teachable Moment   106
   Confidentiality and Consequences   108
   Being Creative with Consequences   109
   Using Conferences before Consequences   111
Working with Parents to Resolve Problems   112
Using Peers to Resolve Behavioral Problems   113
Use of In-School Suspensions   114
Curriculum Design as a Preventive Strategy   116
Teaching Problem Solving   116
Putting It All Together   117

CHAPTER 6

The Nature of and Struggle for Power   120
Power as the Defining Element of the Classroom   122
How Language Can Be Used to Limit or Share Power   123
Power and Its Relation to Multicultural Issues   124
Power and Its Relation to School Cultures   126
Power Relations and Power Struggles   127
Analyzing the Power Struggle   128

Power and Equity   129

The Role of Permanent Value in Diffusing the Struggle for Power   130

Preventive Measures for Avoiding Conflicts   132

    Preventing Power Struggles through Good Communication Strategies   132

    The Fine Art of Backing Off   134

The Relation of Power Struggles to the Physical Environment   137

    Seating Arrangements   137

    Bulletin Boards   139

Reducing Power Struggles with Inclusive Curriculum Practices   139

CHAPTER 7

- -

Those We See and Those We Do Not See: Understanding the Issues of Highly Visible Students and Invisible Students   144

A Paradox   146

Legal Concerns of High Visibility and Invisibility   146

Highly Visible Students   148

    Management Practices That Contribute to High Visibility   148

    High Visibility Is Sometimes a Result of Student Actions   149

    Praising Students Publicly   150

    The Conflict between Public Praise and the Cultural Heritage of Students   151

    Catch Them Being Good . . . or at Least Acting Differently from Their Peers   152

    Memories of Public Punishment   153

    Using High Visibility to Correct Behaviors   155

    The Conflict between Addressing Individual Needs and Correcting Behaviors through High Visibility   156

Invisible Students   157

    Legal Issues of Invisibility   157

    Disabilities That Can Lead to Invisibility   158

    Emotional Causes of Invisibility   158

    Physical Illness and Invisibility   159

    Invisibility and Societal Expectations   159

    Choosing Invisibility: Being in the Closet   161

Effective Strategies for Balancing Highly Visible Students with Invisible Students   162

Managing Students with Severe Emotional Disturbances   162

CHAPTER 8

Creating a Welcoming Climate for Parents   166

Accentuating Differences Can Exacerbate Management Issues   168
Viewing Students as Pieces of a Larger Picture   169
The Legal Rights of Families   169
Personal Histories Can Affect School Attitudes   170
The Quality of Parenting Cannot Be Generalized   171
Management and a Behaviorist View of the Role of Parents   172
Issues Related to Abuse   173
   Physical Abuse   174
   Neglect   175
   Sexual Abuse   175
   Mental Abuse   175
   Legal and Ethical Aspects of Reporting Abuse   176
Parents' Role in Cognitive Management Practices   176
Issues of Diversity: Families and Conflicts with Schools   177
Looking at Religion in the Schools from a Legal Point of View   178
The Role of Compulsory Education in the Separation of Church and State   179
Understanding Issues of Diversity by Taking Another's Perspective   180
The Role of Religion in Schools   180
Cultural Implications as Related to Student Behaviors   181
Maintaining Open Lines of Communication   182
Parents of Students with Special Needs   183
The Value of Parent–School Partnerships   186
Partnership Roles Parents Can Play   187
Keeping in Touch with Parents of Secondary School Students   188

CHAPTER 9

Creating the Democratic Classroom: A Holistic Perspective   190

Developing Consistency between Curriculum and Management   192
Trust: The Critical Element   193
"Yes, but It Wouldn't Work with My Students"   194
Classroom Chatter and the Learning Process   194
Alternatives to Direct Instruction Can Eliminate Concerns about Chatter   196
The Mix of Time, Management, and Curriculum   197

Understanding Who Students Are by Understanding How They Learn   198
Cooperative Learning   200
Effective Curriculum Practices for Students with Special Needs   202
Attention Deficit Disorder or Attention Deficit–Hyperactivity Disorder   203
   Curriculum, Management, and Issues Concerning Students with ADD and ADHD   203
Teaching a Curriculum of Rights and Responsibilities   208
Maintaining the Holistic Classroom When the Players Change   210
The World of the Substitute Teacher   211
   Responsibilities of the Classroom Teacher   212
   Preparations for Being a Substitute Teacher   213
   The Day Begins   215
   The Name Game   217
   Things Will Be Done Differently   217
   Creative Curriculum Options Can Help to Keep Students on Task and Calm   217
   Ending the Day   218
   Long-Term Assignments   218
   A Final Word about Substitute Teaching   219

Conclusion   221
Retaining the Baby and the Bath Water   222
Some Final Thoughts   224

References   227
Index   231

The Art of Classroom Management

Effective Practices for Building Equitable Learning Communities

CHAPTER 1

The Mix of Culture, Law, and Classroom Management

CHAPTER OBJECTIVES

By the end of this chapter the reader should be able to:

◇ Demonstrate an understanding of the basic legal foundation that informs the decisions in public education
◇ Articulate comprehension of the multicultural nature of public school students
◇ Begin to form a comprehensive perspective of how a management philosophy is reflected in rule making, room arrangement, curriculum design, one-on-one interactions, and responses to behavior problems
◇ Understand the link between compulsory education and educators' responsibility to ensure classroom equity.

Scenario

After completing her teacher education program, Claudia had landed her first job, and her dream of being a real teacher was finally coming true. With the luxury of a couple of months to plan, she began organizing materials she had gathered while student teaching and sought out additional resources from libraries, used book stores, and garage sales. A friend asked her one day whom she would be teaching. "Fourth graders," Claudia replied. The friend paused a moment and said, "No, I asked whom you would be teaching." Claudia sat back and thought. It occurred to her that she did not have a good answer for the question. But she did know that who her students were would influence every educational decision she would make.

Questions

What assumptions can be made when teachers learn the location in which they will be working and grade level they will be teaching? Other than the location and grade level, what other information might lead teachers to make assumptions about their students? What assumptions should never be made? Can any assumptions safely be made about students?

Discussion

Let us pretend together that managing a room full of active young people and keeping them focused on a specific task for an extended part of the day was once easily accomplished. Although the reality has always been quite different, that image of a long ago time when teaching was a simple task because all students were well behaved and eager to learn remains in our shared mythology. In that classroom of some distant past, our methods of management were characterized by one of two extremes. Teachers were said to have relied on either parental benevolence and individual attention or liberal applications of the hickory stick. The underlying principles that determined the use of either method had more to do with what suited the teacher's needs and less to do with who the students were. Students were viewed as being members of one group or another, each group characterized by some set of particular attributes. Students were typically not viewed as being individuals with unique aspects of personality, character, and family values.

This view was not based so much on prejudice as on limited information and reflective of a sociopolitical attitude geared toward maintaining the status quo rather than incorporating societal changes into the educational environment.

> Because schools have traditionally perceived their role to be that of an assimilating agent, the isolation and rejection that come hand in hand with immigration and colonization have simply been left at the schoolhouse door. Curriculum and pedagogy, rather than using the lived experiences of students as a foundation, have been based on what can be described as alien and imposed reality. The rich experiences of millions of our students, their parents, grandparents, and neighbors have been kept strangely quiet. (Nieto, 1992, p. xxv)

The rights of the individual to his or her culture were suppressed in favor of establishing and maintaining a school that had at least the outward appearance of homogeneity. And homogeneity seemed to be the means by which teachers experienced smooth sailing in the classroom.

In contrast, teaching in public schools today seems to be an attempt to navigate on an ocean marked by challenging shoals, high waves, and severe undertows. Successfully steering those waters takes quick thinking, creative ideas, and careful application of professional knowledge. Some teachers hesitate to embark on those waters. Other teachers undertake the journey but discern only the difficulties of the voyage. Still others are exhilarated by the struggle required to steer the boat toward an intended destination. Education today is certainly challenging but not impossible. Teachers may not have classrooms filled with quiet, acquiescent children, but classrooms like that have never existed. Teachers increasingly face students with values and beliefs quite different from their own—students who may appear to be enigmatic, difficult, and even dangerous.

Who are the students in today's classrooms? Given the shifting demographics of our country, students in classrooms may well represent a diverse range of cultures, speak several different languages, and have a broad range of special needs that may or may not have been diagnosed or even identified. Teachers no longer have the luxury of viewing students as a group, indistinguishable from one another. Educators can no longer embrace the delusion that they will spend their days in classrooms filled with eager students who submissively respond to any request made of them. Right or wrong, a step forward or a step back, that educational world no longer exists, if it ever did.

The educational world that does exist, though, can be a stimulating environment for professional educators. "Teaching is still a powerful calling for many people, and powerful for the same reasons that it has always been so. There are still young people who need a thoughtful, caring adult in their lives; someone who can nurture and challenge them, who can coach and guide, understand and care about them."*

There is nothing easy about teaching, but the rewards are monumental. And the rewards begin at the point when professional educators acknowledge students as individuals who have the right to expect a fair chance to succeed in school. "A major goal of multicultural education, as stated by specialists in the field, is to reform the school and other educational institutions so that students from diverse racial, ethnic, and social class groups will experience educational equality" (Banks, 1995, p. 3). This basic imperative that all students have the right to a fair chance for success governs every decision the teacher makes. The decisions are quick and constant, and the vast majority of those decisions fall under the general heading of what is called classroom management.

Classroom management is the term used to describe myriad educational decisions, including the ways in which rules are established and reinforced, how consequences are enacted or exacted, how frequently communication with parents takes place, the physical setup of the room, the ready availability of materials, the methods used for resolving conflicts, and the verbal interactions with students.

DIVERSITY AND LAW: TWO COMPLEX INFLUENCES THAT GUIDE MANAGEMENT DECISIONS

In today's public educational environment, two complex influences have been added to the list of issues that are already associated with effective management. The first is the requirement that educational decisions carefully consider and competently address the diverse range of needs, values, and interests represented in any classroom. *Diversity* is perhaps an overused word in today's educational lexicon. However, the term is also undeniably descriptive of the demographics of student populations throughout the United States.

Diversity is not an us–them issue. Diversity is in all of us and is found everywhere. Assumptions based on economics, skin color, religious practices, national origin, or gender are dangerously misleading and do not serve the needs or interests of our students. An example of our rich and diverse nature can be illustrated by the ways in which assumptions are made about students on the basis of their outward appearances.

To understand how diversity resides everywhere and not just in one particular group or culture, people can examine the ways in which each represents some aspects and histories that are different from those around them. Educators (and others) often make the mistake of assuming that diversity is a descriptive term reserved for anyone who does not look as they do; this is particularly true if the educators are Caucasian. Their perspective is understandable given that in many areas of the country Caucasian ancestry represents the predominant culture.

*Reprinted by permission of the publisher from Ayers W., *To Teach: The Journey of a Teacher* (New York: Teachers College Press, © 1993 by Teachers College, Columbia University. All Rights Reserved.) pg. 8

Statistically, Caucasians also make up the majority of educators in our public schools. Accordingly, at least based on outward appearance, Caucasian teachers often assume they are a homogeneous group.

One way to broaden this perspective is to clearly demonstrate how diversity manifests itself even among an outwardly similar collection of individuals. To illustrate the point, a group of people who look similar to each other can be asked to write down the answers to the following questions:

1. What were five favorite foods your family ate when you were growing up?
2. What were some special words you had in your family?
3. What was a special song that you learned in your family?
4. What is a treasure that you have in your family?
5. What is a favorite family tale?

When I apply the questioning strategy during workshops or classes, the answers to the five questions underscore the ways in which each of us represents a unique and special aspect of diversity. Answers to the question about favorite foods range from fried chicken and borscht to linguine and a special family recipe for a holiday cake. The stories include everything from tales of emigration from Eastern Europe to escape persecution to stories about what it was like to cross the United States in a wagon train.

LOOKING AT THE MAIN IDEAS

Exercise: Identifying the Diversity in Any Group

Ask students to share their answers to the following questions:

1. What were five favorite foods your family ate when you were growing up?
2. What were some special words you had in your family?
3. What was a special song that you learned in your family?
4. What is a treasure that you have in your family?
5. What is a favorite family tale?

As participants share their answers to the questions, it becomes clear that even though a group may at first appear to be very similar, its members are in fact quite different. Much cultural diversity often emerges from what may have initially appeared to be a very homogeneous grouping. Diversity is not a consideration only when students live in one or another particular locale or when students with various physical characteristics are present in the classroom.

Using these five questions as an exercise to introduce the nature of diversity can also help educators to understand that categorizing large groups of people under umbrella headings based on skin color or nationality overlooks all people's individual values and interests shaped by family and experience. For instance, there is no single perspective that represents any cultural group. Some perspectives are shared by all people, some are commonly found among members of one group or another, and others represent the unique aspects of each individual.

The second mandate interwoven into the issues of managing diverse student populations is the pervasive influence of law on every aspect of daily school interactions. Although many see the law as a static concept, the law that governs our daily lives is in fact a dynamic composite made up of language derived from the U.S. Constitution, Supreme Court cases, state constitutions, statutes, regulations, interpretations, attorney opinions, and the holdings of boards. And, in addition, what we call the law is often used to include community concepts of morality and ethics. Educators who disregard the professional legal imperatives designed to inform their decision-making processes do so at considerable risk.

The balance of this chapter is devoted to setting out a few basic legal concepts, discussing issues of diversity, and finally bringing the two elements together in a description of democratic classroom management. Because the goal of this book is to present the ways in which law and multicultural issues intertwine to influence management decisions, it is important to begin our discussion with the law that brings students to us in the first place—the law of compulsory education. The army of students filling our classrooms is not made up of volunteers; they have been conscripted.

COMPULSORY EDUCATION

Because students are compelled into the classrooms of teachers, professional considerations must be extended to ensure students' equal treatment. What follows is a scenario to help explain why an understanding of legal mandates in education begins with an understanding of the impact of compulsory education.

Imagine a neighborhood in any area of this country. It might be an urban location filled with multiple-family dwellings or a rural scene with individual homes, each located in the middle of several acres of land. Every home contains family members who may or may not have anything in common with the people who live next door, across the street, or down the road. More typically, these neighbors share some characteristics but not others. They might share a similar economic level but hold very different political views, religious beliefs, and cultural values. However diverse they might be in terms of beliefs and interests, the one common element they share, if they are the parents or guardians of school-aged children, is some form of direct connection to the schools in the area.

Now imagine that we are observing these neighborhoods on a cold morning in September. Many of the homes have young people snuggled in bed who are ruminating and dreaming about what they would like to do with the morning. To some, a cold, crisp autumn morning is a reason to linger in bed, to others it is a call to go exploring in the woods, to others it is a reason to pick the last vegetables out of the garden before they are damaged by an early frost, and to still others it is a motive to go shopping for that new winter jacket. All of them are lying in their beds and interpreting how the weather might factor into how they want to spend their day based on their personal needs, cultural interests, and family values.

Into each of those bedrooms comes an invisible hand, called the law of compulsory education, to pull these young people out of bed. Whether they are in public, private, or home school, our society expects that all will experience some form of education every weekday during the school year. So, whatever else these young people might have been planning to do that day, they will spend part of their time in some form of educational setting with adults who are their certified or noncertified teachers.

If they attend private or home schools, students likely share at least some cultural values with their classmates and educators. In public schools, however, students are compelled into classrooms on a far more random basis and, in fact, may have nothing more in common with their classmates and teachers than where they live and where the teachers have been assigned.

That students are compelled into school is a critical first step in understanding how law and multicultural issues interweave to inform an educator's decision-making processes. Too often teachers hold the expectations that the students who enter their classrooms will all act, think, and look like them. This may have been true at one time in the United States and may still be true in monocultural societies around the world. However, fewer countries in the world today are monocultural than are multicultural. In the United States, our demographics clearly reflect the fact that a vast spectrum of cultures is represented in all parts of the country.

Given our system of compulsory education, it is a safe bet that any public school classroom may well be filled with students who represent a broad sampling of religious, political, and cultural values. How teachers and administrators interact with these students, the curriculum that is designed for them, the philosophical foundation on which classroom expectations are based, and the methods used when correcting inappropriate behaviors must all reflect public school students' diversity in needs, interests, and values.

The unique traits and beliefs that define students as individuals may have little in common with the interests and values of their teachers. Nevertheless, professional educators are responsible for leveling the playing field for every student by accepting them for who they are and creating for them a welcoming and accepting learning environment. According to Ayres, "The school community has straightforward goals that apply to all students and yet are flexible and personalized for each. They find ways to nurture and challenge the wide range of youngsters who actually arrive at school."* To say the least, that is a tall order.

But let us suppose the opposite is true. Let us imagine that we are observing schools and classrooms in which all students appear, on the surface at least, to be homogeneous. Are educators then relieved from having to consider a multicultural perspective in their management and curriculum decisions? As James Banks (1997, p. 4) stated

> Citizenship education must . . . help in the construction of a transformed
> national identity which reflects the hopes, dreams, and realities of all of
> the nation's citizens and to which they can and will be loyal and patriotic.

---

*Reprinted by permission of the publisher from Ayers W., *To Teach: The Journey of a Teacher* (New York: Teachers College Press, © 1993 by Teachers College, Columbia University. All Rights Reserved.) pg. 134

The aim of citizenship education should be to attain a delicate balance between education for unity and nationhood and educating citizens to recognize, confront, and help resolve inequality manifested in forms such as racism, sexism, and classism.

Educators who teach in communities in which cultural diversity carries a more narrow definition can help their students to look beyond the immediate realities and learn that the world is changing. The small community in which these students go to school may not be the same community in which they will spend their lives as adults. Educators can help their students to appreciate rather than fear difference and to see that world cultures are rich with possibilities worth learning about.

Now, let us return to the scenario of that neighborhood on that cold September day. The young people you were imagining are now headed to their particular schools, because the law requires that all of them spend some of their day with an educator. They enter classrooms with notions of what the educational day will bring them that are probably as diverse as their ideas of how they would have spent the day if they did not have to attend school. Again, many of their expectations for their school day are influenced by their personal and family needs, interests, and values.

Because students are compelled into our public schools, educators are responsible for ensuring that these young people be treated as citizens with all the rights and responsibilities that title implies. I devote a good deal of this book to a discussion of student responsibilities, but it is of equal importance to understand their rights. Student rights were underscored and emphasized in 1969 when the *Tinker* decision was handed down by the U.S. Supreme Court. The case stated, in part, that "students in school as well as out of school are 'persons' under our Constitution. They are possessed of fundamental rights which the State must respect, just as they themselves must respect their obligations to the State" (*Tinker v. Des Moines Independent School District, 1969, p. 88*).

STUDENT RIGHTS: A MATTER OF FREEDOM, JUSTICE, AND EQUALITY

Students have rights in school; these rights are not privileges, rewards, or gifts. Students enter our public schools with the rights guaranteed all citizens under the U.S. Constitution. At times their rights may need to be limited to maintain a safe, healthy, and productive school environment, but the rights of students do not depend on the whims of educators. Students possess their rights just as all adults do in our society.

For some educators, the idea of students having rights is at best a nuisance and at worst a threat to the educators' safety and health. However, student rights do not mean that students can do whatever they want. Students do not have the right to disrupt or threaten the common welfare. How to limit the rights of individual students so that they do not interfere with the needs of the group is examined later in this book.

In 1969 the U.S. Supreme Court handed down the *Tinker* decision, a landmark case that established the rights of students in public schools. Justice Fortas, writing for the majority opinion, stated in part that

> State-operated schools may not be enclaves of totalitarianism. . . . In our system, students may not be regarded as closed-circuit recipients of only that which the State chooses to communicate. They may not be confined to the expression of those sentiments that are officially approved. In the absence of a specific showing of constitutionally valid reasons to regulate their speech, students are entitled to freedom of expression of their views. (*Tinker v. Des Moines Independent School District*, 1969)

Before we discuss the ways in which educators can legally limit student rights, it is important to first understand the rights themselves. Some educators think that understanding student rights means memorizing a long list of regulations, case law, and administrative rules. Just as effective, though, is understanding that student rights can basically be reduced to three terms: *freedom, justice*, and *equality*.

Freedom

Students in public schools have the right to be themselves. They have the right to express themselves in terms of their religious beliefs, their dress, their speech, their writing, and their ability to choose whom to spend time with. In other words, freedom stands for the rights included under the First Amendment to the Constitution.

A discussion of the limits on First Amendment freedoms, in terms of dress codes and student speech, appears later in this book. For now, it is sufficient to remember that the symbolic and actual representations of expression are protected rights in our public schools.

> Part of the desired political socialization of students is that they learn that a government official—a school authority in this instance—may not restrict certain types of freedom of expression merely because it may be annoying or somewhat disruptive. Although some school officials may feel uncomfortable with such a doctrine, its rationale is based on the notion that if students are to become full participants in a free and democratic society, they must thoroughly understand that they are free to express themselves on any social, political, or economic issue without undue restraint or reprisal from government. (LaMorte, 1996, p. 92)

Justice

Educators protect student rights to just treatment by ensuring that they experience due process throughout every aspect of their academic life. Due process has two critical pieces—one procedural, and the other substantive: "Procedural due process, in the larger sense, deals with the question of whether or not a person has been accorded fair and proper treatment. . . . Substantive due process essentially deals with . . . the question of the fairness and reasonableness of laws, regulations, and policies in the light of our constitutional heritage" (LaMorte, 1996, p. 6).

When the law compels students into classrooms, the students bring with them not only their freedom to be themselves but also their expectation of justice under their substantive due process rights to be governed by legal rules. Although this may seem a simple concept, it becomes more complex when legal rules are compared with the rules that emanate from personal whim or caprice. In short, the rules that govern students must be reasonable and reflect the common needs of society rather than a teacher's bias. "This is my rule, because I say so" is a difficult stance to support in light of substantive due process expectations.

Students are also entitled to procedural due process: notice, fair hearing, and appeal. Notice should be a continual part of the educational environment, including the specific language of expectations used in student handbooks, parent newsletters, rules posted inside and outside the school building, rules discussed and revisited in individual classrooms, and stated guidelines for specific lessons and activities. Notice should be given in the languages represented among the student population or should be translated into visual images that can be understood regardless of the languages spoken. Printed notices should be enlarged or recorded on auditory tapes for students with visual impairments.

A fair hearing can be a brief conference with a teacher about some issue of concern or a more formal conversation between a student and a school counselor or administrator. The point of the fair hearing is to provide students with an opportunity to tell their side of the story, not for an educator to lecture students about the errors of their ways. Both sides deserve a chance to be heard. Just asking a student about what is happening can set a fair hearing in motion. Such encounters between students and educators usually need not last more than a minute or two. Even a student who is very angry can spend a couple of minutes with the teacher in a corner of the classroom to discuss the problem. Concerns can be heard, and a more convenient time can be arranged for further conversation. Providing students with this brief opportunity to air their grievances can calm difficult situations and allow the class to continue. A fair hearing does not have to be elaborate; even brief encounters help students to know their concerns will be heard.

The right to an appeal is a formal process that occurs if a student is to be expelled. This process can include the presence of legal representatives for the student and the school, witnesses, and a hearings officer. A less formal appeal process is letting students know that if they are unhappy with a decision made by their teachers, they have the right to take their concerns to the principal, and from the principal to the superintendent, and from the superintendent to the school board. Educators should be open about the due process rights of students. Students who exercise the right of appeal are only threatening to a teacher if the rule they are appealing is inequitable or in some way illegal.

Equality

Ensuring equal educational opportunity for all students is the final legal imperative discussed in this chapter. Confusion about what it means to have an equal educational opportunity abounds. The clearest definition of equal educational opportunity is that every student has the same chance to learn and achieve at his or her highest level of capability. Equal educational opportunity does not mean dumbing down the curriculum, giving everyone *As*, or avoiding right or wrong answers; it means that instruction is designed in ways that are appropriate to meet the needs of all the diverse learners in the classroom.

For the purposes of this book, the term *diverse learners* is defined in the broadest terms possible. Although no description can include every imaginable instance of diversity, a more accurate picture of our public school demographics becomes apparent if the term *diversity* is expanded beyond the usual labels.

Equal opportunity is best protected when the focus is on who students are rather than assumptions based on name, outward appearance, or language. Too often students are labeled according to their skin color, physical characteristics, or primary language, and learning as well as behavioral expectations for them are shaped according to that label. Understanding individual students begins by understanding that they are more than any umbrella term assigned to them. For instance, as indicated earlier in this chapter, to speak of African-Americans, Native Americans or First Nation citizens, Asians, and Latinos as groups is to potentially stereotype students according to their skin color, family name, or facial features and miss the rich diversity that exists beyond these broad and often misleading headings.

A student characterized as Asian could be a native-born American whose family immigrated to this country or the student could have been born in Laos, Thailand, Cambodia, Vietnam, the Philippines, Japan, China, Taiwan, Korea, or Sri Lanka. That student may or may not speak English as a primary language and may or may not have much in common with other students who are also categorized as Asian. The term *Asian* will not help a teacher truly understand who a particular student is. The same is true of any classification assigned to people.

Native American is a commonly used descriptor, but under that heading fall a number of diverse people with various tribal affiliations. Many tribes share some common cultural values, but in other aspects they are very different from each other. *African-American* is another umbrella term used for a diverse range of individuals who may or may not share similar values, physical characteristics, economic levels, religious views, or political affiliations. Latino and Latina students may or may not share a common language and cultural values; they may have families who have come from Mexico, Peru, Puerto Rico, or Ecuador, to name a few. Generalizations simply do not lead to understanding.

Racial or ethnic identity is not the only way diversity is represented in our pluralistic schools and classrooms. Diversity can also refer to the differences among the family values students hold, with various religious beliefs being the most notable example of these values. Again, represented in the umbrella descriptors of religious beliefs are many differences. One Christian child may relish the celebration of Halloween, whereas another Christian child would find such a celebration to be representative of satanic beliefs. Some Jewish children come from Orthodox families and practice the strict codes of their belief; other Jewish children come from families who identify themselves as Reform Jews, and their family rituals may or may not be closely aligned to narrower interpretations of Jewish law. As our society becomes increasingly multicultural, teachers will have many opportunities to work with children whose families practice Hinduism, Buddhism, or Islam.

Beyond the categories of race and religion lies more diversity. Minority sexual identity is receiving greater recognition today as an area of diversity. Whatever a teacher's personal views on the subject of sexual identity might be, every student has the right to expect equal treatment in school.

Diversity also exists in terms of economic status. Homeless children attend school with middle-class children. In the same classroom, students who have only known lives of comfort may sit next to students who are uncertain about where they will spend the night. Children who are members of families of migrant workers also attend our schools. They may be with their teachers for only short periods of time, and yet their time in the classroom must be designed to be as educationally meaningful as possible.

Students with disabilities are being assigned to mainstream classrooms for increasingly longer periods of time under the practice of inclusion. The range of disabilities includes physical impairment, developmental disabilities, learning disabilities, brain disorders, and emotional disturbances. In these same classrooms are students who have been identified as academically gifted and students who have been diagnosed with learning disabilities who are also academically gifted. Some students in the classroom may be learning to speak English as a second language and may never have mastered their primary language because of a learning disability; as a result, they may have increased difficulty mastering English.

Other students may look alike, speak alike, and share some common values but have very different preferred learning modalities. Some students learn better when they can touch an object, and some learn better when they can see the object, and some need to act concepts out. Howard Gardner's (1993) work expands our professional understanding of intelligences into several areas, each of which can aid in developing curriculum, management, and assessment strategies. For some students the classroom's physical environment is more or less appropriate for their preferred learning modality. The work of Rita Dunn (1983) has helped educators to understand that the physical environment of the classroom can have a powerful impact on a student's opportunity to be successful. The whole subject of who students are today is difficult to characterize, and generalizations do a great injustice to students' complexities. Decisions based on genuine individual student needs and not the presumption of what students might need based on what they look like or the language they speak build the trust and communication necessary to sustain a safe learning community.

One example of why educational decisions must consider who students are rather than assume things about them based on their outward appearance can be seen in the way the golfer Tiger Woods chooses to identify his ethnic origins. He has selected for himself the label of *Caublanasian,* which stands for Caucasian, Black, Native American, and Asian. His invention of a term that describes the breadth of his cultural heritage speaks volumes about why assumptions based on outward appearances may well be passé in today's society. Woods is also a good example of why one-size-fits-all educational practice is inappropriate for the individual students whom educators encounter in public schools today.

USING STUDENT RIGHTS AND RESPONSIBILITIES TO CREATE A COMMON SCHOOL CULTURE

"We need a language in our leadership programs that defends schools as democratic public spheres responsible for providing an indispensable public service to the nation; a language, in this case, that is capable of awakening the moral, political, and civic responsibilities of our youth" (Giroux, 1993, p. 24). The concepts of freedom, justice, and equality together inform educators about students' rights in the classroom. They have the right to be protected for who they are, to have substantive and procedural due process afforded to them, and to have an equal chance to succeed academically and socially. Decisions concerning the welfare of students must be free from the bias and prejudice of not only their teachers but also their peers.

LOOKING AT THE MAIN IDEAS

An Overview of Student Rights

Freedom: The right to expression through dress, speech, beliefs, and writings

Justice: Procedural due process—the right to notice, fair hearing, and appeal

Substantive due process—the right to legal rules

Equality: Equal educational opportunity—the right to fair and equitable decisions and learning opportunities

---

Freedom of speech does not extend to harming others. Racial slurs, comments designed to sexually harass, and slang terms for persons with minority sexual identities can do great harm to the entire learning community. As Gathercoal (1995, p. 26) states, "When students do not feel safe, they cannot learn." This book not only discusses appropriate ways for educators to interact with students but also provides a number of ideas for how to redirect the intolerant language and behavior of one peer toward another to better ensure equal educational opportunity for all students.

EDUCATIONAL PRACTICES THAT ADDRESS EQUITY AND DIVERSITY

According to Greene (1993, p. 194)

> No one can predict precisely the common world of possibility, nor can we absolutely justify one kind of community over another. Many of us, however, for all the tensions and disagreements around us, would reaffirm the value of principles like justice and equality and freedom and commitment to human rights; since, without these, we cannot even argue for the decency of welcoming.

Maxine Greene's words directly pertain to the spirit of this book. Basing classroom decisions on the principles of freedom, justice, and equality helps members of any learning community to look beyond their own various cultural needs and interests and into the realm of common societal values. Educators and students need not devalue personally held beliefs in favor of the common school culture but rather value and respect both. All students' unique individual natures are deserving of respect, and their due process rights must be protected by providing them with sufficient information to participate in protecting the common welfare needs of the group.

Educators are challenged to develop curriculum that addresses a broad range of individual needs and interests. Equally challenging and perhaps even more important is the acquisition of management skills that can be used as proactive and preventive measures for effectively responding to the problems and concerns brought into the classroom by each student.

> Schools must help youths from diverse cultures and groups to attain the knowledge, attitudes, and skills needed to function effectively in the twenty-first century. To attain this goal, the school must change many of its basic assumptions and practices. School restructuring is essential because the dominant approaches, techniques, and practices used to educate students do not, and I believe will not, succeed with large numbers of students of color, such as African Americans, Native Americans, and Hispanics. Most current school practices are having little success with these students for many complex reasons, including negative perceptions and expectations of them by many teachers and adminis-trators. (Banks, 1994, p. 37)

The negative student perceptions and expectations of which James Banks speaks are not just a curricular issue but a management concern as well. Behavioral expectations should be equally high for all students, regardless of their personal situations. Too often students who display inappropriate behaviors are ignored as if nothing better can be expected of them. In my experience these students typically come from dysfunctional family situations or impoverished backgrounds or hold cultural values different from those of the teacher. Regardless of their circumstances, their equal educational opportunity extends to experiencing the same behavioral expectations as other students. If their early misbehaviors are ignored and the behavior escalates, as it inevitably will, these students are typically suspended or expelled from school. They go from no response to inappropriate actions to a very forceful response without the benefit of any intervening processes. Their due process rights are subverted and their equal protection lost.

This book is designed to provide educators with some very practical management ideas and strategies that reflect best practices as defined by our shared professional knowledge of pedagogy, psychology, developmentally appropriate curriculum, multicultural considerations, and legal issues. In other words, management is addressed within these pages from an educationally diverse perspective to provide teachers and administrators with the tools to better address the diverse needs represented by students in all classrooms.

Although this book focuses on various management concerns, it is impossible to provide an in-depth analysis of every possible management concern and how educators might go about addressing the problem. Accordingly, the chapters that follow examine a broad range of issues and provide a variety of suggestions for resolving the concerns. The chapters also include closing activities that challenge the reader to engage in self-reflection on the strategies being shared.

This book, then, focuses on individual students and the legal, ethical, and managerial practices that can help to ensure each of them fair treatment in all classrooms. Banks (1995, p. 3) states that "a major goal of multicultural education, as stated by specialists in the field, is to reform the school and other educational institutions so that students from diverse racial, ethnic, and social-class groups will experience educational equity." Ultimately, if educators focus on meeting the needs of individual students, then the backgrounds, appearances, and voices of the students will not serve to determine the level of expectation for their learning gains or their behaviors. Rather, educators can invest energy in management and curricular practices that invite all students and provide them with the level playing field to which they are entitled.

BUILDING A DEMOCRATIC LEARNING COMMUNITY

In public school classrooms, with their representative mix of values and cultures, educators are responsible for building learning communities that consist of students who may have nothing more in common than their home addresses. Many students might not like each other, and some may even fear each other. Teachers and administrators must ensure that each student feels a sense of safety and well-being to fully and equally participate in the educational process.

> Those of us who work with children know that our task is complicated; we have to examine the teaching practices we use, the policies we are expected to follow, the theories we adopt. In the end, regardless of policies, philosophies, theories, and methodologies, the success or failure of an individual child—the way that child experiences school—depends on what happens in that child's classroom, what kind of learning environ-

ment the teacher is able to provide, and how well the teacher is able to investigate and attend to the particular needs of that child.*

Given all there is to do during the school day, teachers often seek out approaches to management that are quick and easily implemented. These approaches tend to be more behavioral than cognitive. Students are bribed, coerced, cajoled, and at times threatened into behaving in ways the teacher views as appropriate. Sometimes the preselected behaviors being sought make sense and are helpful to a learning community, but other times they serve only to keep the classroom quiet but not necessarily productive.

Creating rules that reflect behavioral practices can be seen in how a teacher attempts to maintain quiet in the classroom during a learning activity. Educators who use behavioral strategies simply tell students to be quiet and reinforce the behavior when it occurs. How students should demonstrate compliance is predetermined by the teacher; it often has less to do with appropriate voice levels than with the teacher's personal biases for what constitutes accepted responses to the rules.

Educators can tell students how to behave and then reward them for compliance or punish them for noncompliance. But this behavioral approach does not encourage critical reflection by students. Obedience is expected and encouraged. Lists of behavioral rules often include statements such as "Do it the first time you are asked." Students are not invited to participate in decision making but are asked simply to obey any request or demand made of them.

An extreme example of teachers who demand obedience over participation is the middle school teacher who awarded *A*s on his tests when students sat up straight, kept their eyes on the paper, and kept their feet together under the desk. Although this approach may not be the norm, the example illustrates the ways in which a teacher's personal values blur what are meaningful assessment strategies and subvert equal educational opportunity.

Management concerns related to test taking should reflect the needs students have for a classroom conducive to concentration and thinking. Classrooms that are free of unnecessary distractions and that provide students with the opportunity to do their own work (and thus fair assessment) allow all students the chance to learn. But when a teacher stipulates only one way of keeping quiet and doing one's own work without regard to individual learning styles or individual needs, personal judgment gets in the way of equity. Sometimes the drive to maintain control in the classroom clouds a teacher's judgment of what constitutes sound educational practice.

Because behavioral management practices are aimed at external manifestations of appropriate behavior and motivated by extrinsic rewards or punishments, they have little to do with who the individual student is. They are aimed at controlling the group. Behavioral management practices may be quick and work in the sense that they result in students so intimidated by fear or so motivated to get the next treat that they are willing to acquiesce to the rules. However, the practices do little to teach students how to critically examine their own behaviors and make good choices about their behavior that will benefit the common welfare.

*C. Igoa, The Inner World of the Immigrant Child. (1995, p.8). Lawrence Erlbaum Associates, Inc. Reprinted by permission.

Another example of personal bias in a classroom rule might be how some teachers require students to line up at the door; some teachers direct students to line up according to gender. Although this approach may well lead to an orderly procession into the hallway, the expectation itself establishes an arbitrary, as well as discriminatory, standard for lining up. An educator probably would not ask students to stand in separate lines based on other student differences. For instance, it is difficult to imagine students being required to stand in one line or another based on their race or religion.

Lining students up according to gender is just as difficult to justify as any other standard based on personal characteristics. The primary concern of the teacher is to make sure students move safely from the classroom into the hallway, and gender has little to do with that goal. Similarly, a rule that requires students to line up at the door according to height can quickly turn into a rule that separates students based on national origin, disability, or gender.

Instead the purpose for the rule can be the behavioral expectations that will help students make the transition safely and appropriately in a manner that does not disrupt the rest of the learning community. One cognitive management approach to this scenario might be to have students participate in the decision-making process. Educators might state an expectation such as the following: "We need to move safely through the door into the hall. Let us all think about our space and the space needed for others as we do that. Please remember that there are other classes going on around us. Now, tell me, what will it look like? What will it sound like?"

Looking at the Main Ideas

Stating Expectations Will Help Students Focus on the Rules

1. State the issue:

   "We will be working in groups to complete this activity."

2. Ask questions such as the following:

   "What will it look like when we are in groups? Will there be people wandering around? Will there be people just sitting while others are working? What will it sound like? What are the appropriate voice levels for an activity like this?"

Remember: When students are asked about appropriate behaviors rather than told, they are more likely to assume responsibility for the answers.

Stating expectations in this manner is open-ended enough to not be discriminatory and at the same time helps students learn to make good decisions about how to behave. Although the approach might take some time initially, students will be able to apply the information to a variety of situations in which they need to move safely and nondisruptively with only a brief reminder.

Even more problematic are the rules teachers seek to enforce through rewards and punishments, because such responses to student behavior typically reflect teachers' personal values and biases. Demographic statistics documented at the federal and state levels indicate, as mentioned earlier, that the teaching population is predominantly White, whereas the student population is becoming increasingly diverse. When the rules of a classroom are developed to reinforce the personal values and beliefs of a teacher trying to control students who might not share those values and beliefs, the mismatch becomes a source of contention.

> Student compliance with at least the main part of teacher directions and requirements is a major part of the foundation upon which academic engagement and achievement are built. While it is not the only ingredient in the mix that produces student learning, it is certainly a necessary one; and when student resistance to teacher demands markedly outweighs compliance, teaching and learning founder. (D'Amato, 1993, p. 181)

Democratic management, on the other hand, typically centers more on societal expectations that promote the common welfare than on the immediate do-this-in-this-classroom-because-I-say-so approach. Both behavioral and cognitive or democratic techniques can lead to well-ordered classrooms, but the subtext contained in each is very different. Democratic management relies on presenting guidelines and expectations to students and then having students make choices about how to behave appropriately within those parameters.

> I do not want my rules to legislate every action. I want them to encourage reasoned thinking and discussion. I want rules that we "like," not because they give license or permission, but because they help us construct a community that is orderly and safe. And I want rules that have meaningful applications to concrete behaviors, which require not just passive submission but active participation. (Charney, 1991, p. 51)

USING DEMOCRATIC MANAGEMENT TO TEACH DECISION-MAKING SKILLS

When we view the young people in classrooms as representative of all aspects of our society, the importance of educators working to build a classroom climate free of rules that reflect personal biases or prejudice becomes clear. Rather, the rules adopted by teachers and administrators should be based on the common values of our society such as honesty, respect, trust, and the need to be safe. The rules developed for these democratic learning communities can best reflect society's expectations of cooperation when the basis for the rules is derived from the language of individual freedoms balanced against mutual responsibilities. Such a simple premise for classroom management teaches the values of our common democracy and yet does not impose a teacher's personal value system on the students.

One of the foundational principles for having public education is to ensure that our society is made up of an educated citizenry. Because citizenship participation is based in large part on decision making, it only makes sense for students to have many opportunities to learn and practice decision making, particularly when those decisions directly relate to an individual's behaviors.

Democratic management addresses a student's ability to think through a situation, weigh options, review expectations, and make good decisions. In other words, it helps students to assume the responsibilities that characterize appropriate adult behavior. Although teachers may think it is easier and faster to simply tell students what to do and how to do it, by providing students with sufficient information to make decisions, educators can help students become responsible for their own actions.

Although decision making is an important skill for young people to practice, it is equally important that classroom rules be appropriate for the broad spectrum of cultural values represented in our schools. The pluralistic nature of student populations means that the rules for maintaining safe and productive classrooms must be free from bias and inequity. Regardless of the gender, race, religion, sexual identity, or ethnicity of the students, decisions that govern their behavior can be based on the common requirement to maintain safe learning communities and not on who the students are. The values imparted in our management decisions should be those that promote the common welfare while respecting the rights of the individuals.

Student participation in the decision-making process is one essential element of democratic management. Another is the quality of the physical environment in which the students spend their days. Whether educators are teaching elementary students or seniors in high school, arranging the classroom to be welcoming for all students is important. Visual learners do better at any level if the classroom has interesting and appealing items displayed around the room.

Arranging desks in clusters or groups rather than in rows is more welcoming and serves the needs of students with disabilities because they can move or be moved more easily among the desks and around the room. Clustering desks into group arrangements also meets the needs of students whose cultures value cooperative rather than competitive work. Native American students, for example, whose cultures typically value cooperation over competition, often feel more comfortable working with their peers than being isolated from them.

Children who speak a primary language other than English also benefit from desk arrangements that favor peer interaction. Learning English is easier because of the many opportunities to interact with English speaking students. Peer interactions help everyone. Since the range of disabilities is as varied and subtle as the range of diversity present in a classroom, students can benefit from working with peers who have greater or lesser levels of disabilities than they themselves do. Finally, grouping desks rather than arranging them in rows helps teachers manage classrooms more effectively.

> The effectiveness of communication among cooperators, the level of trust built in cooperative groups, the peer tutoring that is available in cooperative learning situations, the student preference for, involvement in, and liking of cooperative experiences—all will contribute to positive peer influence in cooperative situations. . . . Cooperative groupings will reduce your discipline problems, and the cooperative situation is far different

from the one in which you are expected to motivate, counsel, and discipline every student with whom you come into contact. (Johnson & Johnson, 1991, p. 205)

REFLECTIONS ON TEACHER EDUCATION

Educators begin with the best of intentions. Like Claudia in the scenario that begins this chapter, they are eager to start their first year of teaching with the information garnered from teacher preparation programs and the inner passion that first drew them to this profession. The program they choose to attend is typically determined by their location and financial resources, especially if they are making teaching a second career or wish to reenter the workforce after raising a family.

Some teacher education programs are more current than others, and some offer more course options than others. Some programs emphasize content and curriculum over classroom management. Very few teacher education programs include any course work in legal issues. A class in multicultural topics is easier to find, although such classes tend to concentrate more on how to teach about multicultural issues than on the changing demographics of classrooms and how those statistics influence the decision-making processes of educators.

That teachers begin their first year of teaching ill informed about who their students are and with few strategies designed to incorporate all students into the learning community is not their fault. The burden rests with teacher educators to facilitate the learning process of those who enter the teaching profession and to help them understand the nature of the students they will teach. We can look beyond the teaching of a single subject matter to examine the needs and interests of the students.

Many statistics show a high rate of teacher burnout after the first year and certainly within the first five years of teaching. Many teachers who could enrich the lives of students for years leave before they ever realize their potential. Or they stay on, feeling discouraged and always struggling to find just the right reward or punishment to keep students quiet. In desperation, some teachers engage in suspect actions that reflect the rash judgment of a person who is out of ideas and trying to hang onto a job. A student once related a story about her sixth-grade teacher, who had a system of maintaining quiet by hurling items across the classroom at talking students. The teacher would initially throw an eraser, then a stapler, and then a dictionary. "Don't make me get the dictionary" was the continual threat the student remembers hearing from the teacher.

Some students have problems that cannot be fixed in the classroom, some angry students may not be calmed, some discouraged students cannot be reached, and some dysfunctional lives cannot be made whole within the classroom. It would be naive not to acknowledge these hard truths. Yet because such problems exist, teacher education programs must provide their future teachers with, or guide their future teachers toward, as much information about the nature of students as possible. To do less is to increase the likelihood that promising young educators will be forever lost to our profession.

SUMMARY

This book is designed to provide good teachers with additional strategies for building safe and productive learning communities. It is also meant to help teachers who might be uncertain of what ideas and strategies to try next. And this book is for new teachers who find that classroom management is the one aspect of their work that can wake them up at night in cold sweats. The consistent thread running through this book is advocation of an integrated democratic, multi-cultural, and legal approach to classroom management.

Effective democratic management practices can be a source of genuine reward for teachers who go home at the end of the day knowing that their students have been treated respectfully and that their classrooms have been peaceful and productive. These educators have also learned firsthand the one great reality about effective democratic classroom management: When power is shared, there is no management by quick fixes. Equitable, democratic management is a process rather than a series of tricks. It consists of good communication, patience, trust, being willing to try another idea when the last one did not work, keeping calm in the face of anger, and patience. Democratic educators and their students are striving together to reach a consistent level of reasonable human interactions. As with any worthwhile human relationship, our interactions with students require a genuine commitment of our time to establish the trust to address each student's needs.

Any quick-fix approach to management, however inviting the idea might seem, typically values neither the teachers' abilities to effectively problem solve nor the social necessity for students to learn decision-making skills. The ideas presented in this book require an investment of time. Some teachers may initially see such approaches as interfering with the time they have to deliver the curriculum. However, educators who take careful steps to develop democratic management practices at the beginning of the school year consistently report that taking time to establish equitable rules and review expectations that are inclusive and supportive of all students provides them with more time for teaching as the year proceeds. Their classrooms do not fall apart with the approach of a holiday or the end of the school year. These teachers are emphatic that an investment of time as a preventive measure ensures them more time for teaching later. The ideas offered in this book are not designed to take time away from the important work teachers do but to make that use of time more efficacious. And it all begins with an understanding of who the students are.

Some of the topics in this book are more readily associated with issues of management than others. The book encompasses a number of topics as a deliberate attempt to indicate the breadth of classroom management. Welcome to the journey.

APPLYING THE CONCEPTS

Can any assumptions safely be made about students? How would you go about learning who your students are? What are the resources available to you? What information would you still need? Justify your responses to the questions. Once you have given a response, reflect briefly on how you think your answer to each question will affect your teaching.

CHAPTER 2

Why We Need Classroom Rules

CHAPTER OBJECTIVES

By the end of this chapter the reader should be able to:

◇ Establish classroom management rules that are legal and equitable
◇ Develop rules that reflect the multicultural nature of public school students
◇ Teach students how to develop comprehensive classroom rules and apply them to a variety of school and classroom situations

Scenario

Andre was eager to begin his first year of teaching. He had been hired to teach seventh-grade language arts just two months before the beginning of the school year. He spent the rest of the summer reviewing curriculum, writing lesson plans, and setting up his classroom. Now, finally, his first-period students were entering his classroom, and he was ready to go with his opening lesson. He began with a brief introduction of himself, passed out textbooks, and then announced that it was time to begin. He launched into the first lesson and thought later that it had gone fairly well. Based on the way the rest of the day went, Andre envisioned a good year with few problems. He felt certain that all his students would come to share his enthusiasm for language arts because he would present interesting lessons that challenged their minds.

A month later, Andre found himself exhausted at the end of each day. He was spending more time putting out behavioral fires in his classroom than teaching. He still worked hard on his planning, but it was becoming increasingly more difficult to keep the attention of the students long enough to teach anything. As his first month of teaching came to an end, he realized he was feeling discouraged and frustrated. Sitting in the teachers' lounge, he heard another teacher say: "These ungrateful kids. You spend all this time writing good lessons, and they do not quiet down enough to even hear what they are going to be doing." Andre nodded his head in bitter agreement.

Questions

What was missing from Andre's first-day activities? What do students need to know about their teacher, their classroom, and the subject they will be studying?

Discussion

The scenario that opened this chapter is hardly unusual. Unfortunately, Andre's frustrations are not uncommon to new teachers. People make the decision to become teachers for a variety of reasons, and chief among them is often a passion to spend their professional careers fully engaged in academic subject matter. A second premise for becoming a teacher, also commonly heard, is the desire to make a positive change in the lives of students. Both of these positions are laudable. Education needs good teachers who care about students and who want to open young people's eyes to the wonders of science, the physical discipline of athletics, the delightful complexities of mathematics, the ability to express inner thoughts through art, the panorama of history, or the craft and skill of writing. And if a sense of caring about students and a love of subject matter were enough to sustain a productive learning environment, the careers of these people would be an ongoing series of pleasant experiences.

What educators must remember, though, is that the language that shapes and structures our profession encompasses a broad range of disciplines. Educators need to not only understand curriculum design and subject matter but also have some grounding in the theories of pedagogy and developmental psychology. In other words, it is not enough to understand the subject matter to be taught or the lesson plans through which those subjects will be conveyed. It is at least equally important for educators to understand the nature of who will receive the information and the individual needs and cultural perspectives the students will bring to that process.

In the chapter-opening scenario, it was evident that Andre believed his enthusiasm for his subject matter would set such a positive and engaging tone for the classroom that management would not be a concern. Such thinking is not uncommon. Like many midlevel and secondary teachers, Andre is convinced that a mix of interesting lessons and an occasional stern word are enough to keep students focused on a task and attentive for an extended period of time. At the elementary level, teachers often express the conviction that a kind word and a smile occasionally used in combination with "the teacher look" are sufficient for setting a positive classroom tone that will last through the school year. Occasionally, some new teachers enter their first classrooms armed with only one piece of management lore—perhaps the oldest of classroom management myths—"Do not smile 'til December." The common message embedded in all of the mentioned perceptions is that classroom management is the one aspect of education that does not require a great deal of attention. Such thinking can often set a promising career in education on the fast track to burnout.

To function successfully, students need to understand what is expected of them within the school environment. The rules and expectations shared with them should be applicable across the full range of the school day and cover a range of appropriate behaviors applicable to academic basics such as curriculum, assessment, study skills, and other components of the school day that are essential for academic achievement.

THE NEED FOR RULES IN ELEMENTARY CLASSROOMS

The creation of a classroom community designed to function in ways that benefit all its members cannot be left to chance or hope. Developing effective rules and implementing democratic management practices are deliberate processes that require careful thought and preparation. The careful construction of rules sets a tone for how classroom interactions will be orchestrated.

Alfie Kohn (1996, p. 103) describes the child development project (CDP) with which he is involved as follows:

> The CDP study suggests that taking the time to help children care about each other might just affect their enthusiasm about academic learning. That is an insight with the potential to reshape the whole enterprise of school reform, but it really shouldn't be surprising. Students need to feel safe in order to take intellectual risks; they must be comfortable before they can venture into the realm of discomfort. Few things stifle creativity like the fear of being judged or humiliated. Thus, a supportive environment will allow people of any age to play with possibilities and challenge themselves to stretch their thinking. The moral is: if you want academic excellence, you have to attend to how children feel about school and about each other.

Rules that provide shape and structure to the ways students interact within their learning communities offer a necessary sense of security and the knowledge of how to achieve academic success.

Chapter 1 highlighted the breadth of diversity present in today's classrooms. Students come from homes in which people may or may not value following rules, value breaking rules, or understand what the rules are. Students first learn how to interact with their environments within their family structures and among their peers in ways that help them thrive, provide positive feedback, and result in some level of acceptance.

The problem is that the skills they may have developed to successfully survive in their various settings outside of school may be counterproductive to learning appropriate behaviors needed for participation in classroom communities. If their family members typically communicate with anger or even violence, students will view yelling and hitting as the way people get along. If their peers are detached and disinterested, those attitudes will also guide the manner in which students communicate and respond in the classroom. Unless a teacher takes the time to establish appropriate expectations for learning, students exhibit the behaviors modeled for them in their homes or among their friends because that is their paradigm for how to get along in the world. The misguided supposition that these young people know how to act in school can lead to disastrous consequences for all members of the learning community.

Teachers who have self-contained classrooms and work with the same group of students all day have an enormous potential to significantly impact how students learn to communicate and resolve conflicts with each other. Ethical behaviors and moral thinking can be interwoven into all the day's activities, depending on the way rules are phrased and presented. Students have the opportunity to learn socially appropriate behaviors and to see them consistently modeled by their teachers. Through discussions, class meetings, and one-on-one conversations, students can also recognize how those same behaviors can be transferred to other settings and situations.

In self-contained classrooms, typically for kindergarten through sixth-grade students, teachers can establish consistent rules that are developed with the entire class, revisited in class meetings, and applied throughout the school day. Teachers can facilitate peaceful conflict resolution, mediation, and appropriate communication. Curriculum does not have to stop for teachers to build respect and responsibility; rather, the teaching of societal values can be an integral piece of the daily curriculum.

THE IMPORTANCE OF RULES AT THE SECONDARY LEVEL

Students in secondary schools usually have six or seven different classes during the school day, with each class lasting approximately 45 to 50 minutes. Many secondary school administrators focus on the management practices of teachers only when their classrooms are in chaos; preventive policies that establish consistent guidelines for behaviors throughout middle schools or high schools are rare indeed. If behavioral policies have been established, they tend to reflect a reactive posture and focus on the consequences of misbehavior. A philosophical approach to teaching appropriate behaviors is typically absent from any policy statements; teachers are left to invent their own strategies for handling inappropriate behaviors. The result is confusion. As students move from class to class, they are expected to comply with each teacher's different rules. They are expected to shift gears dramatically every 50 minutes, depending on the expectations of their various educators. The result is confusion and the absence of a consistent message about which behaviors best benefit the individual and society.

For instance, in one class students might be considered tardy when the bell rings, but in the next class arriving 5 or even 10 minutes after the bell is not considered late. These daily inconsistencies are difficult for students to handle, particularly in the preadolescent stage when a secure and safe environment is so important to students' sense of psychological well-being.

Research indicates that students have an easier time adapting to variations on a common management theme than trying to comply with each teacher's different expectations. If the rules make sense and students understand the reasons for the rules, they are more likely to follow the rules. Rules that have a reasonable rationale are much easier for teachers to explain and enforce. Secondary educators can work together to create a common vision within their school that includes language for sustaining an equitable and legal classroom environment. They can then share that vision through the rules and expectations established in each classroom. The more carefully and thoroughly they work with students to craft rules that reflect the common vision, the more students will be able to consistently conduct themselves in appropriate ways.

As mentioned earlier, some secondary teachers neglect to engage in any discussion of rules. Like Andre in the opening scenario, they begin to teach without taking the time to discuss behavioral expectations. An interesting exercise for preservice teachers is to observe in classrooms where no rules have been established. When students in those classrooms are asked what the rules are, the results can be startling. Students generally have some knowledge of the behaviors expected by the teacher, but understanding of those expectations varies remarkably from one student to another. Consequently, in classrooms without stated or posted rules, students make personal decisions about what they think their teachers want from them. Teachers face a vast range of different behaviors that are a reflection of the correct or incorrect conclusions drawn by the students about which behaviors are valued. Patiently teaching the behaviors that consider individual rights and group needs protects the common welfare. And, as mentioned earlier, at the elementary and secondary levels, rules should be based on a legal framework.

THE LEGAL RATIONALE FOR RULES

The rationale for creating legal rules is based on students' rights to due process. Students are entitled to know what the rules are and to be governed by rules that are fair and equitable.

> Students seem to feel more ownership of an environment that ensures them their due process. My own research supports unpublished research by C. A. Kelly, cited by David Schimmel and Richard Williams in an article on the use of due process in public schools. In their review of the literature, Schimmel and Williams present evidence that "in those schools that observe due process, students were more likely to have positive attitudes toward the legal system, and toward schooling." (McEwan, 1995, p. 9)

Some educators believe that they should solely determine the classroom's rules, but it is not quite that simple. Public school educators are the tangible representatives of our government. Because public school educators receive their salaries from public funds and work in publicly supported institutions, they are the government in their classrooms. The role of our government is to respect and protect the rights of citizens. In public schools, students, no matter their ages, are citizens, as decided in the 1969 Supreme Court Case of *Tinker v. Des Moines Independent School District.*

The problem is that the concept of students as citizens has not been easily or swiftly translated into daily educational policy.

> To this day, for that matter, there are probably principals and school board members who could not pass a simple test on what Tinker means. Other school officials who knew of the landmark ruling felt no pressure to bring the First Amendment into school life because their students had not heard of the decision in or out of school. . . . In the years since the Tinker decision, however, certain principals have moved to reexamine school regulations in order to make certain that students are being assured their constitutional rights. Others have been forced to comply with the Constitution when challenged in the courts by students and parents who have become very much aware of their rights. (Hentoff, 1980, p. 7)

As representatives of the government, then, educators must seek to ensure that their actions and decisions protect the rights of all their students. A critical first step in the process of ensuring this protection occurs when students are informed of the rules and expectations that govern their classrooms. In legal terms, this is called *notice.*

THE IMPORTANCE OF NOTICE

Notice is the term used to describe the manner in which all citizens are made aware of society's expectations for what constitutes appropriate behavior. The language of notice must be clear and precise, because citizens also have the right to be protected from rules that are unconstitutionally vague. The following scenario may help to illustrate this point.

Imagine two drivers who are trying to find their way around in an unfamiliar town. They most likely are seeking geographic clues about their location and other information that will allow them to drive safely and remain within the law. Now imagine that these two drivers have turned onto unfamiliar streets. Each would quickly want to access certain bits of critical information, one of which is the speed limit. Drivers expect to see speed limit signs posted near corners so that they know immediately the legal expectations for how fast they might drive.

Suppose the drivers in this scenario see no signs for speed limits. In an attempt to compensate for the missing information, the drivers begin to try to figure out for themselves what the speed limits might be. Their guesses are influenced by their past experiences and the clues from their surroundings. One driver might drive 25 miles per hour after thinking about the fact that the two-lane road is in a residential area and has cars parked on both sides. Another driver might think 45 miles per hour on the same road would be just fine, because the road is in a quiet area with little traffic and the driver is in a hurry. Because no expectations have been established for the drivers, both might believe their reasoning to be correct since they are basing their judgments on personal interpretations of the information available.

Sometimes rules are too vague to be easily understood. Imagine that the drivers see a sign that says "We usually like you to go around 25 miles per hour in this neighborhood, but . . . you know . . . if it is late at night and there are not many people around, 35 miles per hour would probably be okay. On the other hand, if the road is wet or icy you might consider keeping your speed at around 20 miles per hour." This notice is not only too vague, but traffic jams would likely result from people trying to read and comprehend the sign's meaning. As citizens who operate motor vehicles, we have come to expect that the frequent notice we receive from our government about speed limits or other health and safety issues will be written in language that is clear and easily understood. Signs that read "Speed Limit 25 mph" posted at precise intervals work best to provide adequate notice.

Although the scenario about drivers and speed limits may seem extreme, educators are sometimes equally vague in communicating rules at the start of the school year. Some teachers do not present or develop any behavioral rules, assuming that their students already have an understanding of expected behaviors and repetition is unnecessary. Other teachers do not establish rules because they want the classroom to seem like a friendly place and fear that imposing rules may not foster the warm ambiance they are attempting to establish. In either case, both groups of teachers have in mind their own expectations for what constitutes appropriate classroom behaviors; by not sharing that information, in effect they are not providing for the due process rights of their students.

Regardless of whether the rules are stated, students who enter such classrooms know there are standards for acceptable and unacceptable behaviors. When the rules must be guessed, students devote a good deal of mental energy on thought processes similar to those of the drivers who turned onto the unfamiliar streets and saw no posted speed limit signs. Students analyze the situation based on a mix of their experiences and the clues from their surroundings and arrive at what they believe to be actions that their teachers will appreciate.

One group of students may fear the possibility of violating some unstated rule. Students who assess the situation from that perspective typically decide to get along as best they can and draw on their previous experiences with rules in other classrooms. They raise their hands when they want to speak, they do not speak out of turn, and they hand in their assignments on the due dates with the hope that they are doing what their teachers expect of them.

Another group of students may enter the same classrooms and think that having no rules means anything goes. They test the limits again and again to see just where and what the limits are. Their teachers spend a good deal of time on management because some students find the limit testing process more interesting than the subject matter being taught.

Some teachers want to be flexible with their students but are uncertain of how to establish behavioral expectations and demonstrate flexibility at the same time. They might attempt to establish classroom rules by saying something like the following: "I want you all to feel comfortable in class, so let us work together to make sure we listen to each other and are polite. I do not care if you raise your hands when you want to speak, but we cannot interrupt each other. So look around first when you have something to say. If no one else seems to want to say anything, then you can go ahead and talk." Students would be forgiven for scratching their heads after hearing expectations stated in such a vague manner.

To meet the legal standard of adequate notice, educators must either give students notice that is clear, easily understood, and repeated at consistent intervals or work with their students to establish rules that meet the same criteria. To do less can lead to confusion, frustration, and anger on the part of teachers and students alike. At the same time, clear notice does not mean classrooms must be governed by rules that are rigid and expectations that are unbending.

CLEAR RULES ARE NOT THE SAME AS INFLEXIBLE RULES

A simple equation helps to explain why giving notice does not equate to being in-flexible. Rules designed to help students know how to function successfully in a classroom contribute to their sense of security. Their sense of security directly con-tributes to their academic success. The importance of clearly stated expectations, then, cannot be overestimated. When students know the expectations, they are more likely to behave appropriately and they are also then free to devote their mental energies to learning.

At the same time, the rules for the classroom must cover a variety of situations and be adaptable to diverse student populations; thus, rules that are unyielding cre-ate as difficult a classroom atmosphere as does the absence of rules. According to Igoa, "Rigid school policies can create disempowering environments. . . . We need to humanize our classrooms to best teach our students and facilitate the development of literacy, which is the most self-empowering skill a child can gain in school."*

One of the arguments for rigid rules maintains that the way to treat students fairly is to treat everyone the same. However, equal educational opportunity has never meant that everyone must be treated the same. If that were true there would be no programs for speakers of other languages or for students with special needs.

Never think that being consistent means treating all students alike. Consistency in education is providing the professional specialization and skills needed to help each student believe success is possible. Students know they have different needs and goals and deeply respect educators who understand that one style of teaching or discipline should not neces-sarily be applied to everyone. (Gathercoal, 1998, p. 45)

Some teachers who create hard and fast rules analogize their role in the lives of their students to that of police officers in our larger society. Consequently, teach-ers justify a harsh response to violations of school rules by warning students about real-life consequences.

There are a few problems with such reasoning. One problem is that although consequences are sometimes appropriate, at other times another resolution to a problem is just as appropriate. Responses to problem behaviors are discussed later in this book. For now it is enough to say that not every inappropriate act requires a consequence. Many other equally effective options are available to educators.

Another problem with teacher statements about harsh consequences for vio-lations of rules is the expectation they establish. When teachers talk about rules but emphasize the consequences, they imply that they expect that the rules will be violated. In that case, rules become little more than the means by which stu-dents eventually and inevitably are punished. Before constructing classroom rules teachers may consider the underlying intentions for having rules.

*C. Igoa, The Inner World of the Immigrant Child. (1995, p.9). Lawrence Erlbaum Associates, Inc. Reprinted by permission

Expectations established are usually expectations fulfilled. When rules are being set up, it is important to emphasize the shared understanding of how the rules relate to the general welfare of the learning community.

The second problem with comparing a teacher with a police officer lies in the words "if I catch you." Democratic classroom rules are constructed to teach appropriate adult behaviors. Accordingly, students learn to follow rules regardless of where they are or who is watching. The well-being of society is ensured when adults behave appropriately regardless of whether their actions are being observed and when they act in ways that are considerate and informed by conscience at all times.

The purpose of rules, in or out of the classroom, is to teach students how to exercise their personal freedoms and, at the same time, act in ways that protect the common welfare. One reason for the existence of classroom rules is to teach the values of our society. With some effort, teachers can design classroom rules to teach personal responsibility rather than ways to avoid being caught.

When teachers say that rules will be enforced when students are caught acting inappropriately, they are also, in effect, assuming responsibility for every behavior that occurs in the classroom. Embedded in the if-you-get-caught mind-set is the idea that students can behave any way they choose as long as they are not observed by an adult. As a result, the teacher not only develops the rules but by default also ensures that students follow the rules. In such a situation, students are excused from personal responsibility because the rules only count if the teacher catches them being broken.

Finally, comparing a teacher's role with that of a police officer does a disservice to both professions. Many teachers justify their inflexibility with students by citing the fact that the police may treat students with similarly inflexible responses. Although the two professions may share some similar responsibilities (and at times work with similarly difficult people), the missions of the two professions are vastly different.

When teachers tell students they must enforce the rules without discretion because that is what police do, both law enforcement and education are seriously misrepresented. Police officers have a great deal of discretion in the field and exercise it. Portraying police officers as individuals who make no discretionary decisions does not accurately teach students about the function of law enforcement in our society.

Rules and expectations reflect the teacher's basic philosophical perspective of education. The fundamental principle governing this process is that the rules teachers develop vary depending on whether they believe their primary role is to teach an area of curriculum or to teach students. If teachers see their primary responsibility as teaching a content area, then their rules will be structured to ensure that the content is viewed as more important than the individual needs of students. The posted or stated rules will focus on expected learning outcomes and what will happen to students who fail to meet those outcomes. On the other hand, if teachers believe that their primary focus must be on understanding and addressing the individual needs of students for learning to happen, then the classroom rules will reflect that point of view.

🌀 LOOKING AT THE MAIN IDEAS

When Developing Classroom Rules Ask Yourself If the Rules

- Support students or support the curriculum (they should do both)
- Set a tone of positive expectations
- Teach an understanding of rights balanced against social responsibilities
- Provide support for students who may lack information about assuming personal responsibility for their actions

---

Classroom rules and expectations can be used as effective ways of teaching personal responsibility.

> The only way to help students become ethical people, as opposed to people who merely do what they are told, is to have them construct moral meaning. It is to help them figure out—for themselves and with each other—how one ought to act. That's why dropping the tools of traditional discipline . . . is only the beginning. It's even more crucial that we overcome a preoccupation with getting compliance and instead bring students in on the process of devising and justifying ethical principles. (Kohn, 1996, p. 67)

Classroom rules can be created with language that welcomes and supports students. They can also consist of language that is blatantly adversarial. The language of rules is critical to setting the classroom tone. According to Giroux (1993, p. 24), "We need a language . . . that defends schools as democratic public spheres responsible for providing an indispensable public service to the nation; a language, in this case, that is capable of awakening the moral, political, and civic responsibilities of our youth."

The language of rules can be designed to push students out of school or to draw students in. Rules can respect or reject. Rules can support students or suppress students.

> Exclusionary practices seemed to be the customary route for teachers, who placed even moderately disruptive children outside the classroom door, banned them from gym, art, music, drama, and special assemblies, or condemned them to a corner of the classroom so they might be denounced and ridiculed. For these children—perceived as "trouble makers," "impossible," "delinquent," or "undesirable"—the school day often translated into rejection and humiliation. (Quint, 1994, p. 20)

Teachers must give some thought to the messages their rules will send students. In a democratic classroom, rules can establish mutual expectations, promote mutual respect, and be stated in ways that assume students will follow them rather than break them.

SUBSTANTIVE DUE PROCESS

To meet the standards of due process, educators consider not only the rights students have to procedural due process and adequate notice but also whether the rule is legal at its inception. This second standard for creating legal rules is called substantive due process, which describes the right citizens have to be governed by legal rules. In a school setting, as in our larger democracy, *substantive due process* becomes a broadly interpreted term applicable to a variety of issues, including rules that protect the common welfare and rules designed to support all the diverse members of a school community.

As mentioned earlier, additional imperatives command the attention of today's teachers; educators must not only be cognizant of the law but also pay attention to multicultural issues. The right to be governed by legal rules extends to all members of our society. For rules to be legal, they must also be equitable. In other words, the rules must be designed to respect the individual values and needs of the students for whom they are created.

Although a speed limit sign might be legal because its purpose is to protect the health and safety of drivers, such a broad and generic rule might not suffice in the school environment. There are some differences.

Before they are issued licenses, drivers, from any cultural and linguistic backgrounds, must take some combination of tests to ensure they understand society's expectations for how they must control their motor vehicles. They prepare for the tests using any one of several methods. Most importantly, these future drivers choose to take the test and to drive. Driving is not a compulsory activity, although it may be a necessity.

Because students from a variety of cultural backgrounds are compelled into the school setting, behavioral expectations cannot be written or stated in only one language and reflective of only one cultural perspective. Such rules, by their very nature, would not meet the standard of substantive due process. For rules to be equitable and legal, they must reflect the needs of the entire school community. The rules should be spoken or written in the language of those who are expected to follow them and designed to include rather than exclude the diverse student population represented in the schools.

Substantive due process is a subtle concept, and one that educators often misunderstand. Educators routinely make many rules, all of which are expected to meet the standard of being legal. Some educators believe that if they have given students fair notice of the rules and what will happen if a rule is broken, they have met the standard of legality. However, rules protect substantive due process, and are therefore legal, only if they are equitable. It is the content of the rules, rather than the ways in which they are implemented, that ensures substantive due process.

When rules are constructed in such a way as to violate the cultural values of students, the special needs of students, or the equal educational opportunity of students, they cannot be made legal through the process of giving notice. One example would be a rule that if students could not speak English well, they would not be eligible to take one teacher's industrial arts class. The teacher's reasoning had to do with health and safety concerns and seemed to be justified because notice had been given to all new students. However, the government cannot discriminate against individuals on the basis of their national origin. In this case the teacher could not discriminate against students who wanted to take his course but who were nonnative English speakers. Notice could never make that rule legal.

LEGAL RULES ARE EQUITABLE RULES

Teachers can construct school rules with language that is respectful of all members of the school community. Addressing the various needs and interests of students is a more subtle aspect of rule making; however, rules that intentionally or unintentionally infringe on the personal or cultural value systems of students can create unnecessary tensions between young people and their schools.

The following story was told a few years ago during a workshop on democratic management practices. The topic being addressed was the need to avoid making rules that put students at risk on the basis of who they are. One participant said that she was reminded of an incident when she was in the sixth grade. Her teacher had a rule that all students must participate in class. The workshop participant went on to say that she is a Navajo and her cultural values did not include speaking out in class but she certainly listened and paid attention. However, her teacher decided to force all the students to participate and ordered those who would not to plan and present a 10-minute speech each week for six weeks. All the students singled out by the teacher were Native Americans.

The woman who related this story said she was so angry and distressed about the prospect of having to stand up and speak in front of her classmates that she decided to use the opportunity to make a statement about how unfair she believed the rule to be. For the first speech, she devoted her time to speaking about the Holocaust of World War II. Her second speech focused on the treatment of Japanese Americans in the United States during that same war. By this time all the students in the class were becoming rebellious, realizing that one of their own was being singled out based on who she was rather than any sound rationale for participation. The teacher backed down and required no further presentations from the Native American students.

As stated in chapter 1, it is of critical importance that the rules developed for classrooms be free from the personal bias and values of the teachers; rather, the rules should reflect values commonly held by all of society. For instance, many teachers and school administrators adopt rules that students may not wear hats in school. Whether students can or should wear hats to school is a frequently discussed issue in workshops and classes on education law. However, it becomes evident that concerns about students wearing hats typically have more to do with personal or cultural bias than with promoting the common welfare.

Teachers often say they require students to remove their hats because it is not polite to wear hats indoors. That reasoning may be sound in certain cultures because for some people such a statement reflects the belief system in which they were raised. However, the belief that wearing hats is impolite represents the thinking of only one portion of society. Many adults always wear hats, particularly caps, both indoors and outdoors. Hats or caps are worn in some cases to demonstrate a commitment to a religion or to show an affiliation to a cause or a devotion to a sports team. Caps, and in some cases the slogans written on caps, reflect an individual's belief system, peer values, or family culture. Hats are worn as symbols of identity and as an act of group bonding. They are not generally worn because the person harbors a desire to be impolite.

Some believe a cap that serves as a means of group identification is one step away from gang dress. Certainly there have been fights in schools over items of clothing. The issue, though, is the fight and not the hat. Educators often respond to the problem of fighting by banning the item of clothing that seems to have caused the fight. The gangs then change the identifying color or substitute one item for another and the problem of violence in the school remains. The problem is not the hat but the behaviors engendered by the hat. It is those behaviors that need to be addressed. Students will not learn strategies for resolving conflicts within socially acceptable parameters if the only efforts made by the educators are aimed at removing the hats and not aimed at the inappropriate actions that may be spawned by the wearing of hats.

Some cultures and religions require that men wear hats, and others require women to cover their heads; many conservative religions believe a modest woman covers her hair. In daily life dressing in ways that maintain modesty can include wearing a shidor, a wig, a scarf, or a shawl, depending on the culture or the religion. Men who wish to show their devotion to God may follow their particular religious dictates by wearing hats, turbans, or yarmulkes. A school that forbids students from wearing hats would either have to make exceptions for these students or ask the students to compromise their religious values to attend school. Neither is an acceptable practice for schools.

Some students wear hats because they are undergoing chemotherapy and have lost their hair. Exceptions cannot be made for them, because their medical history is confidential. If educators make an exception for one student who has cancer, his or her medical history could well become common knowledge. Although that may happen anyway, school rules should not exacerbate an already difficult situation. The issue is to develop policies that respect individual needs and beliefs rather than creating rules that require making exceptions to honor the diversity present in a school or classroom. Again, the rules must be legal at their inception. Teachers or principals may give notice of a rule banning the wearing of hats; however, it is difficult to defend such a rule on the grounds of substantive due process when it has the potential of violating the cultural and personal needs of students.

Educators sometimes justify a rule that bans the wearing of hats on the basis that hats are by their very nature disruptive. The need for a calm learning environment would seem to supersede the individual cultural or religious needs of students. One often-repeated argument is that if one student wears a hat to school, other students will steal it and throw it around, resulting in a serious disruption. There is another way to view that argument, however.

In essence, a rule banning hats on the basis of the potential for students to treat the property with disrespect is difficult to justify. Such a rule goes to the very heart of why educators would choose to implement democratic classroom management. Classroom expectations can be used to promote a sense of personal responsibility or they can be used to discourage students from taking charge of their own behaviors. A rule that bans one student from wearing a hat because of the potential such an action has for generating inappropriate behaviors among the rest of the students has the effect of discouraging personal responsibility.

When a hat is thrown around, the disruption the students create leads educators to ban hats. However, the student who wore the hat did not create the disruption or engage in any actions that demonstrated a lack of respect for the property of others. On the other hand, the students who stole the cap did both. It seems only logical that if any consequences are to be associated with such actions they be directed at those who created the problem in the first place and not at the victim.

LOOKING AT THE MAIN IDEAS

To Ensure Substantive Due Process, the Rules You Have Created:

- Do not cause conflicts between the personal belief systems of students and the behavioral expectations in the classroom
- Do not discriminate against anyone based on special needs
- Ensure equitable treatment for all students

To ensure substantive due process, rules and expectations should protect individual rights and promote social responsibility. Rules should be constructed to help everyone learn the importance of respecting the property rights of others. It is also important for students to have opportunities to practice tolerance evidenced by their understanding that hats are worn as an expression of personal belief systems. Rules about hats can reflect the rights of students to wear them but also that hats must not block the view of students sitting behind them, that hats should not be traded for health and safety reasons, and, finally, that the slogans on hats are written in language appropriate to the school environment. Once educators understand substantive due process and its role in the development of legal rules, the next step is to discuss the language that will best establish and support a democratic climate in the classroom.

ESTABLISHING AND SUPPORTING A DEMOCRATIC CLASSROOM

Teachers can develop rules for a democratic classroom that include, support, and encourage all students. Most important, the language of the classroom rules can emphasize the permanent value shared by all students in their learning communities. Rudolf Dreikurs wrote about the need everyone has to feel a sense of permanent value. Students are no different. They, like their teachers, have good days, bad days, and days when they wish they could be anywhere else. Educators can make it clear with every word and deed that all students are permanently valued. The behaviors of the young people in our schools may at times be troublesome or even dangerous, but the individuals still have value.

The concept of permanent value is directly linked to the way the law describes the status of citizenship. Individuals who live in a free, democratic society are guaranteed the benefits of citizenship; unless an individual decides to relinquish it, that status will always be part of the individual's life. Sometimes citizens' actions might result in limits on personal freedoms, including incarceration, but that is not the same as losing citizenship. Students are citizens in the classroom; teachers can thus value students for who they are rather than fear or deride them for being different from the mainstream culture. This is the essence of what is meant by permanent value.

Democratic rules must be designed to equally support and value all members of the learning community, including teachers, and the rules must also reflect a set of standards with which everyone can feel comfortable. In other words, teachers and students should be able to abide by the democratic structure they are developing; the language of the rules reflects behaviors that both teachers and students can follow.

For instance, if teachers are accustomed to patting students on the shoulder or giving an occasional hug, then a rule about keeping your hands to yourself would be inappropriate. Unless teachers consistently model the expectations established by the class, the message is that adults can break the rules.

Another common rule that often puts teachers and students at odds is that eating and drinking are not allowed in the classroom. Although the rule may seem reasonable, it cannot be enforced sporadically. The teacher who bans eating and drinking by students but keeps a cup of coffee handy is flagrantly violating the rules.

A second-grade teacher addressed this potential problem in a truly democratic fashion. She enjoyed a cup of coffee to start her day, and yet she wanted to have a classroom governed by equitable rules. Because she did not want to forego her morning coffee but wanted to model democratic thinking, she acquired 25 plastic cups from the school's cafeteria and gave them to her students. Before the class began its morning work, the students would line up at the drinking fountain and fill their cups with water. She taught her students how to walk carefully with the cups once they were filled and how to clean up any spills. The result of this practice was that her students would quietly begin their work, sipping their water as they engaged in the morning's activities.

Some say students should not be allowed to drink or eat because of the potential for a mess. However, helping students learn how to clean up after themselves and how to react to spills is a worthwhile lesson that can be applied for the rest of an individual's life. A fifth-grade teacher, like the second-grade teacher just mentioned, permitted her students to drink from water bottles during class. She spent time working with them to learn what to do if a water bottle tipped over. When the inevitable spill did occur, the teacher would not interrupt her teaching for even one minute. While she continued to teach, her students knew where to find extra paper towels and how to mop up the water. The students had been taught how to clean up after themselves, so a spill was not a problem. Students, rather than the teacher, assumed responsibility for their actions.

THE RELATION OF RULES TO THE DEVELOPMENTAL LEVELS OF STUDENTS

Teachers can create rules that are developmentally and pedagogically appropriate. Expecting young people at any age to obey a command without question denies the very human desire to critically examine situations. In addition, asking students to follow directions the first time they hear them ignores the fact that some have auditory processing problems, some are in the process of learning English and have to mentally translate the directions before they can respond, and some may just not be paying attention at that moment. Adult learners in colleges and universities, even those in graduate school, rarely respond to a request or a piece of information the first time they hear it. It is unreasonable to expect children to always comprehend and appropriately react to a direction the first time it is given; democratic rules reflect an understanding that expectations must be appropriate to the abilities of the learners.

THE LANGUAGE OF RULES

Teachers can develop rules that convey not only expectations for behaviors but a standard of civility and tolerance to guide all classroom interactions. The time spent developing rules with students is critically important to everything else that will happen in the classroom for the rest of the year. The role this process plays in establishing a productive academic and moral climate cannot be minimized. In Lickona's (1991, p. 110) words, "Moral discipline seeks to develop students' reasoned respect for rules, the rights of others, and the teacher's legitimate authority; students' sense of responsibility for their own behavior; and their responsibility to the moral community of the classroom."

The process of establishing classroom rules might begin with the teacher talking about the importance of feeling safe during work and play. The teacher could then pose the following question: "What rules do you think we would need to help us all feel safe?" In this way the students are providing input into the rule-making process, but the moral leadership for the climate the rules will support is established by the educator. Although educators are ultimately responsible for each student's safety and success, they are not responsible for each student's behaviors. That distinction is critical to the role of rules in a democratic classroom.

It makes little sense to allow students who are ill-prepared to make sophisticated decisions that consider the needs of others and their own to establish expectations. Respect for others comes from the ability to take on other perspectives beyond our own. The ability to view the world through the eyes of another is a learned behavior that educators can model at every grade level.

USING COMPELLING STATE INTERESTS AS A FRAMEWORK FOR RULE MAKING

Judicious Discipline provides an approach to the development of a democratic, moral classroom environment that encompasses all of the criteria for rule making discussed in this chapter. The approach is based on the universal concepts of human rights and social responsibilities and is specifically grounded in the language of freedom, justice, and equality. A teacher who uses judicious discipline would begin by telling students of their human rights. Of equal importance are their social responsibilities to contribute to a classroom that is safe, healthy, and free from serious disruption. These limits on behaviors are based on the language of "compelling state interests . . . that students are denied their individual rights when their actions seriously affect the welfare of others" (Jones & Jones, 1998, p. 260).

The language of compelling state interests is sufficiently broad in scope to encompass all the activities that occur during a school day in which students, educators, and parents might be involved. The four interests address health and safety, property loss and damage, legitimate educational purpose, and freedom from serious disruption to the educational process.

LOOKING AT THE MAIN IDEAS

Using the Compelling State Interests as a Framework for Classroom Rules

- Health and safety
- Property loss and damage
- Legitimate educational purpose
- Prevention of serious disruptions to the educational process

Rules developed from these state interests are broad in scope. A common rule that students and teachers might develop for the general guideline of health and safety is "Be safe and take care of yourself and others." All-encompassing language easily expands to all situations associated with school life.

This language for rules is particularly useful when creating a classroom climate that supports all members of the learning community. Such language bridges cultures, religions, language, and family values, because it represents the common limits on freedoms that exist in any free society. Accordingly, rules based on the needs of society to protect its common health, safety, and property reflect no cultural bias but rather represent our shared interests.

As mentioned earlier, notice must be precise. The rule about health and safety may seem too vague to be of value; however, the rule is not the only notice students receive. Instead, the rule is discussed, interpreted, and examined for how it applies to a variety of school day activities. Legitimate educational purpose might similarly be interpreted as a rule that states "Do your best work." The teacher then helps students understand what doing their best means and the support available to help them achieve that goal.

After teachers explain the compelling state interests, they may plan a few grade-level-appropriate activities designed to help their students understand how the rules will play out during daily interactions. One idea is to present the compelling state interests and then have the students develop the classroom rules based on the language of the four common needs. After teachers set out the moral criteria for the rules, they can engage their students in a common effort to translate those criteria into guidelines that will sustain the learning environment throughout the year.

At the kindergarten level, teachers might use puppets and other visual aids to help students understand that even at their age they have rights and responsibilities. In elementary classrooms students can draw pictures of what both safe and unsafe classrooms look like. Students can brainstorm all the issues associated with each of the compelling state interests and post their ideas on a bulletin board. The list of issues then would serve as a reminder for appropriate behaviors in place of rules.

One classroom developed the following rules based on the compelling state interests:

1. Always help yourselves and others to be safe and healthy.
2. Take care of your own property and the property of others.
3. Do your best work.
4. Help others to do their best work.

As the students learn to balance their freedoms against the common welfare needs of others, they are learning good citizenship and developing the ability to make appropriate decisions about their own behaviors. The teacher facilitates that process.

THE PROCESS OF DEVELOPING RULES

A variety of activities can contribute to helping students develop rules. What follows are a few ideas for making the process democratic. One idea is to develop rules based on a group brainstorming session. A teacher might ask students to consider what rules would help to support a safe classroom environment. Students might suggest all sorts of ideas from not running to not hitting. Although words such as *no* and *do not* come to mind quickly, teachers can instead help students learn how to state rules in language that is more positive and in terms that are more widely applicable. Eventually students will probably suggest a rule such as "Be safe." That rule covers all activities in the classroom, on the school grounds, or even on a field trip. The teacher helps students understand all the ways in which they can act to be safe.

Kinesthetic learners and those with talent in the visual or performing arts enjoy creating skits or role-playing scenarios to depict all the ways a rule such as "Be safe" can be followed. The role-playing might include demonstrations of how to move safely in the classroom, handle equipment appropriately, and even resolve conflicts peacefully.

For students who enjoy visual arts, teachers can design activities that include drawing pictures of appropriate and inappropriate behaviors. Such pictures can be displayed around the room and used as early reminders of classroom expectations. Some students enjoy creating videotapes that help themselves and others retain information about the rules. Such videotapes can be used throughout the school year as a reminder of the rules and, even more importantly, to help students who transfer to the classroom during the school year.

Another idea is to use the compelling state interests as the basis for a class constitution. The constitution is signed and may be posted. The constitution provides a framework for the classroom based on mutual engagement by students and teachers.

Rules can also be taught through more deliberate structures. Madeline Hunter's approach to establishing behavioral expectations was through the process she called teaching "skills of independence," an approach that might not initially seem consistent with democratic management practices. Although Hunter's work has a behaviorist perspective, its systematic approach to teaching classroom expectations helps ensure the rights of students to clear notice. Hunter's ideas have stirred controversy and are seen by some as passé, but her model for teaching skills of independence (which uses a lesson plan format for teaching students the skills to function independently and successfully in a classroom) can prove to be a helpful tool for new teachers.

DEFINING RULES USING TIME, PLACE, AND MANNER

Rules help to set the tone for a classroom. How those rules play out in day-by-day—and sometimes minute-by-minute—interactions may require further explanation. The nature of the school day is so varied that it would be impossible to provide notice for everything teachers, administrators, and students might encounter. Consequently, teachers can discuss and practice parameters that are applicable to a wide variety of activities. One approach to resolving this dilemma of clear notice that covers the broad range of an average school day is the language of time, place, and manner.

Just as basing rules on compelling state interests can unite the diverse nature of the school population, so can time, place, and manner serve to define rules for a variety of settings. These three parameters can also be used to develop standards that are free from bias and focused on common needs.

One example of how time, place, and manner can be used to define parameters for behaviors is the ways educators limit talking among students. Classrooms typically have rules about talking that address voice levels, when students can talk, when they should be quiet, how students should talk, and how they should take turns, for example.

Many classrooms have a rule about not talking out of turn. Such rules are continually broken or reinforced in the most inconsistent manner. When students get excited, angry, confused, or inattentive they sometimes speak out without waiting to be recognized. Sometimes teachers ignore students' comments, listen to them but remind them of the rule, or accept their comments and say nothing about the rule. The teachers' responses can be attributed to whether the students are making valid points, are confrontational, are nonnative English speakers, are male, are considered to be troublemakers, or any number of other reasons. In other words, the rule of not talking out of turn is impossible to enforce consistently, and a teacher's response to a student who speaks out of turn often has more to do with personal bias than with what students need to learn.

Students speak with their peers and teachers many times and under different circumstances throughout the school day. A rule that students always speak in quiet tones is not applicable to all situations, just as a rule that students must always take turns when speaking might be appropriate in some circumstances but not in others. Rules that are interpreted according to appropriate time, place, and manner preserve the learning atmosphere but are also flexible and can be adapted from one activity to another.

A more reasonable approach to issues of student participation is to define the parameters according to time, place, and manner. Teachers can ask students to engage in a brainstorming activity to determine the times of the school day that require the use of quiet voices, the times that require the use of normal tones, during what times use of loud voices might be appropriate, in what places it is always appropriate to use quiet voices, in what places it is always appropriate to use normal voices, and how to get someone's attention when students are supposed to be using quiet voices.

If teachers tell students the time, place, and manner for appropriate behaviors, then students can once again shift responsibility for their actions to the teacher. As this book proceeds through a variety of management issues, one recurrent theme is the value of asking questions rather than telling students what to do. When teachers ask questions, the student must be responsible for coming up with the solution to a problem.

Accordingly, if a student is in the library and using a loud tone of voice to speak to another person, rather than giving the student a look and a "Shhhhhhh," a teacher can ask whether the library is an appropriate place for that voice level. Such a question usually ends the situation. Students who see such a question as an invitation to a power struggle need further information and interventions. Power struggles are discussed in chapter 6 of this book.

Teachers who use the language of time, place, and manner find that it is useful for explaining the applications of rules, particularly when teachers are working with students who have been diagnosed as severely emotionally disturbed (McEwan, Gathercoal, & Nimmo, 1997). Some teachers display the words *time, place,* and *manner* on their bulletin boards and some have even made themselves T-shirts that read T.P.M. as reminders for their students. If a student is acting inappropriately, the teacher can simply prompt the student with T.P.M. Because the teacher has clearly established the behavioral expectations for the class and discussed time, place, and manner with the students, such a prompt usually quickly resolves a potential problem.

Time, place, and manner establish a simple, straightforward gauge that helps students determine for themselves whether their actions are appropriate, not only at school but anywhere. The three terms are applicable to all students in all situations, regardless of individual differences or special needs.

A FEW WORDS ABOUT CONSEQUENCES

Although I discuss the use of consequences in other chapters, it is important to at least mention them here. As discussed earlier, many teachers think of rules and consequences as being closely linked. Although consequences might be necessary at some point, rules and consequences are two separate concepts. Equitable and reasonable democratic rules establish a safe and productive learning community. Sometimes students need help understanding how they fit within the community, sometimes they test the community, and sometimes they rebel.

Having one set of rules backed by one set of consequences limits the ability of educators to effectively address all the reasons why a classroom rule might be broken. Some teachers believe that rules can only be enforced with consistent consequences. In other words, the same consequence is applied regardless of the behavior students exhibit.

But teachers who are committed to maintaining democratic classrooms know that being consistent does not mean treating everyone the same. At the same time, consistency does mean that all issues and problems are addressed in some fashion, as is any learning problem. Teachers who are helping students learn to read might employ a variety of strategies to reach all the individual needs present in the classroom. Similarly, when teachers are helping students learn appropriate behaviors, there might be a variety of effective strategies to assist students in their understanding of how to respect the rights of others and at the same time be responsible for their own behaviors. Teachers can employ management strategies that include the use of creative responses to the problems that might arise during the school day.

The fear of being perceived as inconsistent often drives teachers to impose consequences that seem inappropriate. To avoid this situation, teachers might share their vision of the classroom with students. Sharing the vision is done partly in the process of establishing rules and partly in letting students know what options will be explored to solve a problem.

Teachers might begin the conversation by talking about how each student is an individual with special needs and particular interests. If students need help with math, the help might take a variety of forms. Similarly, if students need help managing their own behaviors, how the teacher responds might also vary for each individual. Teachers can let students know that all problems will be addressed, but they may be addressed differently because the students are not the same. Equality will lie in the fact that teachers will strive to meet every need and resolve every issue in a manner that manifests respect and protects dignity.

SUMMARY

The foundation for a democratic classroom begins with rules based on law and designed to respect the diversity of individual students. Rules are a means of imparting shared societal values reasonably and appropriately (both pedagogically and developmentally). Democratic classroom rules establish the moral criteria for the learning community in that they are constructed to reflect the common values of a democracy.

In the scenario that introduced this chapter, Andre began his year full of enthusiasm. His error was in assuming that his enthusiasm alone would create a classroom environment in which all his students would be actively engaged. The goal is a worthy one, but as with any goal, it can be achieved only through careful planning and attention to the details. A critical detail in the process is the creation of a caring, safe learning environment supported by reasonable and equitable rules.

APPLYING THE CONCEPTS

Now that we have examined some of the theory and practice of creating classroom rules, develop three or four classroom rules for yourself. Then ask yourself the following:

1. Are the rules legal?
2. Do the rules include any practices that might be discriminatory?
3. Do the rules establish a clear, moral tone of mutual respect?
4. Are they rules you can be comfortable following?

Explain your answers to the questions.

CHAPTER 3

Revisiting Classroom Rules

CHAPTER OBJECTIVES

After you have finished reading this chapter, you should be able to:

◇ Understand the legal rationale for revisiting rules on a consistent, sometimes daily, basis
◇ Apply strategies, such as class meetings, that help educators to revisit rules
◇ Demonstrate the meaning of tort liability and the role it plays in the need to regularly restate classroom rules
◇ Incorporate revisiting rules into a variety of classroom strategies such as stating expectations in lesson plans, structuring one-on-one conferences, and other practical applications

Scenario

Janelle enjoyed developing democratic classroom rules with her fourth-grade class. Together she and her students discussed the reasons for the rules they would have, crafted specific language for the rules, and incorporated them into a classroom constitution. Then Janelle laminated the constitution and posted it on a bulletin board. Assuming that her students all understood the classroom expectations, she launched into her teaching.

Within a few weeks, though, she found that her students were exhibiting more and more disruptive behaviors, including everything from talking out of turn and moving around the classroom to sharpening pencils at inappropriate times. She was having to interrupt her lessons more frequently to quiet the students. To keep their attention, she tried using rhythmic patterns of hand clapping, ringing a bell, and flicking the lights off and on. These strategies each worked a few times but quickly lost their effectiveness.

Finally, she decided to try a few behaviorist strategies, reinforcing appropriate actions with tokens such as stickers and responding to inappropriate behaviors by recording the names of students on the board, followed by check marks to indicate the levels of punishment students would receive. Janelle had not initially intended to use these strategies; although they seemed to give her a greater level of control, she found she had to monitor the students' behaviors even more closely than before to consistently reward appropriate behaviors and discourage inappropriate behaviors. In a conversation with a colleague she expressed her disillusionment: Kids want stickers so I guess that's what I have to give them. "I guess those democratic ideals just do not work in the real world." Although the rules had been carefully developed, Janelle was leaving out an important piece of democratic management.

Questions

What do you think went wrong in Janelle's classroom? What have you seen teachers do or what have you done to prevent these problems?

Discussion

The scenario describes another situation that often occurs in classrooms. The teacher in the opening scenario planned and implemented several democratic practices designed to support a classroom climate built on equity and mutual respect. But Janelle soon felt as if she were forced into using practices with which she was not comfortable. The problem is that after patiently working with the students to develop a framework of expectations and responsibilities, Janelle made the mistake of believing there was no more work to be done in the area of management. The students had given their input into the language of the rules and seemed to understand the rationale behind the rules; the teacher believed that it was reasonable to expect them to abide by the rules.

Missing from Janelle's planning were a variety of deliberate strategies for revisiting rules during the school day. Although Janelle taught a fourth-grade class, there is a compelling need to revisit rules on a regular basis at every grade level. For health and safety and other legitimate reasons, the process of revisiting class behavioral expectations is a basic tool of any sound management plan. Continually reinforcing rules and expectations helps to ensure students will have the information and understanding that supports their ability to make appropriate decisions about their own behaviors regardless of the situation.

PROTECTING THE HEALTH AND SAFETY OF STUDENTS

Chapter 2 discussed the constitutional rights of students, which entitle them to know the rules in the classroom. We begin this chapter by looking at another legal concern associated with rule making: tort liability. As stated previously, teachers are the government's representatives when they are in their classrooms. As such, they are legally responsible for protecting the rights of their students. In part, the rights of students are protected by giving students notice of the rules, ensuring their procedural due process rights, and taking care to craft rules that are legal, which helps to ensure students' rights to substantive due process. Teachers who act in ways that infringe on or interfere with the personal freedoms of the young people with whom they work may be held liable for doing so.

At the same time, teachers are also responsible for protecting the physical well-being of their students and may be liable if they fail to adequately protect students from harm. The legal term for this responsibility is *tort liability*, which is basically the level of personal responsibility an individual carries for an injury. According to LaMorte (1996, p. 373), "A tort is a civil wrong in which one suffers loss as a result of the improper conduct of another. This branch of law is concerned with the compensation of losses suffered by an individual owing to an intentional or negligent act."

People who hear the term *liability* immediately think of lawsuits; teachers may be sued if students are injured or their rights are violated. Some prudent and reasonable practices, if adopted, may prevent teachers from being sued successfully. However, the most important reason to develop and revisit rules regularly is to try to prevent students from being injured. Students can expect that every reasonable step has been taken to protect their health and safety. As mentioned in chapter 2, health and safety is one of the compelling state interests that can be translated into classroom rules that protect the physical and mental well-being of the learning community.

> If student rights are being balanced with a potential student injury, it is far better for educators to err on the side of health and safety. Students will receive lifetime benefits from health and safety rules that are designed with society's welfare in mind. To be effective, these rules should be all inclusive, conspicuous, and rigorously enforced. (Gathercoal, 1993, p. 66)

Educators, by the very nature of their profession, must see protecting the well-being of the students with whom they work as their primary mission.

Courses in educational law often focus on the issues of when, how, and why teachers can be sued for a particular action or decision. Teachers can be sued for the same things as anyone else. If an injury occurs in an educational setting and a lawsuit is brought, the questions asked to determine the facts of the case concern whether the educators involved did everything possible to prevent harm to the students in their care.

Several terms and a body of information are applied to the facts of an injury case to determine how issues associated with tort liability might be resolved. A detailed discussion of the terms and issues is beyond the scope of this chapter. However, we review here some basic legal expectations for how teachers exercise care for their students.

Ensuring the safety of students begins with the simple and sensible steps a reasonable person would take to protect those around him or her, particularly those for whom the person has responsibility. This discussion of tort liability begins with a scene many have experienced.

Imagine that some children have invited other children from the neighborhood to play in their backyard. An adult, who also lives in the house, is in the kitchen preparing lunch. Occasionally the adult looks out the window to make sure the children are safe and might even ask them to settle down. This is a pretty typical scene, and no one would find it curious that the adult present is inside the house and not directly supervising the children outside in the backyard.

But if we change the scene a bit and suppose that this private home is also a day care center and that the children who are playing in the backyard are there because their parents have enrolled them in the center, the expectations for the behaviors of the adult in charge also change. Now it would no longer be appropriate for the adult who is responsible to be inside while the children are playing outside. The adult's expected role has changed, and he or she would need to be in close proximity to the children. The expectations for the adult's actions have shifted from less to more responsibility because all of society draws a clear distinction between the supervision an adult renders in a private home situation and the increased level of supervision expected of day care workers. Although the general setting did not change, the level of responsibility for the children's well-being altered dramatically when their reason for being there shifted. This heightened level of societal expectations for adult behavior in response to the circumstances of the situation and the level of professional responsibility is called duty of care.

Another way to understand the term *duty of care* is to understand the questions that help to define the term. The questions all relate to the role of educators in relation to the children in their proximity. For instance, some defining questions might include the following: What is the duty of care kindergarten teachers should assume when their students are engaged in a variety of learning center activities? What is the duty of care fifth-grade teachers should assume when their students are dissecting owl pellets with scalpels? What is the duty of care seventh-grade physical education teachers should assume when their students are playing soccer? What is the duty of care high school teachers should assume when their senior chemistry students are mixing chemicals for an experiment? What would society expect their various duties to be? What elements particular to their situations would need to be carefully supervised?

To emphasize the importance of the final question, let us return to the scene of the children playing in the backyard of the day care center. When the scenario shifted from describing activities occurring in the backyard of a private home to those of a day care center, the role of the adult changed as well. Society would say that the adult present in the day care situation must be in the backyard, directly supervising the children. In short, it is our shared social conscience that determines duty of care for teachers, doctors, firefighters, lawyers, and others responsible for the well-being of others.

Once the duty of care assumed by the adult present has been determined, how thoroughly the adult fulfills this duty is called the *standard of care*.

> For the most part, the standard of care a teacher must exercise to avoid liability is defined as that of a "reasonable and prudent" person. It is that degree of care a reasonable and prudent teacher, charged with like duties, would exercise under similar circumstances. (LaMorte, 1996, p. 390)

A prudent and reasonable standard of care can be evidenced by the pains teachers take to make sure their settings are free from hazards and their students understand how to operate within the classroom in ways that preserve their health and safety. A prudent standard of care can also be seen and heard in consistent, daily reminders of classroom expectations.

But sometimes teachers omit these careful reminders because they do not want to seem heavy-handed or too structured. In one case, a fifth-grade teacher began the school year with a written getting-to-know-you activity that would immediately proceed students' first recess of the school year. Before going to recess, the students would clean up the room. The teacher carefully reviewed the expectations about how paper should be recycled in their classroom. She had her students practice recycling with the paper used in the activity. The teacher even had one student model walking to the recycling box and putting the paper in it.

Then it was time to go to recess. The teacher had students practice how to line up at the door. She also mentioned that there were rules for the playground but then said there was no need to review them because the students already knew them. Her statement may have been an attempt to not overburden her students with too many rules; however, the potential for injury on the playground would make the review of recess rules perhaps the most important information shared that morning. Given the age of the students, assuming that they had retained all the expectations for safe playground behavior over the course of the summer and have the ability to act appropriately if they get angry or feel hurt was at best optimistic. Teachers can establish a reasonable standard of care only if they carefully address all aspects of the school day and take steps to ensure that students understand the information.

DEVELOPING A REASONABLE STANDARD OF CARE

Three practical steps can be followed in constructing a prudent standard of care, and they all require careful planning. A reasonable standard of care, at the very least, expects teachers to make plans, share their plans, and stick to their plans. Although these three steps are critically important for the safety and well-being of students, they are often absent from curricular and extracurricular planning in the educational setting.

Step One: Make a Plan

Educators make health and safety plans for their classrooms that cover both routine and special school activities. A little forethought is a good thing because a range of activities and actions occur on a regular basis. Students move around inside the school building, arrive at and depart from the building, play on the surrounding grounds, eat food on the premises, and engage in a number of activities, some of which are more dangerous than others, on a daily basis. Although the school day may not always go as planned, educators usually can develop reasonable and prudent plans that encompass the majority of actions likely to occur.

Plans that cover health and safety should be comprehensive, which means they should be sufficiently inclusive to protect students from their environment and to protect their environment from them. As mentioned earlier, plans vary depending on the subject matter, the classroom conditions, and the range of students' activities.

Teachers can create plans that reflect students' developmental levels and their breadth of activities. Specific plans help teachers to deal with any reasonably expected situations. A high school agriculture class that requires several field-based activities must have a plan that covers activities in both the classroom and outdoor settings. A sixth-grade language arts class requires a plan primarily focused on moving safely in and around the classroom. A second-grade self-contained classroom must have a plan that covers a broad range of curriculum projects but also extends itself to such things as safe behavior during recess and snack time. The plans have some common elements, given that they are all designed for educational settings, but the plans also contain unique aspects that reflect each grade level's particular needs.

Before educators greet their students on the first day of school, they spend some time brainstorming all the information students need to function safely as they go about their daily activities at school. The initial planning should be open, because the items can be pared down or condensed later as the plans begin to take on their final forms. One way to begin formulating a plan is by asking questions such as the following: How will the students move around the room? How will the students enter and leave the room? How will materials be distributed? How will students have access to classroom materials? Will students be eating in the room? Will students have their own desks or need to access materials from a locker? Will students be handling potentially dangerous equipment?

Looking at the Main Ideas

Protect Health and Safety by Taking the Following Actions:

- Make a plan that is developmentally appropriate for the age group you are teaching and specific to your classroom circumstances and subject matter requirements.

- Share the plan in a manner appropriate to a variety of learning styles and in as many languages as are represented in your classroom. (Remember to share the plan with all the stakeholders, but especially with students, parents, and administrators.)

- Stick to the plan; a spontaneous romp in the snow should be carefully weighed against the responsibility of teachers to protect the health and safety of students.

At this point some readers may be wondering how teaching fits into the day with so many rules and expectations to be reviewed. Because most of the rules overlap, once students understand the concepts of health and safety, property loss and damage, serious disruption, and time, place, and manner, they can more easily make decisions that support the learning environment and their peers.

Step Two: Share the Plan

Although these plans are initially shared as part of notice, review on a regular basis meets a prudent and reasonable standard of care. I mentioned in chapter 2 that it is not uncommon for teachers to have a vision for how their classrooms will work but fail to share that vision with students. Carefully imparting information about rules not only ensures notice has been given to students but also helps educators to be prudent and reasonable professionals. The processes of developing, sharing, and sticking to a plan are three essential components of a pragmatic, systematic method for protecting the health and safety of students. If a student is injured in a classroom or in any other setting in which a teacher is in charge, everyone experiences emotional trauma. Unfortunately, subsequent litigation is possible. A thoroughly articulated plan for protecting students during a variety of school activities, as well as the documentation showing how completely the plan was shared and how carefully the plan was followed, should certainly help to mitigate against successful lawsuits.

All potential stakeholders have the right to see and hear the plans. The list of stakeholders would, of course, begin with students, administrators, and parents. Depending on the nature of the plan it may also be shared with classified personnel, the librarian, the school counselor, the school nurse, bus drivers, and school board members.

Sharing the plan with parents may take a variety of forms and meet with various levels of success. Newsletters or individual memos designed by teachers or school administrators are one way to provide notice and share the plan; however, relying on this method as the sole means of communication between families and the school may not be sufficient to adequately share the plan.

If the only method teachers use to communicate with parents is through the notices sent home with students, educators have to hope that the information reaches its destination in one piece, is given to parents, is found by parents, is read by parents, and is written in the parents' primary language and that parents have the ability to read and understand the material.

Another option, of course, is to mail the information directly to the students' homes. Mail can be an effective way to communicate with parents, but there are potential problems. Families may move frequently, and mail will take time to catch up to them, students may intercept mail before parents get home, or mail coming from schools may look unimportant and, as a result, not receive the attention it deserves. Phone calls are effective because teachers know conclusively that they have communicated directly with parents. However, some parents do not have a phone, do not speak English as a primary language, or need telecommunications device for the deaf/teletypewriter (TDD/TTY) equipment to communicate.

Teachers may need to schedule home visits for parents who do not have phones. Home visits may be a rich opportunity for educators to bridge cultural, economic, or language barriers between the home and school. Parents who do not speak English as a primary language still have a right and need to know about their students' education. Teachers who have experience in teaching nonnative English speakers, who speak second languages, or who are themselves nonnative English speakers may be effective at breaking through language barriers with parents. If teachers lack these skills, they might be able to locate a person within the community to serve as a translator. In addition, some school districts make TDD/TTY equipment available to teachers.

Parents' nights and open houses, special school events typically scheduled in the early fall, provide excellent opportunities to share the plans. It is best to write down rules and expectations so that parents or guardians who are visual learners will be able to follow the information being presented. Written information translated into the languages spoken by nonnative English speakers is helpful. The written material can also be sent home to parents who were unable to attend the open house. If combinations of the mentioned strategies have been employed, educators have done their part to share the plan with students' family members or guardians.

Teachers can share plans in ways that meet the diverse needs of the students in classrooms or other settings by translating or interpreting them for students who speak a primary language other than English, who have auditory or visual disabilities, or who have learning disabilities that take the form of auditory processing difficulties. The professional imperative to protect the rights of students extends to equitable practices of notice.

Step Three: Stick to the Plan

Sticking to the plan is often the most difficult step to remember and the one probably violated most often. One Oregon teacher, a creative and imaginative person whose students enjoy being in her class, has a sign outside her classroom that reads "The Curriculum Is Subject to Change Depending on the Weather, the Time of Day, or the Bird on the Windowsill." It is a lovely thought and certainly reflects the desire teachers have to take advantage of their inspirations and explore the teachable moments that present themselves.

However, the spirit of inspiration must be tempered by prudent and reasonable decision making. For example, a sudden, unexpected snowfall might provide a reason to abandon the lesson plans for the day and instead explore snow through children's literature, writing activities, or a historical perspective on the effects of snow on migration or war. In social studies it might be a reason to spend the day exploring the influence of snow on culture, dress, and foods. Estimating the number of snowflakes falling per minute might help reinforce mathematics concepts. All of those ideas fall within the realm of curriculum, are adjustable to grade levels, and are well within the parameters of an appropriate educational plan. Less appropriate is abandoning whatever lesson is in progress and inviting the students to go outside and play in the snow. If an injury occurs while the children are outside playing in the snow, it would be difficult to show an educational purpose or that an educator's plan for health and safety was followed.

Some educators believe the need to stick to plans means that they must abandon spontaneity. Although that is not necessarily the case, the desire to abandon a plan in the excitement of the moment must be tempered by the compulsory nature of the students' presence in the classroom. Just as students are compelled into a teacher's classroom, so are the parents compelled to relinquish their students' physical, emotional, and academic well-being to the teacher for a considerable time during the school year. Parents thus have every right to expect that educators will view the compulsory nature of their students' presence with a sense of solemn responsibility. The law requires students to spend weekdays in a public school setting, and parents can certainly expect that health and safety concerns will be the motivating force behind most decisions made by educators.

Plans can be tailored to the needs of each situation. These plans are based on the relative certainty of what happens on an average school day. Other events, although infrequent during the typical school day, may well be anticipated. Snow will fall, wind will blow, news events of all kinds will occur, and daily schedules will change. Teachers can reasonably imagine that the odds are as much in favor of the unexpected happening as the expected. A file of what-if activities can be brought out when new and unusual events occur.

Accordingly, educators can share a plan that includes some what-if information, such as what a self-contained fourth-grade class might do when snow falls, or how a sophomore social studies class might address the unexpected death of a major political figure. Sticking to the plan does not have to mean a rigid response to unexpected events. Alternative plans allow educators to respond to unusual occurrences in ways that are thoughtful and do not put students at risk.

No plans or strategies will ever prevent some students from being injured, even though educators try to keep that from happening. There is also no guarantee that a lawsuit will not be brought against a teacher whose student has been injured while in the teacher's care. However, a sound and comprehensive plan shared with all the stakeholders and carefully adhered to will go a long way toward preventing unfortunate outcomes.

To summarize, then, substantive due process requires that the rules address the needs of all students and do not discriminate against any. Notice means students have the right to know what is expected of them in all situations. Tort liability can be the unfortunate outcome of not acting in prudent and reasonable ways that protect students from harm. Carefully crafted rules that are continually reviewed and discussed can help students to be safe, healthy, and productive.

ANY MANAGEMENT SYSTEM MUST INCLUDE FREQUENT RULE REMINDERS

Classrooms rooted in democratic educational theory would involve students in making behavioral management decisions all of the time. However, achieving that ideal requires not only thoughtful planning but also careful consideration of the students' developmental levels and cultural and family values. All of these conditions are pertinent to whether students can successfully exercise thoughtful control over their actions in ways that preserve and protect the general welfare. Given that so much is at stake and so much diversity is present, a safe and productive classroom can only be ensured if the expectations are revisited in a variety of ways and on a regular basis.

The more teachers rely on classroom management practices derived from behaviorist theories, the more likely they are to regularly revisit rules as part of their daily interactions with students. They must do so because their management practices are successful only if they assume responsibility for the behaviors in the class. It is up to the teacher to catch students being good or breaking rules, to tell students when their voices are too loud, and so forth. Students are left with only two options: to follow the rules or not. The reminders about the rules are constant.

Behavioral judgments are left to the discretion of teachers, and students are required to obey or suffer the consequences for their failure to do so. When praise or punishment is based on the teacher's judgment of what is appropriate, then the teacher is saying that he or she is the sole determiner of which behaviors meet classroom standards. Because the teacher is in charge, the reminders of the rules must occur frequently.

Cognitive or democratic management practices, on the other hand, provide a framework in which students can learn to make appropriate behavioral decisions. Unfortunately, teachers are sometimes misled into thinking that the framework they have developed has provided students with sufficient information for managing their own behaviors and, once it is in place, will serve to help everyone make appropriate personal decisions for the rest of the year. Teachers must remember, though, that these students are learning to be socially responsible individuals just as they are learning to be mathematicians, scientists, gymnasts, or authors.

Teachers engaged in explaining academic skills would probably not rely on a single expository lecture to ensure that students understand a critical piece of curriculum. The more likely scenario is that they will initially share the information and then consistently revisit it during practice activities, laboratory work, additional lessons, and other curriculum exercises designed to help students grasp the concepts being taught. It seems only reasonable to approach the teaching and learning of management skills in exactly the same fashion.

A democratic classroom begins with the premise that students can make good decisions about their behavior if the information they need to accomplish that task is readily available. Once the classroom rules have been mutually agreed to and, depending on the age of the students, prominently displayed on a bulletin board, the real work begins. In some classes, such as the one described in the opening scenario, the rules are never mentioned again. But continually revisiting behavioral expectations is a critical part of any good classroom management approach. A teacher who has decided to use democratic management strategies must be willing to devote the same amount of time to reviewing classroom expectations as the teacher who uses behaviorist strategies. The difference lies in the manner in which the teacher reviews the expectations.

REVISITING RULES THROUGH A VARIETY OF STRATEGIES

Students may feel more or less inclined to conform to classroom expectations regardless of which strategies are being used. When using democratic practices, the single most important element for maintaining a safe, caring learning environment is to revisit rules before beginning any activity. Then, if a rule is broken, teachers can ask students to gauge their behaviors against the previously stated expectations as opposed to telling students to stop the behavior.

Sometimes teachers review the rules only after a serious disruption; then the rules are typically reviewed at the same time consequences are meted out. Classes can get out of control because some students are having very bad days or because the teacher tries to ignore inappropriate behaviors when they first occur and might be more quickly and easily corrected. Instead, the teacher waits until the minor problems incite anger and a major response is required to settle the situation.

Such teachers seem reluctant to be thought of as mean or bad. However, their hesitation to quickly redirect students who are not making appropriate behavioral decisions can easily be interpreted as a lack of authority. Teachers may stop, look in the direction of the disruption, wait, try to make eye contact with the students who are not paying attention, and perhaps even smile; however, they are not providing clear redirection, and if students are not attending to the class activities, they are unlikely to pick up on their teachers' body language.

Some teachers hesitate to stop behaviors because they do not want to single students out—a worthy consideration. Students who are singled out in front of their peers for behavioral or academic corrections often feel the sting of that embarrassment for years. However, another approach to resolving the interruptions would be to say: "Let us please look again at the rules for our activity. I want all of you to ask yourselves if you are doing what you said you would do. We will take a minute for a self-check." In most cases this sort of general reminder is enough to settle things down. The point is that inappropriate behaviors should not be ignored until they become worse and the student is in real trouble.

ONE-ON-ONE PROBLEM SOLVING

In addition to redirecting the entire class when a disruption occurs, teachers can personally meet with the students who were misbehaving to solve the problem one-on-one. Although it is more expedient to review rules with the entire class, it is sometimes necessary to privately review rules with individual students. (Consequences for inappropriate actions are discussed in a later chapter.) Sometimes taking students aside for a private review of the rules can help to keep problems from recurring and prevent future difficulties. Sitting down with students during a time when the other students are working on some task would allow a measure of privacy for the conversation. The teacher could begin by discussing the problem from his or her perspective and then ask the students about their perceptions of the problem. The teacher listens to students' comments respectfully, without dismissing or judging them.

After both teacher and students have talked about the problems from their perspectives, they review the rules that were broken. The teacher needs to know if the students really grasp the purpose of the rules or if they are having trouble understanding what is expected. Then the students and teacher can reach an agreement about how to handle such situations in the future. The students can be expected to commit to behaving in ways that are helpful to the class and not disruptive. It may be useful to record the students' comments as contracts and to serve as visual reminders of the agreements reached. The teacher may use this discussion time to learn why the students were disruptive and make some changes in the procedures for future meetings. These one-on-one conferences are not meant to place blame but to provide a time for both parties to work together to resolve a problem. The issue is not who is at fault but rather how to help students learn to assume responsibility for their own behaviors.

REVISITING RULES TO REINFORCE HEALTH AND SAFETY

Given the need to protect the health and safety of students, teachers must sometimes intercede quickly to stop the actions of students. A physical education teacher shared the following story about her sixth-grade class. At the beginning of the lesson, her students were each asked to get a piece of equipment from the gym's storage cupboard. The students immediately broke into a run. The teacher blew her whistle, a signal to freeze that students had been taught at the beginning of the year. When the students stopped, the teacher quietly asked them to walk back to where she was standing.

Once they had gathered around her she said, "We are having a health and safety problem. I want you to think about what that problem might be. Do not say anything right now. Just think. When you have an idea, raise your hands." Hands began to go up a few at a time. When most of the students had raised their hands, the teacher asked one student to talk about the problem. The student said that everyone was running, which was not safe. The teacher thanked the student and then asked the class to try it again. This time they walked quietly to the cupboard and selected the necessary equipment. The teacher was relying on the cognitive abilities of the students to remember previous discussions about health and safety. She did not lecture or scold and kept calm and quiet. She refocused her students, resolved the problem, and acted appropriately within her duty of care.

PREVENTING SERIOUS DISRUPTIONS

Some classroom concerns relate to health and safety, whereas others relate to preventing serious disruptions of the educational process. One fifth-grade teacher had a classroom located off a large common area in one wing of the elementary school. She had planned to take her students out into this larger area for some scheduled presentations. However, four or five other classrooms were located in the vicinity, so excessive noise in this central location would have disturbed the other students and teachers nearby.

Before the teacher took her students out of their classroom, she asked students what they needed to remember about being out in the court. Students quickly offered that they should all listen while others are speaking, keep their voices low because classes are going on around them, and stay together in a group. The teacher thanked the students for their input, and they went out into the common area. After about 15 minutes, some of the students began to engage in side conversations. The teacher immediately stopped the activity to remind everyone about the expectations to which they had all agreed. She asked for volunteers who could restate the three rules that had been discussed before leaving the classroom. Students quickly restated the rules, quieted down, and continued with the presentations.

The teacher did not wait for the situation to escalate to a serious disruption but handled the problem early so that the activity could go on and trouble could be avoided. The strategy she used was only effective because she had taken time to review the rules before they left the classroom. As a result, everyone knew what they were expected to do, and the teacher only had to remind students of their earlier conversation. This same technique is equally successful before any class endeavor, whether it is moving from one area to another, retrieving items from a locker, going out on the playground, taking a field trip, or participating in any other activity.

REVISITING RULES THROUGH LESSON PLANS

The practice of revisiting rules can be embedded in lesson plans. If a class is about to engage in a group activity, the teacher might begin by saying the following: "We will be working in groups on this research activity. Here are some roles for group members that I thought would be helpful. Can you think of other roles? When we are working in groups, what do we need to consider in terms of our voice levels? How do we act in our groups if someone has an opinion different from ours? How do we resolve a conflict in ways that do not hurt each other's feelings?"

In this example, the teacher is revisiting some important management strategies embedded in how the groups will interact. Individual roles within the group, the rationale for soft voices, and respecting different opinions were addressed when the class set expectations in September. The teacher is just taking a few minutes in this situation to review the expectations. Then, if voices begin to rise, the teacher can stop the class and remind students of the behaviors they previously discussed.

There are many effective strategies for revisiting class rules during lessons. One middle school teacher used her own behaviors to help students revisit rules and expectations. The teacher helped her students form groups for an activity she had planned. Before the class began to work, the teacher reviewed rules the class had developed together for appropriate group behaviors. About six rules addressed issues such as noise levels, cooperation, and respect. One rule was that group members should stay with their groups and not wander around the room. After this brief review, the teacher joined one of the groups and the activity began.

◈ LOOKING AT THE MAIN IDEAS
Revisiting Rules through Lesson Plan Design

- The more equipment students will be using during a lesson, the more a teacher needs to carefully review all health and safety concerns associated with the tools and instruments required.

- If students are working in groups, rules for group behaviors should be reviewed—even if the review is very brief.

- Teachers cannot assume students will remember the rules, no matter how late in the school year it is. It is always wise to spend a minute or two reviewing expectations applicable to a particular lesson.

The next day, the teacher reviewed the rules again and had the students use the rules to assess how well they had done in their groups. When she reached the rule about staying with the group she recalled that during the activity she had been called to the door by another faculty member. She commented to the students that she had not been a very good group member and did not follow the rule. The students agreed, and the conversation went on. By not drawing a distinction between her reasons for leaving the group and reasons a student might use for the same behavior, the teacher was making certain that the students understood that everyone in the class was an equal member of the learning community and mutually responsible for the success of everyone else.

REVISITING RULES TO SUPPORT A MORAL CLIMATE

The time spent reviewing rules can also be used to reinforce the moral climate of the classroom. Even a situation as mundane as giving a spelling test can be an opportunity to emphasize moral values such as caring and respect. A teacher could transition into the spelling test by saying, "We all work hard to be successful. Please think about how to listen so each of you and those around you can be successful." Then, if students start to talk, a teacher can stop the review and ask students if they are helping themselves and others to succeed. Students may need a minute or two to consider this idea and then continue with the activity.

Consistent behavioral reminders can be part of the normal daily interactions rather than intrusive. One example of how to incorporate reminders is the technique used by a teacher of a blended fourth- and fifth-grade class of students who are culturally, economically, and academically diverse. They take a great deal of nurturing to help them achieve and focus on the various learning tasks included in their day. The fourth graders in the class continue, or "loop," with the same teacher for their fifth-grade year.

The teacher initiates the school year with an activity that invites student interaction while carefully reviewing all the classroom rules. She draws on the expertise of students who have been with her for the previous year to review the rules and to reestablish the moral tone for the classroom. The teacher begins the activity by asking the new students if they have any questions about what will happen over the course of the year and incorporates expectations for appropriate behaviors into her answers.

For instance, one question she is often asked is whether students can write on their desks. The teacher's response to that question will cover a number of property issues and moral and ethical principles. She typically begins by saying that writing on the desks is fine but then goes on to discuss the property loss and damage issues. Desks can only be written on with pencil, the tops of the desks need to be cleaned each Friday, no holes can be gouged in the desks, and existing holes should not be enlarged.

Then the teacher reminds students of the moral structure of the classroom by discussing appropriate and inappropriate words and pictures for students to include in their desktop drawings. She also discusses some guidelines for students who might want to use the names of other classmates in their doodles. The teacher makes it clear that using the name of another person is appropriate only if permission had been granted by that person. This last item helps to protect the confidentiality of students and their emotional well-being. The teacher carefully reviews several classroom expectations in this manner, talking about all aspects of the classroom and how students will be interacting with her and each other throughout the year.

LEARNING TO WATCH STUDENTS

New teachers are often so excited to teach their first lessons that their energies are entirely focused on what they are going to say next. Sometimes they are working from a written lesson plan and paying attention to the scripted words rather than the students. Although reviewing expectations before a lesson is a sound management strategy, it is of equal importance to scan the class on a regular basis to see whether students are paying attention. If they do begin to drift, the lesson may be confusing, boring, or frustrating.

If teachers see that students are becoming inattentive or restless, it is appropriate to stop the lesson and talk about the fact that the students seem to be off task. Then a teacher can ask students if they are following the material. One way to do so is to pause and ask students in a friendly tone "How are we doing?" It is important to follow that question with a pause to indicate to students that an answer is expected and that their input is welcome. Students usually say that they are okay and the lesson can proceed. However, sometimes students have questions about the information being discussed and may have been reluctant to ask questions for fear that questions would seem silly or unimportant. Giving students an invitation to respond encourages them to ask about information they want to review or about which they are uncertain.

BEGIN WITH A QUESTION

A common thread runs through all of the examples given: the strategy of reviewing rules by asking students about the expectations rather than telling them. Although lecturing students might be a faster, easier way of imparting behavioral information, asking questions is a much more effective way to help students assume responsibility for the information. The students already have the information because they participated in the process of developing the classroom rules and expectations. Now the questions asked of them will help them to assume responsibility for remembering what they have already agreed should happen in the classroom.

LOOKING AT THE MAIN IDEAS

Ask Students about Expectations Rather Than Telling Them

Some questions might be the following:

- Is that a safe and healthy way to _____?
- Is that action helping others around you to learn?
- What should you be doing now?
- How are you doing?

If students cannot recall a rule, they might not have heard the information the first time or misunderstood what was being asked of them. By asking questions the teacher can ascertain whether there is a problem with communication or comprehension. If the teacher simply repeats the original expectation before a lesson or after a problem has occurred, misunderstanding will remain. Unless teachers ask students for the information, there is no way of knowing where the communication has broken down. The process of asking questions can be successful at any grade level if it is approached in developmentally appropriate ways. The simple strategy of asking questions rather than telling students what to do places the accountability for knowing the rules on the students rather than on the teacher.

USING CLASS MEETINGS TO REVISIT RULES

Democratic classrooms are supported by democratic practices. That may seem obvious, but many classrooms initially set up to run in a democratic fashion lack an appropriate forum that supports and invites opportunities to openly discuss respect, responsibility, and mutual caring among students. One way to encourage an honest discussion of such issues is through a class meeting. A class meeting occurs at the same time every day or every week, depending on the age of the students and their needs. It can also occur whenever an issue needs to be addressed immediately.

As with any other process, establishing expectations for class meetings helps them to run smoothly. A few basic criteria include making sure everyone has an opportunity to share opinions, everyone is listened to with respect, and issues, not people, are the topics of conversations.

Students at every grade level from preschool to high school can benefit from participating in class meetings. Regardless of cultural heritage, class meetings reinforce the importance of dialogue and discussion when trying to solve problems—necessary skills for those who want to live and work together in a peaceful society.

Young students require class meetings that are short and focused on one or two topics. Given their developmental levels, discussions should emphasize concrete examples of problems. Structured role-playing, storytelling, puppets, and flannel board figures are useful for conveying behavioral expectations. One kindergarten teacher begins the first class meeting of the year by introducing her students to a puppet of Felix the cat. Felix has special things that he likes to wear such as suspenders and special things he likes to bring to school in his pencil box. The teacher explains that it is all right for Felix to do that.

Felix also has to remember that there are times when he might not be able to do whatever he wants. He has to be careful not to hurt himself or others. He has to help himself and everyone else to do their best in school. The children talk about Felix and eventually come up with rules for Felix and themselves. Whenever problems arise, the teacher can ask the students how Felix might react to what is going on. Sometimes she brings Felix out and has him "talk" with the students. The lessons on behavior and the subsequent meetings are fun and at the same time filled with meaningful content for the students.

Visual aids are still important for older students, as are the other sorts of prompts that can stimulate discussion. Although puppets may be inappropriate for older students, pictures or brief role-playing exercises that depict a problem might be a good way to begin a class meeting. Problems can be discussed in greater depth, topics that pertain to the larger community can be shared, and moral dilemmas can be wrestled with. "How do you find the time for these meetings when they cut into the already scarce hours allotted to academics? You make the time. Apart from the invaluable social and ethical benefits of class meetings, they foster intellectual development as well, as students learn to reason their way through problems, analyzing possibilities and negotiating solutions" (Kohn, 1996, p. 90). Regardless of the educational level, class meetings provide excellent opportunities for developing and discussing goals, expectations, and relationships.

Class meetings provide a forum during which students can air grievances and discuss concerns that arise during the daily give and take of classroom interactions. "Class meetings are an integral part of a program designed to involve students in solving their own problems. Class meetings not only support the use of individual problem-solving conferences but can also provide students with opportunities for improving their social and problem-solving skills" (Jones & Jones, 1995, p. 331). Although no one student's name should ever be brought up in a class meeting, issues that affect the tone and tenor of the classroom are certainly acceptable topics. Including regularly scheduled class meetings in a plan ensures that the teacher and students will be able to revisit rules or share the plan on a daily or weekly basis. According to McEwan, Gathercoal, and Nimmo (1997, p. 29),

> Democratic class meetings work to share power; and, as a result, they can play a significant role in reducing the likelihood of power struggles occurring between teachers and students. When students know that the power they have in class meetings is an opportunity for genuine input, they are less motivated to seize power through means that disrupt the learning opportunities of the entire community. Class meetings provide institutionally sanctioned opportunities in which students are able to openly, yet appropriately, express their frustrations, anxieties, and joys in a fair and equitable manner.

LOOKING AT THE MAIN IDEAS

Basic Rules for Class Meetings

1. Have an agreed-upon agenda. Students or the teacher can generate the agenda. If it is teacher generated, then students should have the opportunity to add items if needed.

2. Never use the names of students. Discuss issues, not people.

3. Keep the meeting focused on one topic at a time.

4. Do not dismiss the ideas students contribute. If their suggestions are not practical, explain your concerns and ask if there is a way to modify the original idea so it can work.

The trust and communication skills developed as a result of class meetings can dramatically impact the classroom. One third-grade teacher had to be absent for two days. When she came back to work, she learned that the substitute teacher had a very difficult time with the students and they with the substitute. The teacher decided she needed to begin the day with a class meeting.

The teacher called the students over to a corner of the classroom set aside for class meetings. The teacher deliberately created a casual atmosphere to help students feel more comfortable discussing problems and general class business. The teacher began this particular meeting by bringing up the problems that occurred when she was gone. She then directed students to spend the first five minutes of the meeting discussing what they felt happened with the substitute teacher. The students were upset because the substitute teacher told them they could not wear caps, which were allowed by their regular teacher. Students were also used to speaking quietly among themselves when they were working, but the substitute teacher told them that they could not do that either. The students were very upset and frustrated by what had occurred, and they responded to the conflicts with the substitute by being inattentive, confrontational, and disruptive.

The teacher listened to the students without comment or judgment. When the five minutes were over, she told her students that she could not promise them she would be in school every day and they might have another substitute sometime. Then the teacher asked the students to think quietly about how to act if a similar situation arose again. After thinking for a few minutes, students began to offer suggestions for how they could manage their feelings more appropriately the next time something similar happened. One idea put forward was to use their journals as a safe and nondisruptive way to vent their feelings. Then, when their teacher returned, they could discuss their journal entries with her. The teacher listened carefully to their suggestions and wrote them down on a large piece of paper. When they were finished she thanked them for their input and the meeting ended. The teacher never scolded the students about their behavior or threatened consequences if they acted the same way again; instead, she was respectful of their feelings and appreciative of their ideas.

Regardless of whether the class meeting served to resolve all future problems with substitute teachers, the process of learning to manage their anger even when they felt they were being treated unjustly was an important lesson that would serve them well not only in their classroom but in life. The students were more likely to handle difficult situations well because they had come up with the solutions themselves. The teacher had an opportunity to demonstrate the trust she had in the students' abilities to critically examine issues and apply their problem-solving skills.

Class Meetings and Flexibility

Class meetings can take any form and occur at any prearranged time. In a self-contained classroom they can be held every day if necessary. In a classroom that meets for 45 or 50 minutes a day, class meetings can occur weekly or every other week. The schedule should be whatever works best for the teacher and the students. According to Jones and Jones (1995, p. 333),

> The length of class meetings will vary according to the students' attention spans. Most primary-grade teachers find that their meetings can last between 10 and 30 minutes, and intermediate-grade teachers find between 30 and 45 minutes optimal. Middle school teachers or specialists in elementary schools who meet with a class five hours or fewer a week often choose to hold class meetings on a biweekly basis or to limit weekly meetings to 15 minutes so that meetings will not take up a significant portion of instructional time.

Sometimes the sheer numbers of students seem to make conducting class meetings impossible. However, one useful strategy is to form a representative group of students responsible for gathering topics of concern and interest from their peers. Teachers can meet with the representatives and use the meeting to set an agenda for a weekly or biweekly class meeting. Other items can be added to the agenda as time allows, but this format ensures that the time used for class meetings is focused and produces results.

Class meetings are an excellent time to reteach moral values and revisit rules. One self-contained classroom has a weekly class meeting. A variety of issues are discussed, including how to schedule time on the computer so each student can have a fair turn to how to organize parents' night. In addition, time is also used during class meetings to problem solve about any rules that do not seem to be working well.

This class devoted one meeting to issues of property. One of the class rules, based on the compelling state interest of property loss and damage, was that students would respect their own and others' property. The students, however, were having trouble following the rule, and property was being taken without permission. Students were asked to contribute ideas that would help solve the problem; their solutions included asking to borrow items and helping to fix items that got broken. The teacher patiently recorded their ideas and read their suggestions back to them; the class agreed that the students would abide by those ideas. Regardless of whether they were always able to do so, they learned the value of coming together in a peaceful manner to resolve an issue of conflict.

Some Ideas for Organizing Class Meetings

There is no one right way to conduct a democratic class meeting. The best structure for teachers and students will probably emerge in each classroom as the year progresses. However, some elements work well to facilitate and democratize class meetings. The following elements could be helpful for teachers who are organizing democratic class meetings for the first time:

- **Determine who can call a class meeting and when it should be held according to standards of appropriate time, place, and manner.**   Some teachers allow any student in the class to call a meeting whenever the individual feels one is necessary. Other teachers determine a specific time, place, and manner for meetings. Either approach, or some combination of the two, works well as long as the meeting schedule includes students and ensures that they have some power and control over what is happening in the classroom.
- **Students and teachers should be seated so they can see the faces of all other class members.**   How we position ourselves says much about power relationships. Seating arrangements are often a circle either on a rug or, for older students, desks arranged into circles. The physical environment in the classroom should be as inclusive as possible. A more formal arrangement, such as sitting in rows, can exclude students or allow them to exclude themselves.
- **Establish the expectation that names will never be used in class meetings.** The purpose of class meetings is to discuss issues, not students. Using names casts an accusatory finger at the person being named and has the effect of putting that person on the defense. It also causes ill feelings. That names will

never be used in class meetings should be clearly stated and its rationale understood before any meeting occurs.

- **Establish the expectation that the meeting will stay on topic.**   Meetings are not the time for students to tell personal stories about themselves or their families. Again, the meeting is to discuss an issue of common concern to the classroom community. If students have personal problems, they need to have an opportunity to speak with the teacher privately.
- **No student should be forced or coerced into participating during a class meeting.**   Every student should have the opportunity to pass when he or she feels the need to do so. However, students will often pass if they know they can. It is important, then, for the teacher to not pass. Participation needs to be modeled. It is also helpful for the teacher to engage in a brief exchange with students who participate. Teachers can make a brief comment or ask a question or two, which might help students to make a comment or suggestion.
- **Students and teachers should maintain a class meeting journal.**   All members of the learning community, including the teacher, should take a few minutes to write in a class meeting journal immediately after the actual meeting. The purpose of the journal is to help the class meetings move the class forward in its democratic process rather than repeatedly discussing the same issues. Topics for journal entries might include concerns, clarifications, delights, topics for future discussion, topics to work on, and things that are going well. These entries then can help shape future meeting agendas. (McEwan, Gathercoal, & Niemo, 1997, pp. 32–33)

Class meetings can be used to air grievances, review rules, make decisions about ideas in a classroom suggestion box, discuss what the class has accomplished or the point toward which it is headed, or touch base at regular intervals. If the class is off task, it may be appropriate to stop an activity and tell the students that the problems will be discussed in a class meeting. If class meetings are used in this fashion, a few ideas will help make this process successful.

First, change the seating arrangements. In a primary classroom teachers may want students to gather on a carpeted area. At the upper grade levels, students might draw their desks into a circle. A change in the seating arrangement signals students that a different sort of process is about to occur. Second, the purpose of these meetings is not to lecture students about off-task behaviors but to hear the students' concerns just as students are hearing those of their teacher. Teachers should be ready to either explain the rationale for what is happening or change what can be changed to better suit the students' needs.

SUMMARY

In the opening scenario, Janelle's planning was good and her intentions were honorable. However, revisiting rules through stated expectations and during class meetings is critical if class-

rooms are to function smoothly. Even if rules were developed by students and have been revisited many times, the one time they are not is the very time the lesson might well fall apart. When that does happen, it may help to know that every teacher has had the same experience and has learned from it.

Asking students a few questions at the beginning of a lesson, while moving into a transition, or before beginning another activity helps students and teachers to be successful. Furthermore, this simple strategy helps to preserve safety and prevent serious disruptions. A simple way for teachers to remember to include a review of rules in the lessons is to ask themselves what they would really like to be sure their students know before beginning an activity.

APPLYING THE CONCEPTS

Think of a lesson you have taught recently or one you would like to teach. Consider all the various parts of the lesson. What behavioral information will students need to have to be successful? How would you write or rewrite a lesson to include that information?

CHAPTER 4

The Art of Equitable Assessment

CHAPTER OBJECTIVES

By the end of this chapter the reader should be able to:

◇ Understand the role assessment plays in creating a democratic classroom environment and how grades can impact students' behaviors
◇ Articulate comprehension of the various legal, personal, and pedagogical issues involved in developing equitable assessment practices
◇ Create assessment practices that are, as much as possible, culturally neutral

Scenario

Sam surveyed the grade book for his ninth-grade social studies class and shook his head over the number of missing homework assignments. He sighed as he recorded *F*s in the blanks. Then he turned to the stack of papers on his desk. The first paper in the stack was from a student who had handed in the work one day after its due date. "Too bad," Sam thought. "Yesterday she probably would have had an *A* on this. Now, the best she can do is a *B*."

Questions

Based on your experiences in classrooms as a student or teacher, what connections have you seen between the grades students are given and the behaviors they exhibit in class? How do students respond to receiving low grades? High grades? How do students react when they think they have received an inflated grade? How do students react when they think they have received a deflated grade?

Discussion

How students are assessed, who assesses whom, how grades are recorded, whether grades are publicly displayed, and practices of grade inflation or deflation are just a few of the controversial topics in education. They are also some of the most contentious. Students, parents, and educators all have an enormous emotional, financial, and educational investment in what grades represent, who eventually sees them, and how they will be interpreted. The basis for the concerns associated with grading is primarily the lack of agreement among the stakeholders as to what grades mean.

BASICS OF ASSESSMENT

The principal role of any educator is to design learning opportunities and then to assess those activities fairly and accurately. Assessment ideally begins at the start of each school year when teachers evaluate their students' levels of understanding in areas such as math, reading, writing, athletic skills, vocal abilities, and artistic proficiency. As the school year proceeds, teachers continually assess student progress through a variety of activities such as written projects, oral reports, paper-and-pencil tests, and other practices that yield evidence of learning.

Throughout the school year, educators provide students with frequent and objective feedback on completed assignments. Teachers also collect anecdotal data on students by observing how they approach and complete tasks. In addition, interviews can help teachers to know more about individual students' progress. Ideally, assessment is interwoven throughout the daily curriculum so that teachers know what students have or have not learned and can adjust their lesson plans to accommodate both students who are ready to move on and students who need additional time with some lessons.

CONTROVERSIES OF ASSESSMENT

As with all the other topics discussed in this book, there are legal implications for how educators assign grades, just as there are cultural values that help to shape the lens through which students and their families interpret those grades. Students' future opportunities are undeniably intertwined with the grades they receive in school. Given the enormous impact of an *A*, a *B*, or a *D* on the lives of students, how those grades are derived and what they represent are at the heart of legal concerns related to assessment.

Ideal assessment practices mean teachers provide their students with only fair and balanced feedback on the work completed for each academic subject. However, in reality, grades have come to reflect much more than what students know about any given area of academics. Today grades are used to reflect anything a teacher might want to include in the assessment milieu. Grades can reflect whether students are viewed favorably by their teachers. They can also reflect whether students were chewing gum in class, came to class with surly attitudes, handed in the work on the due date, put their names on their papers, put the papers' headings on the right or left side of the papers, used pens or pencils, or any number of other issues teachers might choose to include. Because grades have come to represent so much, they are increasingly perceived by the general public to represent nothing. Many employers believe that it is impossible to know what grades represent anymore; therefore, standards such as grade point averages (GPAs) carry less weight in hiring decisions.

Although grades might be viewed as a means of controlling students' behaviors, students are less intimidated by grading processes than perhaps they once were. They, too, have learned that grades can mean any number of things and that there is little consistency among teachers as to the significance of particular grades. If grades are important to students, they either play the game and do what is necessary to get good grades or they find ways to cheat. A polite student who smiles and hands work in on time is likely to get the benefit of the doubt when decisions are made between an *A*, an *A−*, a *B+*, and a *B*. Students who are withdrawn or angry may well see their lack of social interaction with teachers reflected in lower grades on their grade cards.

Assessment policies based on these sorts of arbitrary standards have the effect of putting students at risk because of who they are rather than what they have learned. Although some teachers may justify grade inflation or deflation based on student behaviors, the grades they assign must always be seen in light of the powerful repercussions those decisions will have on the rest of a student's life.

> As a motivating force in our children's lives, the success and failure game may have had some utility at a different time in our history. In an expanding, full employment economy, for example, the consequences of the game may be minimized. . . . But when an arbitrary device for encouraging motivation becomes reified into a classification schema defining social statuses, not just in school, but far beyond into the adult work lives of the children, the nature of the game has been transformed. Success and failure are now used to ascribe social status early in life, and these statuses are documented in school records that follow the children from school to other institutions, effectively locking them into particular tracks. (Smith, Gilmore, Goldman, & McDermott, 1993, p. 211)

The degree of intellectual and emotional security students experience in their learning environments is in large part influenced by and a reflection of their educators' assessment strategies. The classroom rules may advocate mutual respect and a community spirit of fairness, but an educator's assessment strategies determine whether students feel protected and supported by the adult in charge.

> Students' grades may be perceived as rewards if they are high and, conversely, as penalties if they are low. Teachers should try to convey to students that grades are indicators of achievement as their primary function, even though high grades may secondarily have the effect of a reward. Students are more likely to own a grade when they perceive it as a measure of performance not as a gift dispensed by a benevolent teacher. High grades, while they are ordinarily prized by students, should not be exploited as discipline ends by teachers in place of the learning outcomes the grades purport to measure. (Hoover & Kindsvatter, 1997, p. 112)

Assessment practices that discourage, minimalize, and exclude do not fit within the spirit of a democratic classroom. Democratic assessment is characterized by practices that are equitable, provide encouragement, manifest inclusion, and reflect high expectations for all students.

LEGAL IMPLICATIONS OF GRADING

The Fourteenth Amendment, as discussed earlier, protects the procedural and substantive due process rights of all citizens. The Fourteenth Amendment states, in part, ". . . nor shall any State deprive any person of life, liberty, or property without the due process of law nor deny to any person the equal protection of the laws." The Fourteenth Amendment is related to every action educators take with students, especially with regard to how teachers assess the work of students. The process of evaluation is closely tied to the liberty and property protections guaranteed for all citizens.

The term *property* has been broadly interpreted to mean all the tangible and intangible possessions of a person. Property includes a person's real estate, clothing, money, and intellectual property. Everything a person owns or knows or has up to this present moment in time falls under the heading of property. *Liberty,* on the other hand, is defined in terms of an individual's future: everything a person will become, will do, will own, and will know.

GRADES AS ISSUES OF LIBERTY

In light of the definitions, consider how grades are used. Grades are used, in part, to determine the grade levels to which students will be assigned, the tracks in which students will be placed, the reading and math groups to which students will be assigned, whether students will be able to participate in school-sponsored sports teams, whether students will be admitted into honorary scholarship associations, students' employment opportunities, the college or university opportunities open to students, the financial scholarships for which students might be considered, and the graduation honors students may earn. In addition, grades can also affect aspects of students' lives that are seemingly outside the range of education such as the cost of their car insurance.

Beyond these tangible effects of grades are emotional and psychological effects. Although perhaps less obvious, the affective results of assessment are nevertheless just as real. How students view themselves in terms of their peer relationships, their ability to be successful in life, their potential for financial security, and their sense of their own capabilities for academic achievement is inseparable from the grades they receive.

LOOKING AT THE MAIN IDEAS

Grades as Liberty Issues

- Grades impact the present and future grade placement and course opportunities open to students.
- Grades impact the colleges and universities open to students.
- Grades impact the employment opportunities available to students.
- Grades impact peer and family relationships.

Because one grade is capable of so dramatically affecting a student's life, the process of assessment is a solemn responsibility for educators. When students receive low grades, they typically begin to see themselves as incapable of succeeding in school. On the other hand, students who receive high grades generally begin to see themselves as capable learners. Both examples may be either accurate or inaccurate reflections of a student's academic ability. Depending on how the grades were derived, they may have less to do with academic capabilities than with the nature of the relationships students have with their teachers.

SUBSTANTIVE DUE PROCESS AND ASSESSMENT

What emerges from even the most cursory examination of grading practices is the enormous impact they have on the liberty issues associated with the lives of students. Once liberty issues are understood, it is important to explore how liberty issues and grading practices relate to substantive due process. To meet the standards of substantive due process, the rules that govern how grades are determined must be legal. How grades are determined must ensure the equal protection, or equal educational opportunity, of all students.

Equitable grading practices are designed to assess only the level of academic understanding students have achieved for a particular course of study. Although that would seem to be an obvious statement, grades have the potential for being the most discriminatory aspect of education. Grades based on due dates, tardiness, absences and whether those absences are excused, or a compendium of other issues often relate more to the personal lives of students than to the level of scholarly achievement attained. According to Fischer, Schimmel, and Kelly (1995, p. 266),

> if a student can show that a grade was lowered for disciplinary reasons or that the teacher acted out of prejudice or malice the courts will listen and help. When an eleventh-grade student on a field trip to New York drank a glass of wine while with friends in a restaurant, she was suspended for five days and expelled from the cheerleading squad and the National Honor Society. When the student and her parents challenged the grade reduction policy, the court struck it down. According to the court, reduction of the grade would misrepresent academic achievement and such misrepresentation would be both improper and illegal.

Enforcing rules that discriminate against who students are rather than assessing what they know can infringe on students' rights to substantive due process and equal educational opportunity. Accordingly, such rules may be questionable in terms of their legality.

> The use of academic penalties for nonacademic reasons raises complex legal issues. The practice also raises serious educational issues. . . . The practice of lowering grades as an automatic penalty, such as "each day missed is a zero," is suspect. The courts would be sympathetic to

extenuating circumstances, which the student is entitled to tell the teacher. "Blanket" policies for lowering grades, regardless of the reasons, are also open to court challenges (Nolte, 1980, p. 71). Generally, the courts have held that teachers have considerable discretion when evaluating student work. The courts will intervene in this process only if a student can show that a grade was lowered for nonacademic reasons or can verify that the teacher acted maliciously or arbitrarily. (Froyen, 1993, p. 419)

ETHICAL ASPECTS OF ASSESSMENT

As indicated, the matter of academic equity has legal implications for educators, even without a history of legal action or court cases associated with the topic. Equitable assessment practices relate as much to professional ethics as to the law. In fact, no body of case law definitively establishes whether a particular teacher's grading practices can stand up to legal scrutiny. The rationale for providing students with an equal opportunity to be successful emerges from a sense of professional ethics that informs the practices of democratic educators.

Students should at least be able to expect to have a level playing field on which to experience their education and an equal chance to be successful. The problem is that school policies on tracking, assessment, attendance, and other issues often quickly intervene to separate students by economic class and culture. According to Eisenhart and Graue (1993, p. 176),

> We have also demonstrated that the processes of cultural differentiation occurring at school take several forms. Some children arrive at school with little that differentiates them, yet the school's policies of assessment, grouping, and ranking may create its own set of different groups and orientations. Other differences are produced primarily by the students, as they respond to the way the school treats them or they work out their own social identities among their peers.

LOOKING AT THE MAIN IDEAS

Ethical Aspects of Grading

- Grades reflect what a student knows, not who a student is.
- Grades do not victimize students because of their personal or financial circumstances.
- Grades are viewed as a means of informing students as to their academic achievement rather than as a means of gatekeeping.

The use of equitable grading practices does not mean all students earn *A*s but that all students, regardless of their needs, interests, circumstances, or learning styles, have the chance to succeed.

WHAT DOES A GRADE MEAN?

When examining issues of assessment, then, it is important to begin with an understanding of liberty and its application to assessment practices. It is also critical to grasp the ethical aspects of assessment. Having done that, we can move ahead to an examination of not only what grades mean in general, but what grades mean to the person viewing them.

In the scenario that began this chapter, Sam responded to a variety of issues associated with learning and assessment in much the way most other teachers would. He records *F*s when no work has been submitted and lowers the grades of students who submit work after the due date. Teachers often feel that doing otherwise means ignoring missing work, and they fear students will not understand the importance of the tasks if there is no consequence for late or incomplete work.

Schoolwork is essential for many things but primarily as a useful measure of whether students understand the course content. Sam would certainly want to know if his students understand what he is teaching and would need to provide his students with feedback about the levels of understanding they are demonstrating. Part of that process involves recording grades or check marks in his grade book to indicate how well students comprehend the subject matter. Sam also tries to make sure that the records he maintains in his grade book specify which assignments have been handed in and which are missing. All of these practices are appropriate.

More problematic is Sam's practice of accounting for missing assignments by lowering grades or recording *F*s in the grade book, practices that have probably been encouraged and endorsed by many of his colleagues. However, the people who will eventually view a student's grade card to determine college admission, employment, or grade level have no way of knowing what the *F*s mean in this case. To the disinterested observer, an *F* is commonly understood to mean that a student has failed to understand the subject matter. Missing work is not the same thing as a failure to understand; it simply means that the student's level of comprehension has yet to be determined.

The practice of grade deflation based on late or missing work often fails to consider the variety of cultural, economic, or pedagogical reasons that students would submit work after the due date or not submit the work at all. Teachers' responses to this spectrum of compelling family and personal needs are as varied as the needs themselves. Teachers may respond with compassion to any excuse from a favored student, but they are just as likely to respond harshly to a troublesome student with a valid excuse written by a parent. Students learn quickly that their future opportunities, governed by the grades they receive, depend heavily on whether they can successfully pitch an excuse for a late paper.

To illustrate the constant erosion of norms in the low-income school, let us consider the apparently innocuous tendency of teachers to use different grading policies. Almost all teachers follow policies which, to some degree, are different from their colleagues in the same school. In most schools, a degree of uniformity and coherence is present, if only because students generally understand what is expected of them, thereby making it likely that deviance will be singled out and punished. In the low-income school, however, common understandings of this sort seldom are developed adequately. Nowhere in American education does an observer encounter so bewildering a confusion of grading norms as in a high school in a slum neighborhood. In many such schools, a resemblance between the grading practices utilized in any two classrooms seems entirely coincidental. (Levine, 1972, p. 279).

TEACHERS ARE NOT EMPLOYERS, AND GRADES ARE NOT EMPLOYEE EVALUATIONS

Grades are inseparable from the liberties to which they can potentially lead or the liberties that can be so elusive, depending as much on what grades are received as how they were derived. Some educators believe that they are protecting the liberty interests of students when they deflate grades for late papers; they then justify their policy by saying that the need to meet deadlines is as or more important than the mastery of academic subject matter. Arguing that students will have to meet deadlines as adults in the workplace, some educators believe that deflating grades will teach students about the real world. However, Gathercoal (1993, pp. 140–141) says that

> Lowering achievement grades for misbehavior does not always teach responsibility, but it always does pass on misinformation. . . . [Students] should not be experiencing an employer/employee relationship with their teacher; indeed, in the workplace such relationships are often adversarial. Instead, students should be experiencing a professional relationship with their teacher/mentors, who are using educational strategies designed to develop and change attitudes. Furthermore, students in public schools have liberty rights, but employees in the private sector do not.

In addition, business managers are increasingly aware that supporting their workers through difficult times by providing them with counseling opportunities or other tangible demonstrations of support benefits the company in the long run. In other words, employees who know they will receive managerial support for personal and workplace problems are more loyal and more devoted to their tasks. Justifying the use of grades as punishment because it is thought to be good preparation for the workplace simply does not hold up to even the most cursory examination of the business world today.

Although it is important for most people to complete work in a timely manner, the skills associated with that ability are learned in a variety of ways; the strategies that prove to be most effective often vary dramatically from one individual to another. The use of a blanket policy that reduces grades for late work to teach students to meet deadlines more often results in discouragement, anger, and frustration than in a meaningful learning experience.

WHEN FAMILY ISSUES ARE NOT COMPATIBLE WITH SCHOOLWORK

Late papers are often more a reflection of a student's family circumstances than of an insolent or lazy attitude. Depending on their circumstances, some students may never be able to meet a due date; as a result, they may frequently find themselves at odds with their teachers and families over the conflicts between the personal issues that interfere with schoolwork being completed and the classroom penalties for late or missing assignments. Students at any point along the cultural or economic spectrum may come from families who greatly value schoolwork or who see it as an intrusion into family time, work schedules, extracurricular activities, or any number of other special needs and interests. According to Quint (1994, pp. 13–14),

> Students and their entire families often share one small room when residing in hotels or motels, or experience noisy barracks-like conditions in overcrowded shelters. Frequently, access to and use of community medical and mental health services are undermined by lengthy paperwork, inadequate payment coverage, or plain fear. Potential recipients often forgo such necessary treatment as prescription drugs, immunizations, and therapy. This lack of physical and mental health care often accounts for poor school attendance. When children do attend class, they are often stressed out, hungry, exhausted, and dressed inappropriately for the weather. Emotional or socialization problems may show up as depression or aggression in class. These transient and frightened students are often embarrassed to tell anyone at school about their lifestyle and the stress and turmoil they experience. (U.S. Department of Education, 1989, p. 158)

These examples are not uncommon or extreme. They are, however, just a few of the numerous and complex conditions that mitigate against some students completing schoolwork in class or at home. If grades are determined according to such standards as deadlines, attitudes, and the neat, attractive appearance of the papers, then educators may be imposing rules that discriminate against students based on their family situations. Although homework is important, its grading does not enhance its educational value. More appropriate uses of homework are discussed later in this chapter.

Assessment must, as much as possible, be separated from the attitudes and circumstances of students. When family issues impinge on liberty issues, such as those related to grades, there is an enormous potential for turning students into victims of their own circumstances.

An Alternative Perspective on Due Dates

Classrooms function smoothly when the curriculum is planned so that educators can provide their students with ongoing feedback. To provide that feedback, work must be handed in; the use of due dates is a reasonable organizational tool to assist with that goal. The problem lies not in the use of deadlines but in how deadlines are enforced, particularly if grade reduction is a means of enforcement.

Hard and fast rules about due dates have the effect, by their very nature, of discriminating against students with learning disabilities, difficult home situations, illnesses, and the like. Instead, teachers may tell students when work is to be handed in and explain how feedback enhances a student's ability to succeed. Beyond that, punitive measures too often interfere with the purposes behind the due dates and the assignments themselves.

Due dates are problematic in part because they are often set as much on the basis of the teacher's schedule as the amount of time students require to successfully complete the work. Another problem with enforcing due dates with punishment is that, although teachers say the dates are fixed and unbendable, in fact the dates are often moved to accommodate the needs of teachers, students, or both.

Teachers sometimes find themselves in personal situations that interfere with timely grading of papers and extend due dates to accommodate their circumstances. Students have less flexibility available to them, although that does not prevent them from requesting more time. When students have not completed their work by the due date, they attempt to negotiate for more time. Whether their requests are granted typically depends on whether the excuses given are deemed worthy of consideration. If the teacher believes the student has a good excuse, more time is typically granted; if the teacher believes the student has a poor excuse, the student is denied extra time and suffers the consequences for missing the due date. However, both good and poor excuses could be fabrications.

Students might invent a tale of woe to explain why an assignment is not finished and be rewarded with additional time to complete the assignment. Other students might offer no excuses or vague excuses because telling the truth about why the assignment is late would reveal personal information, such as dysfunctional home lives, that students would prefer not to share. Educators then have to determine whether excuses for late work have any truth. And regardless of whether they decide to extend the due date or deflate the grade, teachers still have to determine whether the student has learned the course content.

The practice of giving *F*s for work that is not turned in is another common example of grades being used as punishment. Educators justify this practice by saying that if the work has not been done and a grade must be given, then a grade cannot be anything except an *F*. This argument misses the purpose of the failing grade, which is to indicate that a student does not understand the subject matter.

The absence of work is not the same as a lack of understanding. Missing work indicates that students have not done the required tasks, but their level of understanding has not yet been assessed. When an assignment is missing, the only information a teacher has is that an assignment has not been completed. Whether the student comprehends the subject is still in question. Giving students *F*s for missing work leaves the issue of understanding unresolved.

Once a teacher has entered a grade into a grade book, the problem of missing work might appear to be resolved. In fact, record keeping has become more important than discovering what students know; the responsibility for students to learn the academic content has been removed. Students may not have understood the lesson content, and once the grade has been entered the student may never be given the opportunity to learn the material. The teacher and the class simply move on. Students who receive *F*s for missing work in all likelihood will fall farther and farther behind. These students are never held accountable for their own learning progress. Recording an *F* when the work has not been handed in has the effect of giving students permission to fall through the cracks.

Another approach to late or missing assignments is to treat every learning opportunity as part of an educator's legitimate educational purpose. Then, no matter why a student has not completed the work, the teacher can say "If there is something you didn't understand about the assignment, I will be glad to help you as soon as I can. Maybe we might need to find some time together during the day or after school. In order for me to do my job, I need to assess your progress in this class. So, when can I expect your work?"

It does not matter if the assignment is at home, in the student's locker, lost on the playground, or in the stomach of the family's dog. When a teacher ignores the excuses and instead focuses on why the assignment is necessary, the deadline can be renegotiated in terms of the learning needs of the students rather than in terms of how to punish students for not doing the work in the first place.

Students, not teachers, need to assume responsibility for completing schoolwork. In the scenario at the beginning of this chapter, Sam is recording *F*s in the empty spaces of his grade book without knowing why the work is missing or expecting his students to be accountable for completing the work. Students may not complete assignments because they do not understand what has to be done, they do not appreciate the need for the work they are being asked to do, they have learning disabilities that prevent them from addressing the task effectively, they have jobs that conflict with the time needed to do homework, they do not have the language skills to understand the assignment, or they just ignore the assignment. They also may be too young to understand the liberty ramifications inextricably woven into low grade point averages.

HELPING STUDENTS LEARN RESPONSIBILITY

Few students at any grade level truly comprehend the connections among grades received in elementary school, expectations for success in high school, satisfying college or university experiences, and intellectually and financially fulfilling careers. Although teachers may try to make students aware of these connections, students, along with their families, usually make their own decisions about their levels of engagement in course work. Educators can focus on examining and assessing student learning and adjust their curriculum accordingly to guide students to the next level of activity.

Sam's policies are never going to help him know why papers are missing or late. The problems may occur for several reasons, but when Sam records the grades for the missing or late work, he ends the possibility of further explanations.

Sometimes the reasons for not handing in work can reflect a sense of success rather than a sense of failure. One university professor tells many stories of the coping skills he developed to handle his dyslexia. Sometimes his coping skills resulted in positive outcomes, and sometimes they resulted in outcomes that were harmful to his future. After a school career marked by failure, he enrolled in a geometry class during his eighth-grade year; he quickly discovered that he loved the subject matter. The visual aspects of the work were very appealing to him.

Despite the fact that this was the first class in which he felt confident about the subject matter, his method of coping with this new success was dramatically negative. Every night he would do the homework but then throw the assignments away. He got the right answers, but, at the same time, he feared the ways his teachers might react if he were to suddenly become successful in school after so many years of struggling. His fear of their skepticism or praise caused him to avoid the problem by never handing in his work. He received an *F*. The grade did not reflect what he knew about geometry but rather demonstrated the teacher's desire to punish him for not handing in homework. Had the teacher investigated the reasons why his work was missing, the two could have developed alternative ideas for handing in the work without any unwanted attention.

THE PERILS OF GRADE INFLATION

Examination of liberty issues and other associated topics that relate to grade deflation and the impact of that practice on all the future decisions students will make is warranted. Given the widespread nature of grade deflation, its potential ramifications deserve exploration. It is equally fitting to spend time discussing the equally devastating outcomes of grade inflation.

Grade inflation has become a politicized term and is currently used as an argument against curriculum strategies that are mutually inclusive rather than selectively exclusive. "Dumbing down the curriculum," a common expression for grade inflation, has been derided by educators and politicians alike. The intent of this chapter is not to address the problems or strengths inherent in the debate but rather to focus on the liberty issues associated with grade inflation and its potential damage.

It is not uncommon for some students to be awarded top grades throughout their school careers even though their actual academic skills may be wanting. These students are often elected to school offices, are listed on the honor role, and receive other sorts of academic and social recognition. Teachers typically give these students first consideration in recommendations for academic scholarships for college. These same students are often members of the mainstream culture—they look like and act like the teachers who teach them and share a similar lifestyle. Such students have discovered that being pleasant and polite to everyone results in favorable teacher responses and high grades that are more closely linked to their demeanors than to their academic understanding.

College or university faculties often encounter these students, who have arrived on campus with high expectations but lack some necessary academic skills. It soon becomes clear that students who received inflated grades in primary and secondary schools are more likely to be at risk in higher education. They have often been passed along from one grade to the next because they were nice, they were well behaved, they were physically attractive, or all three.

At the university level, these students become little more than numbers in large first-year lecture classes with few opportunities for the sort of one-on-one contact they experienced with their high school teachers. Their grades typically plummet because the students cannot meet college-level expectations for writing, reading, and math. As a result, their liberty interests, like those of students at the other end of the continuum, are violated. They may end up on academic probation or flunk out of college. Even if they stay in school, their average grade records, although acceptable, can bar their entry to graduate schools.

Looking at the Main Ideas

What Grades Are and What Grades Are Not

- Grades are one way to reflect the academic progress of students. Grades are not a means of punishing negative student behaviors.
- Grades are one way to let students know when they are achieving well academically. Grades are not a means of rewarding good student behaviors.
- Grades are one key element of a student's future. Grades cannot be viewed in terms of only one classroom, one course, or one grading period.

Additional points for extra credit work, visually attractive work, effort, or pleasant demeanors are potentially damaging to students, however well meaning the gesture may seem. Students are much better served by honest assessment accompanied by support and commitment from a trained professional.

MIXING MESSAGES: SCHOOLWORK AS PUNISHMENT

Exacerbating the controversies associated with schoolwork is the practice of punishing students not through grade reduction but by giving them additional or unplanned assignments. Some teachers require students to write essays or complete extra math assignments if they break a rule. Such punitive measures send students a mixed message about the value of homework and the learning process. According to Jones and Jones (1995, p. 282), "using such activities as writing sentences, assigning additional homework, and lowering a student's grade as punishment may create a negative attitude regarding these activities. Activities and settings in which one is involved when receiving punishment tend to become aversive. Teachers do not want this connection made with homework or writing." It is important for students to understand that in-class and homework assignments have a value of their own and are designed to further academic subject mastery.

Using class work for any other purpose, particularly as a means of punishment, may lessen the value students place on all assignments.

When educators use additional assignments as consequences for inappropriate behaviors, students may feel turned off to education and believe their grades essentially have no meaning. Although some educators respond that these practices teach their own lessons, assignments should always be used to improve subject mastery, just as grades should only reflect academic understanding.

DOCUMENTING BEHAVIORAL ISSUES

Given all the reasons why grades should accurately reflect the learning that has occurred, teachers might wonder if there is any way to reflect some of the behavioral issues that impact the learning environment. One of the most common methods to do so is the use of a citizenship grade. Citizenship grades let teachers reflect behavioral concerns while at the same time allowing the academic grade to stand alone as a reflection of subject area mastery.

Another avenue for recording behavioral issues is through narrative assessment. With this system, teachers can record grades for academic understanding and then write a brief statement about the students' behaviors, such as submitting papers before or after the due dates, their pleasant or belligerent attitudes, the amount of effort students displayed, and the improvement or lack of improvement evidenced by comparison of past and current grades. All of this information is important, but how it is reported requires attention.

When writing about the academic achievement levels of students, teachers can use objective rather than subjective language and describe rather than characterize behaviors. For instance, describing students as difficult and unpleasant does not reflect what teachers have seen but the conclusions they have drawn from observations. When using narrative assessment, the language reflects specific information that will help families to work with their students to solve any problems. Narratives should include specific information about the ways students approach tasks, the difficulties or successes they experience with the tasks, and other useful information that will help to encourage and inform students.

CONCERNS ABOUT TIME

In any discussion of appropriate assessment practices, concerns about time, or the lack thereof, often arise. Whether teachers are trying to manage a large self-contained classroom of 30 students or attempting to work with 150 or more students a day at the secondary level, the time involved in grading papers, recording grades, and speaking with students about missing assignments can be considerable. In addition, teachers can spend a great deal of time listening to the concerns and complaints of students, and their families, who believe their teachers' policies will prevent their success. Time constraints are legitimate concerns. They are not, however, satisfactory justifications for infringing on students' right to liberty.

Sometimes the solutions to these seemingly insurmountable problems can be found by altering perspectives. Blaufaus (1995, p. 36) states

> My old emphasis on discipline and deadlines has been replaced with compassion, understanding, and the best interest of the individual. It's remarkable to me how much I am suddenly enjoying teaching and how much my students are finding me to be an adult to whom they can turn for understanding. There have been times in my years of teaching when individuals have known that I genuinely care about them, but with a few alterations in my approach, I now have 125 students who feel I am really working for them.

Time constraints can be lessened if educators work with students to resolve problems rather than creating situations that will inevitably lead to confrontation.

Some teachers envision that at the end of the term some students may have handed in no work. They fear that by not responding to missing work with a lowered grade, the students will think it is acceptable to avoid assignments. Guarding liberty interests, however, is not the same as ignoring work that is missing. When work has not been handed in, teachers should immediately ask students when it will be finished. Rather than letting students off the hook by recording an *F*, teachers can persistently request the missing assignments from students.

It may seem that keeping track of many students precludes this sort of personal contact. However, a brief conversation to ask each student about the missing work is usually all that is needed. If more information is required to resolve the problem, a longer conference can be scheduled at a time convenient for both the teacher and student.

One middle school English teacher in New York State has few problems with students not turning in assignments. At the beginning of each school year, he tells students that all the work he will ask them to do has a purpose and needs to be completed so that he can assess their progress. He goes on to let students know that if their work is one day late he will ask them when he can expect it. If it is two days late, he will require students to stay with him for a study period. He has chosen to schedule these periods after school, but other times might better serve the needs of other teachers. When students attend these sessions, the teacher sits down with them and provides whatever help they need with the work. He also speaks with students about the reasons the work was not completed on time.

As a result of one of these conversations, the teacher discovered that one student's family was in hiding to escape an abusive parent. The student was living in the back of a pickup truck outfitted with a camper canopy. When the sun went down, the lights went out. The teacher remarked that if he had never asked her, he would never have known how to help her. The situation was resolved by the teacher working with the student after school to help her catch up.

HOW TO HANDLE LATE PAPERS

Papers should be accepted and graded whenever they are submitted. If papers are late once or are late consistently, the issues need to be resolved with students, their families, and any other available resources. Some teachers express the concern that students who hand in papers late are getting extra time. Yes, they are. But all students get extra time when needed; the only source of contention is the reason extra time is required. Extra time for a student who has a broken arm or leg would seem reasonable, whereas extra time for a student who is angry and just does not seem to care about school might seem unreasonable. But leniency toward one student and not toward another results in arbitrary judgments based on personal likes and bias, which is why inconsistency is so problematic. When teachers accept late papers, every student has the option of handing in a late paper when circumstances make that option necessary. To resolve the underlying problem, teachers can ask why the work is late and engage in some problem solving with students to assist them in meeting deadlines in the future.

The idea of accepting late papers always leads to the concern that if late papers are accepted at any time, teachers inevitably will be burdened with a flood of papers to grade at the end of the term. One solution to this problem is to immediately ask students about when the missing work will be handed in. Another helpful practice is the use of an incomplete grade. Teachers can encourage students to complete assignments in a timely manner, but work missing at the end of a grading period can be given an incomplete grade.

Teachers who accept late work tell me that students are more likely to complete their assignments if they know it will not be graded down, thereby learning and benefiting more from the course work. It also communicates to students that all class assignments have a legitimate educational purpose that must be fulfilled. Many educators are also discussing due dates for assignments with students based on how much time they feel the student will need to complete the work. Taking into account the students' needs and interests gives them some ownership in the deadline. (Gathercoal, 1993, p. 143)

THE ROLE OF CULTURAL PERSPECTIVES

Although teachers may not intend to act in ways that are culturally biased, they tend to base grading on their own histories of academic successes without reflecting on the personal variables that influenced their school experiences. The mind-set that if teachers could do it then so can students can become a powerful influence when determining how to respond to issues of late or missing papers. However, this sort of thinking can lead to a lack of sensitivity toward the personal realities of students' lives. Punishing students for circumstances that are often beyond their control only serves to turn them off to education. After all, they may not be in a position to drop out of their personal circumstances, but at the age of 16 they can drop out of the other source of discouragement in their lives—their schools.

Teachers have a personal standard in mind for academic success that often reflects cultures that value following rules and adhering to deadlines. These values come into play in the assessment process because teachers have come to believe that meeting deadlines is at least as important as demonstrating subject matter mastery. The two are not synonymous but are often thought to be.

On the other hand, lowered expectations should never be equated to a sense of professional empathy toward the personal, cultural, familial, or special needs of any students. Expectations must be equally high for all students. However, what must be clarified is the exact nature of what teachers are assessing.

Too often, grades are lowered for missing work because teachers, at some conscious or unconscious level, believe students are not capable of doing better and the grades they assign reflect that belief. Rather than working with students to complete the assignments, teachers rationalize that little more can be expected of the students given their personal circumstances of social class or culture. The cycle set in motion by such thinking is one of increasing discouragement for students, who incorporate the notion of failure into their sense of self.

The issue of missing assignments can be viewed from a different perspective that, at its core, maintains high expectations for all students. All students must be held to the expectation that they can succeed to the best of their ability. Although not every student will emerge as a scholar, each student has the right to be viewed as someone who can understand the academic content of any course, without regard to race, class, or gender. That expectation is underscored when educators hold to the standard that work must be completed for it to be given a grade.

Reducing grades for missing work has the effect of lowering that expectation and giving students permission not to do the work rather than fostering personal and academic responsibility. Once the grade of zero or *F* has been recorded for a missing assignment, the issue of subject matter mastery becomes moot. The teacher has instead assumed the responsibility for filling in the grade book while the students have been permitted to avoid learning the necessary material.

Reducing grades for late or missing work may seem a significant consequence to teachers who come from cultures that value time lines and adhere to mainstream standards of what it means to succeed. In reality, though, the practice of grade reduction may not hold the same level of significance for their students. Teachers must not confuse academic achievement with a specific set of cultural behaviors. The capacity to comprehend mathematical equations is not the same as the capacity to submit a paper by a due date. A level educational playing field depends on an understanding of that distinction.

Few areas of educational give and take are more laden with the potential for personal bias than determining grades based on deadlines. Such rules are most likely to place the personal lives of students in direct conflict with the personal bias of their teachers. Students who believe they have not been treated fairly are turned off to the educational process as a result. When we view the statistics on illiteracy and dropout rates, we see that as a society we cannot afford to lose so many young people as productive, self-actualized citizens.

If grades are viewed as a means of reflecting what a student has learned and not as a tool of punishment, then teachers can take a more proactive approach to assessment and student work. Classroom rules related to responsibility should include language that encourages students to be responsible for their own learning. Then, when an assignment is not handed in, a teacher can approach a student and ask when the assignment will be finished. The only issue is that the teacher cannot assess the work if it has not been submitted.

GRADING HOMEWORK

Further complicating the role of families and culture in assessment is the practice of grading nightly homework. Simply put, when homework is graded teachers can never be certain whose work they are grading. The assignment might have been done with the assistance of peers, parents, grandparents, a friendly manager at work, or any number of other people. Someone else may have done the work for payment. Students may have accessed Web sites and copied from them appropriate assignments. There is no doubt about the potential value of homework as a way to provide students with extra time to learn subject content and to develop study skills. It may also be an effective means of helping teachers know which students are progressing smoothly through the subject matter and which need some additional help. However, grading homework assignments is far less defensible as an educational practice.

Some parents truly enjoy helping their children with homework assignments and projects. They think nothing of spending time and money to help create projects that are visually appealing and academically outstanding. Some families view completing academic assignments together as a special time for them to gather and share in an important activity. The problem is that educators are then uncertain about who did the work to be assessed. When assignments, large or small, are completed outside the school environment and graded, the integrity of the grade is always in question.

Nightly homework assignments can be checked for accuracy and recorded as complete. Any additional information concerning comprehension or progress can be noted anecdotally. In that way teachers can monitor whether assignments are being completed and how well the content is understood.

Teachers can monitor students' progress on long-term projects to keep abreast of any problems that might be arising with the assignments and to have a better chance of ensuring that students themselves are doing the work. Such systematic checks also help students with organizational skills. If students know that their progress will be monitored at specific time intervals, they can plan to have that work done on schedule. If it is not done, the teacher may need to help students with the skill of developing and adhering to a schedule.

WORKING TO KEEP IT CONFIDENTIAL

Maintaining the privacy rights of students is an issue that arises frequently when discussing how grades are reported and how records are kept. Unfortunately, when it comes to grading practices, confidentiality is often subverted in the name of motivating students. Students who have missing or late work often see reminders of the assignments they still need to complete posted on bulletin boards or written on chalkboards next to their names. Some teachers stand in front of the room with the grade book open and call out the names of students who are missing work and which assignments are missing. Teachers may have a misperception that if students give their permission for such information to be read aloud maintaining confidentiality is unnecessary. However, minors cannot give up their rights to privacy, particularly when the reasons an assignment is missing are reflections of students' home situations. Teachers can instead meet privately with students to let them know that some work still needs to be completed. Some teachers hand out folded slips of paper with that information.

Students do not need to know about the academic performance of their peers, yet such information is typically made public by some teachers in the spirit of trying to motivate students to do their work, work better, or continue working well. One elementary teacher routinely began her day by asking students to stand on their chairs. Then she would call out the names of the students who had handed in their homework from the night before. As each student's name was read out loud, he or she could sit down. At the end of this exercise the students who remained standing on their chairs were those who had work missing. The teacher explained that her rationale was to embarrass students as a way to motivate them to do their work in the future. Regardless of how the teacher justifies her actions, the need to protect the confidentiality rights of students mitigates against its use.

Another issue of confidentiality arises when teachers ask students to switch papers and grade each other's work. Assessment is a professional, not student, responsibility. Having students grade each other's work creates enormous difficulties for students struggling with some content area, such as spelling, when that struggle becomes common knowledge. Teachers sometimes reward well-behaved students by letting them become assistants in the classroom. One privilege associated with being an assistant is grading and recording other students' grades; in legal terms, such practices could represent a serious breech of confidentiality. Student helpers can perform a number of useful classroom activities, but the teacher is responsible for grading.

Similarly, parent volunteers can participate in classroom activities unrelated to assessment. The potential for backyard conversations about students' academic performance makes allowing parent volunteers to grade papers at least questionable. Graded papers should be passed out with discretion. Teachers can write the grades on the backs of papers and not publicly display them as papers are returned. Teachers must be particularly careful if students are handing back papers to each other in rows or retrieving their papers from a stack of graded work on the teacher's desk.

◈ LOOKING AT THE MAIN IDEAS

Keeping Grades Confidential

- Write grades on the inside or the back of student papers.
- Record grades yourself. Student and parent aides can perform other important activities in the classroom.
- Never post student work on bulletin boards without their permission. Be sure to cover their names when the work is displayed.
- Use private notes or conversations to notify students about missing assignments.

Public praise for good work can be just as difficult for students to handle as public humiliation for incomplete work. Students can experience encouragement and compliments privately from the teacher without the embarrassment of being singled out in front of their peers. At the same time, students who were not successful on an assignment can choose whether to share that information.

Graded work should not be posted on bulletin boards unless the grades are written on the back of the paper and the student's permission has been obtained. Rather than displaying only work with high grades a teacher could ask a student to display a paper because it is a good example of an essay with a topic sentence and summary statement. The reason for displaying the work is that other students might find it useful.

Peer relationships are often difficult for students to manage. Contributing to the problems students have is the continual competition often imposed on them. Teachers may be quick to compare students. Young people already judge those around them by many standards and do not need adult influence to give them any more fuel for those judgments. This issue is particularly important for teachers who are trying to build a classroom based on trust and mutual respect. It is equally difficult for students to find their niche with their peers if they are either struggling academically or excelling at their studies. They have the right to decide whether to make information about their grades public.

ALTERNATIVE ASSESSMENT PRACTICES

A democratic classroom cannot be separated from democratic curriculum strategies or democratic assessment practices. Several educators have recently written about alternative assessment, portfolios, and scoring guides. These alternatives to traditional grading practices are unique in that they invite students to participate in, rather than be the recipients of, assessment.

As discussed later in this book, teachers who want to address student needs and interests across the spectrum of learning styles and abilities have available a number of democratic curriculum strategies. Democratic curriculum, democratic management, and democratic assessment practices comprise the basic components of classroom equity. Teachers may begin with one of the three elements of democratic education and then add the other two. The more compatible the three elements are, the more synergistic the classroom.

Democratic assessment involves students in the process of understanding how to measure their own progress in a content area. They maintain portfolios of their own work, which provide them with benchmarks against which to judge any subsequent efforts. Rather than asking teachers if their work is good or acceptable, students can learn to examine their previous efforts and compare them with their current work. They can learn to judge for themselves whether their work is poor, adequate, or first rate.

> In a democratic classroom, the teacher and his/her students are accustomed to functioning as a community that works collaboratively on classroom rules and other decisions that affect them all. Following this philosophy, it is only natural that students should be empowered to have a say in the criteria with which they will be assessed—individually or as a group. This ownership will improve the quality of all assessment tasks and is an important part of the assessment process often left out in many classrooms. (Higgins, 1995, p. 22)

One second-grade teacher introduced democratic assessment to her students by saying: "I have been thinking a lot about how we approach grading in this class. I realized that I need to be involved in how your grades happen. But do you know what else I realized? Who else should decide what grade you get?" Students offered guesses such as their parents, the principal, and finally themselves. The teacher agreed that students were capable of evaluating their own work. Because she was just introducing the idea, the teacher did not spend time discussing the particulars of scoring guides, journal entries, or narratives as alternative assessment forms. Instead, she handed out folders for all of the students and asked them to keep all their work in these folders. She went on to say that after they had three or four papers in their portfolios, they could begin to determine which were their best assignments. She explained to them that portfolios would allow students to look at all their work, compare how well they did on various assignments, and determine their strengths and weaknesses.

The teacher still determined the letter grades her school required for grade cards, but she used a variety of alternative assessment options for providing her students with feedback. According to Higgins (1995, p. 23),

> It is important to keep in mind that numbers, or letters, do not have to be assigned as a final grade on [a] project/product. But, if these techniques are used for assessment purposes, teachers need to somehow communicate the learning gains their students have made to their parents and other interested parties—even if it is just a written narrative which addresses the established assessment criteria.

Students at all grade levels can learn to develop scoring guides against which they will judge their work. Teachers can lead students in a discussion about aspects of their class work that would best demonstrate subject area mastery. Those identified elements can then become the basis for scoring guides on which students would rate their progress on scales of, for instance, one to five. Scoring guides can also be used to assess how effectively students work together in groups and the level to which students have individually contributed to the success of their groups. Many states are developing and adopting standards designed to reflect subject mastery at various grade levels. If students are to be judged against state standards as requirements for graduation, then it only makes sense to develop in-class scoring guides that are written in language that reflects those standards.

LOOKING AT THE MAIN IDEAS

Developing Scoring Guides

- Students and teachers can work together to develop scoring guides that reflect academic achievement at any grade level and for any subject matter.

- Scoring guides can be used to reflect state or national standards for subject matter at any grade level.

- Scoring guides can be used to assess cooperative behaviors in groups, because they do not directly impact the grades students receive but can help to underscore expectations for appropriate interactions.

Relying on a variety of alternative assessment strategies also helps to protect the confidentiality and substantive due process rights of students who have individualized educational plans because of diagnosed learning disabilities or other physical or mental impairments. An inclusive curriculum enhanced by alternative assessment practices means that a teacher can meet the special needs for these students without greatly altering the mainstream curriculum. When students are given a variety of ways to demonstrate their understanding of a topic and work together to develop scoring guides based on a variety of criteria, their needs, interests, and differences can be served without calling attention to students' individualized educational plans. The more options a teacher can provide in learning opportunities and assessment strategies, the easier it will be to avoid management problems and effectively address the special needs of the students.

SUMMARY

Assessment is the primary responsibility of professional educators and therefore must reflect what students know and not who they are. It is not a means of punishment or a way to reward students with pleasant demeanors. An *A* in math means that the student understands computation and number relationships at an outstanding level.

An *F* in science means that the student fails to understand the principles and concepts presented in the course.

The connection between assessment and classroom management is real and tangible. Students who are made to understand that they are not and never can be successful in school have little reason to avoid disrupting others' learning opportunities. Schools typically respond to the disruptions these students create rather than the learning problems that might be causing them. Constantly responding to only the problems themselves rather than focusing on the reasons the problems are occurring may turn students off to education and not sufficiently prepare them for the challenges of the workplace. In short, equitable assessment is not just an issue for any one teacher or student; rather, it is a societal issue that impacts our economy and our social welfare. The liberty issues associated with grades effectively impact all of us.

Because assessment practices touch on every aspect of a student's academic life, they must be equitable and ethical. They can be the source of bitter contention or the foundation for profound professional influences on the lives of students. Letting students know they are in the presence of professionals who have their best interests in mind provides them with a powerful message of support and encouragement.

APPLYING THE CONCEPTS

After reading this chapter, consider how you might discuss these ideas with students in the grade levels you teach or will be teaching. How would you explain your strategies to third-grade students? How would you explain them to a senior-level advanced placement physics class? How would you explain them to a seventh-grade language arts class? How would you communicate these ideas to parents? What common elements would you address among all of the mentioned groups? What would be some particular concerns for each of these groups?

CHAPTER 5

Democratic Consequences

CHAPTER OBJECTIVES

By the end of this chapter the reader should be able to:

◇ Demonstrate understanding of the difference between being treated equally and being treated the same
◇ Comprehend the necessity of incorporating due process into how educators respond to behavior problems
◇ Apply a variety of strategies designed to help students recover from a mistake and learn ways to make better decisions for controlling their own behaviors
◇ Adapt consequences to effectively address students with special needs or students from a variety of cultural backgrounds

Scenario

Early in the school year, Suwana wanted to make sure that the students not only understood the rules for the classroom but also that if they failed to follow the rules, there would be consequences. She decided that if the consequences were to be fair, they would have to be predetermined and uniformly administered. Two rule violations would receive the next and more severe consequence and so on. In explaining this policy to the students, Suwana said, "I want to be fair to all of you. So, it is important that you all receive the same treatment. All your consequences will be identical and that way you cannot say that I am treating you any differently from the way I treat anyone else."

Questions

Does being treated fairly mean always being treated the same? Think of some examples where this may or may not be true in society. Is everyone treated the same? Is everyone treated fairly? What would be most important to you if you faced a consequence?

Discussion

Consequences are imposed in an attempt to quickly end a behavioral problem, teach the offending student a lesson, and convey a message to the rest of the class that inappropriate behaviors will receive stern responses. In an attempt to gain control over students, teachers can find themselves being diverted from the genuine cause of a problem and scrambling to find a consequence severe enough to end the offending behavior. However, instead of imposing consequences that are capable of frightening their students into compliance, teachers may well find themselves trying to sustain a management system that is perceived as being a game to be played rather than a moral structure to be learned.

The ramifications of consequences as games to be played are evident at all grade levels. I was once in the front office of an elementary school when a teacher walked in leading a young child by the hand. The teacher explained to the school secretary that the student had been disruptive in class and needed to be sent home. The child seemed very happy, and my professional curiosity led to my asking him questions about how he viewed his circumstances and how his day was going. "I got suspended," he said. I responded: "Oh, that is too bad." "No!" he replied. "I wanted to get suspended. I have two new toy cars at home and I want to play with them. I knew I could go home if I was noisy." After chatting a little longer, he revealed that he planned to be disruptive often so that he could stay home and play.

It seemed obvious that a considerable distance separated this child from his classmates. I observed that if the child were absent for a number of days, he might be missed. The smile faded from his face for the first time. He looked away as he said, "They do not care about me, so I do not care about them."

The act of punishing this young person by sending him home may have seemed a reasonable response to the disruption he was causing, but a quick question or two from the teacher might have led to a very different, and far more appropriate, resolution to the problem. Any number of interventions, including a conference with the child's parents, would have constituted a much more effective response to the disruption the student had caused.

The encounter in this school office contained echoes of the Uncle Remus tale about Br'er Rabbit in the Briar Patch. Br'er Rabbit begged and pleaded to be punished in any other way than to be thrown into the briar patch. Br'er Fox and Br'er Bear wanted to teach Br'er Rabbit a lesson and threw him into the Briar Patch anyway. Once Br'er Rabbit landed among the briars, he leapt about in joy because the Briar Patch was his home. In the case of this student, the adults who decided to act quickly and decisively in response to his disruptions gave him the very outcome, some might even think reward, he was hoping to receive.

Tragically, this student seemed to have learned at a very young age that school was not a welcoming place and that if he acted in a disruptive manner, he would not have to stay there. He had determined that no one at his school cared about his welfare. One can only imagine how different things might have been if his teacher had tried to resolve the problem in a more positive and productive manner. As it was, this incident seemed to be the first step on a very slippery slope for this student. Unless he encounters a caring professional educator somewhere in his school career, he may become another dropout statistic.

THE NATURE OF CONSEQUENCES

Consequences—what they are, when to use them, and who should receive them—constitute a contentious area of classroom management because they represent yet another measure of what educators believe their roles to be in the lives of their students. As a result, consequences are applied to a broad spectrum of ed-

ucational problems and vary among students and classrooms. The inconsistencies among consequences occur because their severity is often linked to a
teacher's level of tolerance.

Any discussion of consequences must include an examination of what is often
a dichotomy between what teachers are hoping to accomplish when they admin-
ister consequences and what is actually being achieved. In the situation described
earlier, the first-grade student's teacher seemed to believe that sending the child
home would result in feelings of contrition and apology. The teacher may have
even believed that a suspension would cure the student's disruptive behaviors. Instead, the results of the suspension were yet more evidence for the student that no
one at his school cared about his welfare.

When educators discuss consequences, they typically justify whatever strategy they select by saying that it works. This chapter is primarily devoted to an
examination of consequences from the perspective of moving beyond the statement that it works and challenging each reader to consider toward what end the
consequences work. What is being accomplished with the consequence used?
Does the consequence achieve what teachers are hoping to achieve?

Consequences typically accomplish one of two things: they help students learn
from their mistakes or they push young people out of school. The teacher sends
students messages by how classroom rules are fashioned, whether class meetings
are held, how assessment data are collected, and how the physical space of the
classroom is used. Those messages can be inclusive or exclusive. Consequences are
yet another powerful means to tell students whether educators emphasize inclusion or exclusion. It is only logical that students will feel a greater sense of being
welcomed in school if efforts are made to keep them there rather than subjecting
them to persistent threats of being suspended or expelled.

Too many educators use suspension as a first rather than a last step when
trying to resolve problems with students. Discipline policies in public schools
often contain a laundry list of actions that can result in suspension or expulsion.
Students have been removed from school for wearing caps; chewing gum; running in the hall; talking in class; coming to class late; skipping school; not bringing paper, pencil, or textbook to class; and many other reasons. If educators are
looking for reasons to suspend students with behavioral problems, the students
are quickly removed for any infraction that falls outside the behavioral expectations of a classroom or school. There is also a sense among educators that punitive responses to inappropriate behaviors must occur to teach other students
about acceptable behavior. But many students do not view suspension as something to be avoided. Quite the opposite, in fact, was evidenced in the earlier
story.

Granted, students may sometimes need a break from their classrooms to re-
group and get back on track. The time students spend away from their regular
classroom settings may take many different forms; some of the options are discussed later in this chapter. Teachers may choose from many strategies to keep
students in the classroom environment and, at the same time, teach them how to
manage behaviors so that the same problems do not recur.

ATTENDING TO RATHER THAN IGNORING BEHAVIORS

Teachers too often ignore minor misbehavior because they think that if they do not respond to some actions, the actions will disappear. However, if students receive no information about their inappropriate actions, they usually continue to exhibit the behaviors. If the student is seeking attention, the behaviors may become even more exaggerated in an effort to get the teacher to notice. Teachers who have been trying to ignore the behaviors will find themselves becoming irritated, and the inevitable confrontation is characterized by anger and hostility.

When inappropriate behaviors mushroom out of control, many schools quickly move to suspend or expel students from the learning community. But just as with the first grader in the earlier story, the motivations for acting out in school are as diverse and complex as the students. Students act out in schools for any number of reasons, only some of which can be easily discerned and very few of which will improve because of a quick response. This is particularly true if the root causes for disruptive behaviors lie in students' home environments. Throwing students out of school only ensures that they will spend more time in the very environment that may be the source of their problems in the first place.

A 1993 study took a hard look at behavior problems and consequences that are being handed out in schools:

> Students who faced disruption, violence, substance abuse, or conflicting obligations to school and family were understandably distracted, uncooperative, or truant. Manifesting those symptoms of broader social ills, however, brought them into contact with the discipline office. There, troubled students were rather easily reconceptualized as troublemakers. And troublemakers were readily seen as undeserving of the school's services. This process is all the more disturbing when we consider that inner-city African Americans and Hispanics are disproportionately likely to suffer from such social ills. (Bowditch, 1993, p. 506)

Although this study is specific to one high school, its results are common to other schools throughout the country.

Some educators blame parents for the problems seen in students, but educators rarely attempt to reach out to the families for information or offer help or support. Yet students often get into trouble for exhibiting behaviors that are learned and even encouraged in their homes. The result is a no-win situation for students, one that ultimately can make dropping out of school, in the student's mind, a desirable and defendable alternative.

SOME LEGAL CONSIDERATIONS

Legal concerns are associated with fixed rules and consequences but are not necessarily issues of equity. Students who are in classrooms governed by behaviorist rules and predetermined consequences have little or no due process.

The [Supreme] Court [in *Goss v. Lopez,* 1975] invalidated [a student's] suspension for lack of a due process hearing. The Court stressed that the hearing need not unreasonably burden school functions and resources, and could, in minor disciplinary cases, be satisfied by [an] immediate informal conference between the student and school principal or faculty supervisor in which the student received oral notice of the charge and an opportunity to respond to the charge. (Valente, 1998, p. 169)

Procedural due process gives citizens the right to notice, fair hearing, and appeal. In a behaviorist classroom, as discussed earlier, there is certainly notice, but fair hearings and appeals are rare or nonexistent. In some classrooms students who try to exercise their right to a fair hearing by offering explanations for their behaviors often receive additional consequences for "talking back." Taking a few minutes to hear students' side of the story often gives teachers good information that may offer more responses to correct problem behaviors. But when teachers do not take the time to hear students' sides of stories, they can find themselves responding to difficulties in ways that further exacerbate the problem.

Failure to provide for due process rights can also result in teachers failing to address the underlying cause of a problem. It is too easy to get caught up in trying to get a student to stop tapping a pencil, throwing paper, eating food, or engaging in some other taboo activity. Teachers tell students to stop, students say no, and the power struggle is engaged. A reasonable approach is to simply ask students if they understand the expectations and help them get back on track.

LOOKING AT THE MAIN IDEAS

Procedural Due Process before Removing Students

1. Notice: Students have a right to know the rules and how to meet those expectations.
2. Fair hearing: Students have the right to tell their side of the story before an educator makes a decision about removing them from the classroom.
3. Appeal: Students have the right to a full appeal, including legal representation, if they are facing expulsion.

When the right to due process is not protected and there is no opportunity to be heard, students become more covert in their actions to avoid being caught. Then, if they do get caught, they can choose to act as passive receptors of the consequence or they can challenge the teacher and attempt to invoke the due process rights by protesting what is happening. With either of those outcomes, the strategies being used do not require students to assume responsibility for their actions. Instructional time is lost in the back-and-forth arguing between teachers and students.

Concerns about equal educational opportunities are also linked to the applications of consequences. According to Bowditch (1993, p. 493),

Dropout research has found that a disproportionate number of inner-city Hispanic and black students leave school before graduation and has identified a series of factors that place such students "at risk" of dropping out: students are least likely to complete high school if they come from a low-income background, are frequently absent or truant, have a record of disciplinary problems, are failing classes, and are overage in grade (Borus & Carpenter, 1983; Ekstrom et al., 1987; Peng, 1983; Rumberger, 1983). Dropouts are also more likely to feel alienated from school and less likely to get along with their teachers (Wagenaar, 1987).

Teachers employed where student populations are diverse often become aware of who is and who is not receiving punishments and consequences. It is not uncommon for a disproportionate number of students from diverse cultural backgrounds to be punished, including, one might say especially, corporal punishment in states where it is still legal. Students of color sit in school halls, receive paddlings, are removed from school, and are placed in in-school suspensions much more often than their Caucasian peers. Given the statistics on cultural representation among the teaching population, the majority of the students who are punished do not share the same culture as the teachers who are meting out the punishments. Professional conscience and a sense of ethics, in addition to concerns about equity, demand that educators carefully examine their motives when considering who will face what consequences and why.

FAIR TREATMENT DOES NOT MEAN THE SAME TREATMENT

Classroom rules and how they are developed reveal the fundamental philosophy of the teacher, as does the manner in which consequences are developed and employed. For instance, a behaviorist teacher typically uses consequences that have been established well in advance of problems occurring. When there is a behavior problem, the predetermined consequence is applied regardless of whether it effectively addresses the particular situation that is unfolding. The consequences are the same for everyone and for every infraction. However, their uniformity does not provide for any meaningful educational value. Little learning can be associated with having to remain at school for an extra 15 minutes when that is the consequence of speaking out of turn, staying too long in the bathroom, chewing gum, yelling across the room, not doing an assignment, or any other infraction of the rules.

If five students are having problems learning a math concept, they may need five different approaches to help them understand the material. If five students are having problems following the rules, there may be five different reasons why those problems are happening and five different appropriate corrections. However, if teachers commit themselves to employing only one response for all misbehaviors, while ignoring the reasons that may underlie the problems, they are much less likely to fix the difficulty and far more likely to have to correct the same students over and over.

Students' inappropriate actions might occur for many different reasons, but if the consequences are the same for every infraction, there is no real opportunity for educators to effectively address, understand, and perhaps correct the individual needs at the heart of behavior problems. "Researchers have found . . . that children who are severely punished at home are more likely than their peers to act out when they are away from home. I have yet to find an educator who is surprised by this finding, which suggests that we have all noticed something similar going on in schools. The problem is that we have trouble acting on this recognition." (Kohn, 1996, p. 26)

Even when schools have stated policies about the nature of consequences and when to apply them, the anger and frustration experienced in a difficult moment can lead to consequences that are made up on the fly and lack any grounding in reason. As a result, students can experience a great deal of variance in the kinds of consequences they receive in different classrooms. Inconsistent responses create confusion and inequities in any school community. According to Morgan-D'Atrio, Northup, LaFleur, and Spera (1996, p. 192),

> Overall, it was found that 45% of the disciplinary actions taken by the [large urban high school] did not correspond with any of the disciplinary consequences of the written school disciplinary policy. Approximately 20% of all suspensions violated the written policy. That is, a student was suspended when the school disciplinary policy did not include suspension as an administrative response to the student's behavior.

CONSISTENT CONSEQUENCES CAN RESULT IN TATTLING

When students feel they have been treated unfairly, they often want everyone else in the class to receive the same treatment. Tattling is common because students try to catch each other's misbehaviors and report them to the teacher. Individual needs are not a part of such classroom cultures, and students quickly learn that it can be entertaining to complain about the actions of other students and who is doing what to whom. Teachers often complain that students tattling on each other takes too much of their instructional time, yet the climate established by behaviorist rules and consequences can have the effect of encouraging just such student actions.

One fear associated with not using punitive measures is that if other students do not see severe consequences for misbehaviors they will think nothing is happening. A teacher from Australia told the following story about his first experiences with democratic management practices:

> I am reminded of one of my second-grade students who wrote and submitted an article to me for final editing and inclusion in our first class newsletter that was to be sent home to parent[s]/caregiver[s]. In the article, the student expressed concern that there was a lot of fighting going on in our classroom and that I was doing nothing about it. It was early in

the year, after we had addressed the principles of Judicious Discipline and established our class rules, but had yet to talk about consequences. As a result, my way of dealing with the behavior problems in the classroom was seen, at least by this student, as doing nothing about it. This was probably because the strategies I used were transparent to students who were not involved. This particular student saw no names on the board, heard no warnings being issued, and observed no public ridicule being meted out. There were, however, quiet talks that resulted in negotiated and commensurate consequences assigned to the offending behavior. All of this remained confidential, and so was not obvious to others until we talked about appropriate consequences as a class. It was quite some time later that the concerned student approached me and requested that I not publish the article "about the fighting in our class." (Gathercoal, 1994, p. 25)

Teachers who use specific consequences in response to all rule violations can avoid tattling only if they become responsible for consistently catching all students in the act of violating rules, keeping track of which consequence needs to be imposed when, and making sure that all students get the same consequences. Clearly, doing so would take superhuman abilities.

On the other hand, if the classroom expectations established at the beginning of the year revolve around mutual respect and effective ways of addressing individual needs, tattling can be quickly diffused. An Oregon teacher was supervising his fifth-grade students during a game of kick ball. The teams were taking their places when a student ran up to him to say that someone had cut in line to kick. The teacher looked at the students and said "What needs to happen so everyone can have a turn?" The first student and the student who had cut in line both shrugged their shoulders and looked a little sheepish. The one who was attempting to tattle got back in line and the other one moved to the end of the line. There was no problem, and the teacher was able to turn back to watching the game, which was where his attention needed to be.

SOME BEHAVIORS ARE NOT CHOICES

One common consequence is keeping students from going to recess, lunch, study hall, or home on time at the end of the day as a response to academic or behavioral problems. Students typically hear their teachers say "Since you are choosing to not work now, you can stay and work later" or "Since you have chosen to disrupt my class for this period of time, you can pay me back that time." This practice is seen at every grade level.

Teachers believe such consequences to be appropriate reactions to conscious decisions made by students. Another perspective, though, is that students who are having difficulty in school often feel out of control, with little or no sense that they are making any conscious choices. As a result, when students are told they have chosen a particular consequence, they understandably might feel confused. In Dreikurs, Grunwald, and Pepper's (1971, p. 34) words,

> Nobody is fully aware why he behaves as he does. Only a few of our intentions reach the conscious level. When you ask a child why he did something wrong, he simply doesn't know. Parents and teachers often become furious when the child openly responds to their questions of why he did it, with "I don't know," which is actually the truth. If the child gives an explanation, it is usually a rationalization; the child is actually not aware of his own motive.

Students might be disruptive because they missed breakfast, because they are feeling no sense of permanent value in the classroom, or because of a problem they are having at home or with their peers. They may be having a bad day, a bad week, or a bad month, and their ability to handle their problems is not well developed. The same conditions can be seen in adult behaviors.

If a teacher needs to speak with students about misbehavior or negotiate time during which students can catch up on missing work, one approach might be to say: "It is very important that we have some time to work this problem out together. Would recess, silent reading time, our break time after lunch, or after school be best for you?" The students might well choose to give up recess or study hall, depending on grade levels, but the difference is that they are making conscious choices. Needless to say, recess is an important time for elementary students to socialize and get fresh air. Study hall is an important time for older students to finish work or read a good book. Neither should be taken away on a regular basis.

LOOKING AT THE MAIN IDEAS

A Process for Developing Meaningful Consequences

1. Ask questions to find out what might be motivating the student's behaviors.
2. Determine a time to meet and speak with the student to reach a mutually agreeable solution to the problem.
3. Use a follow-up conference to see how the student is doing and to continue building a trust relationship with the student.

Providing students with an opportunity to recover from problems and learn strategies for avoiding the same problems in the future should be the framework for an educator's decisions about consequences. It is not necessary to make young people feel worse than they already do or to immediately isolate them from their learning communities. Other, more effective, options are explored later in this chapter.

WHAT ARE DEMOCRATIC CONSEQUENCES?

A democratic classroom makes use of consequences that are developed out of a consistent philosophical perspective advocating the importance of addressing individual needs over the utilitarian response of imposing predetermined punishments. The consequences used in a democratic classroom are designed to sustain every student's sense of permanent value in the classroom while teaching alternative ways to express anger, frustration, and sorrow. Consequences employed in democratic classrooms can teach students the importance of responsible decision making and how to make restitution for damages that have occurred.

Once the principles on which consequences are based have been established, the actual responses to problems are developed as situations occur because educators need to understand motives and circumstances before determining the most effective way to address the behaviors. A teacher who uses democratic practices might begin the school year by saying something like the following: "We all have some days that are better than others and times when we feel better than at other times. When any of you are having a bad day, I will want to help you get back on track and try to find a way for us to work out the problems together. That means I will be speaking with you if there is a problem in class and we will find a way to resolve it. But that also means that each of you may be resolving your problems differently. So, you will not be treated the same, but you will all have the same consideration when there is a problem and you will all have the same opportunity to work out the problem in a way that will help you and everyone else."

Democratic consequences work to protect students' procedural due process rights because it is impossible to tailor a response to a behavioral problem without affording a minimum of a minute or two for considering due process. The response can be as straightforward as asking a student what is happening. To choose consequences that focus on addressing individual needs and helping students make restitution for inappropriate actions, it is essential that teachers first know the nature of the problem; the inquiry required to understand the problem ensures that due process rights are protected.

Democratic consequences also protect society's need for a safe and respectful community by teaching students the skills required to be responsible and self-motivated. The response students receive when they act inappropriately speaks volumes as to whether a classroom is operating in a true democratic fashion.

Consequence as a Teachable Moment

As mentioned earlier, students often act out in school because their home lives are characterized by tumultuous human interactions. These students come to school feeling frightened, depressed, or angry and have little or no basis for understanding what constitutes appropriate behavior. They may well respond to frustration by hitting or yelling because it is the behavioral model with which they are most familiar. Removing these students from school without providing information about anger management and conflict resolution ensures that this cycle of violence will continue. These students may grow into adults who take this same level of anger out on their spouses, children, and coworkers unless they are given some opportunity to learn alternative strategies. If educators can structure consequences into opportunities to teach lessons about responsible behaviors and help students learn how to make appropriate decisions for the common welfare, both teachers and students can retain their sense of dignity.

A teacher from New York State shared the following story. One day, after the school day had ended, the teacher was walking past the girls' restroom when she heard laughter and shrieking echoing out into the hall. She stepped inside the bathroom and was greeted by the sight of wet toilet paper and water everywhere. Wads of wet toilet paper decorated the ceiling and walls, and water was all over the floor. The teacher looked at the three female students standing there, their hands full of more wet toilet paper, and asked the students what they were going to do about the situation. The use of a question rather than a lecture gave the students the responsibility for solving the problem: "We probably need to clean this up," the students replied.

The teacher supervised the students while they got a ladder and set about wiping down the walls and drying the floor of the bathroom. When they were finished, the teacher told me, the bathroom was sparkling clean. Then the teacher talked with the three students about the health and safety dangers of a wet floor and the potential for property loss and damage from the water. That ended the incident.

The teacher speculated that many other teachers might have walked into the bathroom and automatically suspended the three students. But the teacher wondered what the students would have learned from being suspended when they would have been gone for two or three days and someone else would have had to clean up the mess.

This teacher's story makes a powerful point. A fixed policy of suspensions sometimes known as a zero tolerance policy for misbehaviors has the effect of excusing students from having to make restitution for their inappropriate actions. Restitution can be immediate, as in the situation described here, or it can happen later in some form of community service. However it occurs, though, teachers can give students the opportunity to learn how and why to make things whole after peace and order have been disrupted.

> An educator's approach to shaping consequences should reflect the basic principles of empowerment and students' responsibility and avoid as much as possible forcing explanations from students about what is already past. Students should know that when rules have been broken, their discussion with educators will center around two important future aspects: (1) What needs to be done? and (2) What needs to be learned? (Gathercoal, 1994, p. 117)

Rather than using consequences as the tools with which to embarrass, humiliate, or exclude students, educators can respond to behavior problems in ways that help students learn how to assume responsibility for their own actions. Learning to be responsible is a process that requires time and patience. Responses to inappropriate student behavior can be the most powerful means by which educators establish themselves as professionals who are working to keep students in school rather than moving to exclude students from their learning opportunities.

Sometimes educators cannot immediately think of the most appropriate response. In such circumstances teachers can demonstrate how to make use of time to enhance good decision making. Even if the time consists of counting to 10, the use of that time models for students that there is another way to respond when they feel angry or frustrated. Educators who take time to think before speaking model a critical component of resolving issues peacefully and avoiding power struggles. Gathercoal (1994) mentions three organizers that can help teachers move past their initial frustration with a student's behavior and toward understanding what might be causing the problems.

> The following are some mental images I use that help me gain a broader perspective:
>
> 1. If I am this student's educator and mentor, I had better listen and act as his or her loyal friend and advisor; and
> 2. I must keep in mind that this student is not finished yet, but is in the process of growing to adulthood; and, therefore,
> 3. I must decide what I can do now to help him or her recover and learn something from an error in judgment. (Gathercoal, 1994, p. 105)

This approach of responding to problems from an educational rather than punitive posture allows educators more flexibility for resolving conflicts peacefully while at the same time teaching lessons about appropriate decision making.

When a student disrupts the learning environment, a primary focus of concern is what form the response will take. Educators should carefully consider what steps will be taken to ensure that the consequence is handled in a respectful and confidential manner. They can also consider what will be learned from the experience to help students to do it differently the next time.

Confidentiality and Consequences

One of our paramount responsibilities as educators is to maintain the confidentiality of issues surrounding the abilities of students to learn and to behave. Confidentiality is a valued human right and a critical component to the development of consequences that are both legal and psychologically appropriate for students. Consequences in response to behavioral problems are no different from any other personal information, especially because many inappropriate behaviors originate from students' personal problems or learning disabilities. Unfortunately, some educators believe that if students create disruptions, confidentiality has already been breached and so rights to privacy are suspended.

There is another way to view this issue. Educators are ultimately responsible for setting and maintaining a respectful, responsible tone for daily interactions. Perhaps a metaphorical scenario can best explain this point. Imagine that you have gone to the doctor and are very sick. You are sneezing, coughing, and blowing your nose. It is obvious that you are running a fever because you are glassy eyed and flushed. When you sit down in the waiting room, others around you get up and move away. You are publicly displaying your health situation, which is confidential information.

However public your illness might be, though, the doctor will respond to your needs in a professional manner. She will not walk into the waiting room and lecture you about your failure to take vitamin C, put your name on a blackboard, or tell you that she is tired of seeing you in the office so often.

LOOKING AT THE MAIN IDEAS
Keeping Consequences Confidential

1. Move close to students who are acting out to speak quietly with them.
2. Find a time and place to continue the conversation, if necessary, that is away from the eyes and ears of other students.
3. Keep behavioral information off of the chalkboards and bulletin boards.

You may or may not be making good decisions about your health. Nevertheless, any conversation concerning your health practices will take place privately in an examination room away from other patients. Teachers can view how they respond to student behaviors in the same way. Young people have the right to expect privacy, and educators serve their needs much more effectively when they do not make a public display of students' problems.

Educators cannot let inappropriate behaviors determine their own levels of professional behavior. Students may be experiencing trauma and distress that affect the classroom community in any number of ways. Regardless of how public students make their behaviors, educators can still take the time to speak quietly to students and not attempt to publicly embarrass them as a means of controlling behavior.

Being Creative with Consequences

After trying all the best preventive measures, educators may still be faced with recalcitrant students for whom consequences would be appropriate. The primary goal of a consequence should be restitution rather than shame. How can students learn to restore what they have harmed or make amends for ill-considered deeds? Community service is one option. Students can work with their teachers to develop appropriate community service activities for themselves. One example of how to use community service as a consequence is the sentence handed down for the captain of the *Exxon Valdez*. After the oil spill that resulted from mistakes and poor decisions, part of his sentence included having to participate in the cleaning of Prince William Sound's beaches. He did not do this by himself, but by contributing to the efforts of restoring the natural environment of that area the captain assumed some responsibility for the decisions he made.

Consequences are usually less related to specific misbehaviors by students. Educators send students home or away from the problems they have created. Although the approach may seem justified, in fact, the effect of such decisions is to remove the responsibility for actions from the students and shift the burden elsewhere. Students can participate in restoring things to the way they were, even if their participation consists of handing appropriate and necessary tools to an adult who is actually fixing the situation.

Other possible consequences might include the following:

- **A sincere apology.** As with other consequences, the apology should be developed with the student's participation. A mumbled "I am sorry" in response to an adult's command to apologize can hardly be considered sincere. However, a reasoned statement (either written or oral) asking forgiveness for an action can provide students with time to reflect on what they did and how their actions impacted their classmates.
- **Time-out.** Taking time to cool down and gather one's thoughts is an important anger-management skill. Educators can help students learn how to know when they need some time out to collect themselves and calm down. Educators who provide their students with the option of taking a time-out help students learn to assess their own levels of anger and handle problems in ways that do not hurt themselves or others.

  However, students may need some help understanding the purposes of a time-out. A student attending a middle school in New York State was instructed to take time out and "get himself together." This student walked into the hall, gave himself a brief shake, pivoted around, and walked back in. Perhaps something more was needed. A teacher in South Dakota provides students with a corner that contains a comfortable chair, some ocean pictures, and a tape of soothing ocean sounds. A teacher in Oregon provides students with drawing and writing materials. The equipment educators choose to use is not as important as the lessons they are teaching: that calming down takes some time and a little work.

  Students can be offered the opportunity to take time out or they can opt for it themselves. A student who announces that he or she needs some time should be congratulated for good decision making. Students cannot go to a quiet corner for the entire day, but they should be allowed a reasonable amount of time to recover from stressful events.

  A time-out should never mean sitting in the hall. The humiliation that accompanies this practice negates any value the student might gain from a cooling down time, and this practice raises serious confidentiality issues. Anyone walking past the classroom can see who is sitting outside. If school personnel often see the same students sitting outside, they quickly earn a reputation of being troublemakers. Teachers who may teach those students in subsequent years quickly develop some negative expectations about them that will inevitably affect their future interactions.

  Serious health and safety concerns are also associated with placing students in the hall. Students may or may not decide to remain outside the classroom door. If a student decides to leave, there is little a teacher can do to stop that from happening. One adult remembers her middle school experience of being placed in the hall; because most of the teachers in her school used the practice, being sent out into the halls for a time-out became a way of socializing with friends. Students would often disrupt their classes just so they could stand in the halls and catch up on the latest peer gossip. Time-outs are important and useful strategies, but only if they are structured appropriately.

- **Loss of privileges.**   On an occasional basis, taking privileges away from students may be an effective response to behavioral problems. However, some events in a school day are neither privileges nor academics. Recess, lunch, and field trips, to name a few, are as important to a student's equal educational opportunity as are math and spelling lessons and should not be taken away arbitrarily or routinely. Educators may need some time to speak with students. When that need arises, as suggested earlier in this chapter, they can ask students what times would be best for a conference. The options likely include lunch, recess, or after school. Teachers do not have to place an undue burden on themselves in terms of how they use their time, but it is important to realize that peer relationships and fresh air are vital needs for all of us.

- **Counseling.**   Because a troubled student may need help far beyond what the teacher can provide, educators should not hesitate to recruit other skilled personnel to assist them. Teachers can only do so much, and it is imperative to our shared sense of professional responsibility to know when to refer problems to those who have the expertise to better help students. In-school resources are one option. If the problem is something like substance abuse, help may be found in the community. Diversion programs can be recommended to families before students become truly addicted or experience legal problems. Parents decide how such a problem is handled; the role of the educator is to notice the problem and see it in terms of how it affects the student's educational opportunities.

Teachers are not police officers, but they cannot ignore violations of the law. Rather, educators can work with parents, counselors, and law enforcement agencies to help students recover from substance addiction or other severe problems that may destroy their futures. Suspending students who abuse controlled substances but making no effort to refer the problems to other professionals or parents very likely results in students not getting the help they so desperately need.

Using Conferences before Consequences

One effective strategy for working through problems with students is a strategy called a fairness conference (Lickona, 1991). The conference has six steps but is designed to be flexible and adaptable. Not all steps need to be used all the time, and a great deal can be accomplished with the use of only one or two steps. It is also possible to interrupt the steps, completing some of them at one time and finishing the rest at another time.

The steps consist of the following:

1. **State the problem.**   Using an I message, the teacher tells the student what he or she sees happening: "I see you moving around the room and talking when others are working. I see that other students are having trouble getting their work done."
2. **Ask for the student's perspective of the problem.**   Listen carefully and without judgment to what the student says in response. Remember that this is an opportunity to get more information and to ensure that the student's due process rights are protected. Educators gather data; they do not entrap.
3. **Listen actively.**   Active listening means teachers nonjudgmentally restate the explanation offered by the student: "So, the reason you are walking around is that you do not understand what you need to be doing now."
4. **Problem solve.**   What possible solutions fit within a teacher's professional responsibilities and, at the same time, meet the student's educational needs? You might ask the student whether this is the appropriate time to speak with other students. Is this the most effective manner to seek out the needed information? Is the student's manner appropriate for what is happening in the class?

   Remember that asking questions is a powerful tool for engaging students in solving the problem. The student has created the problem, and so the student, with a teacher's guidance, must solve it. Educators might be tempted to impose a solution, but then they, not the student, would own the solution.
5. **Agree to the terms.**   Agreeing to the terms applies to both teacher and student. If the resolution is inappropriate for educational or legal reasons then the teacher, as the adult facilitator, needs to state the concerns and keep working on a suitable solution. Once a solution has been reached, teachers can ask their students if the agreement should be written or if there are other ways to help both parties remember what was discussed.
6. **Follow up.**   Teachers can check in with students later and ask how their solutions are working. If educators see that the agreements are not effective, they should work with their students to find a more useful solution. Students then own the problem and can learn from the process of having to rethink what might have initially seemed like a good idea.

The fairness conference is not meant to be used as a rigid formula for problem solving. Educators may choose to use only the first three steps for a very brief problem-solving session or break the process off and pick it up again as needed. The fairness conference is a flexible structure.

WORKING WITH PARENTS TO RESOLVE PROBLEMS

Parents are partners in the process of developing consequences and restitution options for their students. Teachers often threaten students with a call to their parents, but pitting families against schools makes little sense pedagogically. Parents can be included in management decisions just as they are in other educational decisions.

Regardless of the home circumstances, parents are in charge of their students' education and have the right to be kept informed of what is happening at school. Suspected parental abuse should be reported rather than used as a reason to keep parents in the dark about their students' problems. Putting parents in an adversarial role may mean the loss of the most powerful partner a teacher has. Waiting until a minor problem becomes an issue over which a student is suspended or expelled angers parents, who feel they were left out of the initial processes that might have more easily corrected the misbehaviors. Parents have the right to know about their students' problems in school and a right to be involved in problem resolution.

Educators stand a much better chance of receiving helpful responses from parents if they consistently attempt to reach out to and work with family members from the beginning of the school year. No one knows the student as well as the parent does. Input from parents is an invaluable resource. Granted, some parents care more than others, some parents want to be more involved than others, and some parents have more useful information than others. Whatever the situation, parents should at least have the opportunity to participate in conversations directed at trying to solve students' problems.

Parents who are nonnative English speakers feel particularly closed out of the system. Their inability to speak English or to speak it fluently is too often used as justification for excluding them from conferences or talking around them rather than to them. Although educators are not expected to be fluent in every language represented within a school community, teachers should invite parents who are nonnative English speakers to conferences and make a reasonable effort to communicate concerns.

USING PEERS TO RESOLVE BEHAVIORAL PROBLEMS

Some schools have implemented systems whereby a group of students is charged with determining an appropriate punishment or consequence for other students. Although this approach might seem to be fair, its potential to violate confidentiality may exacerbate rather than alleviate problems. First, students are in the process of developing their own levels of moral reasoning and are typically not sophisticated enough to consider something other than punitive measures to correct misbehaviors. Teaching students to problem solve among themselves is appropriate, and sometimes students can serve in peer mediation roles after receiving some training. However, simply assembling a panel of students to hear behavioral issues and mete out punishment only serves to further exclude the student who is having a hard time in school.

The other potential problem with allowing students responsibility for behavioral corrections is the issue of confidentiality. If a misbehaving student acts up because of trauma at home, the only people who should be hearing about the problem are the adult professionals responsible for working with the student.

Given all the private reasons that might be involved in a student's misbehavior, the search for solutions through peer trials is simply not appropriate. Teachers, as the educational leaders in classrooms, take the lead in determining the best way to help a student recover from a problem. Adults cannot relinquish that responsibility to young people, who have not developed the same level of moral reasoning professional educators possess.

USE OF IN-SCHOOL SUSPENSIONS

As stated earlier, people sometimes need a break from each other; time away from a problem can be a healthy thing. Rather than suspending students, however, a more reasoned and educationally productive approach is to keep students in school in some form of alternative setting. In-school suspension can be a useful way to provide students with individual attention when there are few other options. The goal of in-school suspension is much the same as that of a time-out. It is not so much a punishment as an opportunity to help students recover from a problem and get back on track. Schools might choose to staff their in-school suspension or problem-solving rooms with retired people who are volunteering their time. Students who spend time in this room could receive help with their homework, work through some problem solving with the adult present, and consider ways that they can best repair their relationships with their teachers. Some educators resist in-school suspensions for such activities, thinking that good students will resent the attention a misbehaving student receives. However, as long as all students have access to help with their problems, all are treated fairly.

In-school suspensions also provide students with opportunities to fill out problem-solving forms. Problem-solving, or behavior, forms are not ends in themselves but can be used to help students cool down, think about the problems that have occurred, and initiate a conversation with the adult assigned to the in-school suspension room. Depending on their needs and developmental levels, students can write or draw their responses to the questions on the forms. After the problem has been resolved, one copy of the form is kept in the student's file for future reference, in case problems recur, one copy goes to the teachers, and one copy is sent home to parents. The form might look something like Figure 5.1.

Plans developed during in-school suspensions should be written down and reproduced in triplicate, one copy each for the student's file, the teacher, and parents. This way, all parties are informed about the decisions made and any contracts that have been developed.

If the focus of consequences is to keep students in school rather than to find ways to exclude them, an in-school alternative placement is one appropriate way to address behavioral concerns. But, as with all things, the effectiveness of in-school suspension depends on how the strategy is used. Therefore, it is also necessary to explore in this chapter some of the misuses of in-school suspension.

FIGURE 5.1 Behavior Form

Behavior Form

Name _____   Date _____

Today I _____

_____

_____

_____

Next time I will try to _____

_____

_____

I will help myself to remember by _____

_____

_____

(After you fill this out, another member of our school community will speak with you about the incident. Thank you for helping us help you to resolve the problem.)

Student Signature _____

Postconference:

_____ (Student's Name) and

I _____ (Problem-Solving Partner's Name)

spoke about the problem. The following decisions were made:

_____

_____

_____

Some in-school suspensions consist of putting students in very small rooms where they are isolated from adults and peers. Sometimes students are given work to do and sometimes they are told to just sit and think about their behaviors. In either case, they receive no support or adult redirection. When they return to their classrooms they are behind in their work and sometimes are not allowed to make up the work they missed. The purpose of the in-school suspension is to provide everyone with a chance to cool down and, in particular, with a structured opportunity to get back on track.

CURRICULUM DESIGN AS A PREVENTIVE STRATEGY

Most of the inappropriate behaviors teachers face are just the natural outcome of gathering social beings in one place for a long period of time. As students pass through the various stages of physical, emotional, social, and sexual development, they do not always react to their peers in ways that are conducive to a quiet learning environment. Teachers can demonstrate understanding of this natural process by ensuring that students have opportunities during lessons or during the school day to interact socially with other members of their class, such as through regularly scheduled group activities and class meetings. Planning curriculum that addresses these social needs often helps prevent the need for consequences because the expectations are developmentally appropriate to the needs of the students.

Carefully planning the details of how lessons will be presented can also go a long way toward preventing behavioral problems. Teachers can introduce and explain each new activity in such a way that all learners can get to work quickly. Introductions include reviews of expectations for behaviors as they pertain to the various activities. For instance, if students will work in groups, then teachers can revisit behavioral expectations for group work before the lesson. If students begin to get off task, chat, and move around, teachers can immediately stop the activity and remind students to think about the expectations established earlier.

Sometimes teachers find that students are restless and begin to engage in side conversations, which disrupt the educational process. Rather than trying to talk over the growing noise, teachers can refocus their students with a direct question or two. Instead of singling out any one student, the teacher can let the class know that he or she is aware of the disruption and wants to solve whatever problem might be at the source of the talking.

Questions can be used to obtain information from students about their behaviors rather than quieting them at the expense of learning what aspects of a lesson they do not understand. For instance, a teacher might ask in a friendly tone of voice, "Why do I think you are not understanding this information?" Students will probably answer honestly; after all, they know they have been talking. Follow-up questions should pertain to the information to assess students' understanding of it. Or, perhaps they are just off task. Teachers could say, "Some of you think there is too much talking going on. Please ask yourself if this applies to you." These types of questions can be used for students from kindergarten through grade 12. The result is a reduced need to impose consequences because the problems are mitigated before they create serious disturbances.

TEACHING PROBLEM SOLVING

Curriculum strategies can be effective for helping to reduce inappropriate behaviors. Sometimes the lesson content itself can also be an effective tool for reducing disruptions. Time can be spent in every classroom teaching students what our society views as behaviors that contribute to the common welfare. This concept is more thoroughly discussed in a later chapter on curriculum.

It is also important to teach the behaviors expected in safe and equitable classrooms. The following model for problem solving was developed by David Johnson and Roger Johnson (1995):

> The heart of conflict resolution training is teaching students how to negotiate constructive resolutions to their conflicts. It is not enough to tell students to "be nice" or "talk it out," or "solve your problem." All students in all schools need to learn how to engage in problem-solving negotiations. . . . The steps in problem-solving negotiations are:
>
> 1. **Describing what you want.** "I want to use the book now." This includes using good communication skills and defining the conflict as a small and specific mutual problem.
> 2. **Describing how you feel.** "I'm frustrated." Disputants must understand how they feel and communicate it openly and clearly.
> 3. **Describing the reasons for your wants and feelings.** "You have been using the book for the past hour. If I don't get to use the book soon my report will not be done on time. It's frustrating to have to wait so long." This includes expressing cooperative intentions, listening carefully, separating interests from positions, and differentiating before trying to integrate the two sets of interests.
> 4. **Taking the other's perspective and summarizing your understanding of what the other person wants, how the other person feels, and the reasons underlying both.** "My understanding of you is . . ." This includes understanding the perspective of the opposing disputant and being able to see the problem from both perspectives simultaneously.
> 5. **Inventing three optional plans to resolve the conflict that maximize joint benefits.** "Plan A is . . . Plan B is . . . Plan C is . . ." This includes inventing creative options to solve the problem.
> 6. **Choosing one and formalizing the agreement with a hand shake.** "Let's agree on Plan B." A wise agreement is fair to all disputants and is based on principles. It maximizes joint benefits and strengthens disputants' ability to work together cooperatively and resolve conflicts constructively in the future. It specifies how each disputant should act in the future and how the agreement will be reviewed and renegotiated if it does not work.

PUTTING IT ALL TOGETHER

What, then, might be some appropriate ways to respond to students who are having problems following the rules? Once educators decide that consequences should not embarrass, humiliate, exclude, or further exacerbate the problem, the possible responses are endless. The goal of any response to a behavioral concern is always to protect a student's sense of permanent value in the learning community and to convey the idea that the problem can be resolved amicably.

Regardless of the consequence, some time should be spent finding out why the problem is occurring. Everything from a quick "What is happening?" or "How are you doing?" to a more lengthy conference as time permits can be considered as part of the standard process when responding to behavior problems. A consequence, if necessary, might take the form of community service or restitution, which allows the student a chance to restore things to the way they were before the problem occurred.

A teacher in Minnesota used problem solving and mediation to resolve an incident between two students, one of whom had a history of defiant behaviors. The defiant student was physically larger than his peers and tended to dominate other students on the basis of his size. The teacher was committed to helping this student understand that he was a valued member of the class and had responsibilities toward other class members.

One day the student damaged another student's backpack. Because of the groundwork that had been laid, the student sought out the teacher, admitted what he had done, and offered to make restitution. The student who owned the backpack admitted that he should have taken better care of the item. The two students agreed that it would be fair to split the cost of purchasing a new backpack. The teacher now feels he can gauge the success of using reasonable consequences on the basis of such situations.

SUMMARY

There is no magic formula for determining the perfect consequence. Depending on the circumstances, teachers may need to use consequences only rarely. But if it is an appropriate step in helping the student learn from a mistake, then the consequence should reflect a spirit of creativity and flexibility on the part of the educators involved. Most important, students should walk away from these experiences with their dignity in place and an understanding of how to avoid the same problem in the future. Educators can focus on helping students recover and acquire new skills. Teachers and students can work together to develop consequences that best suit their needs and the interests of the entire learning community. Confidentiality is vital; students have a right to expect privacy, and teachers must do everything they can to help protect that right.

APPLYING THE CONCEPTS

Now that we have reviewed various aspects of consequences, please give some thought to how you might establish consequences in your classroom. How would you present these ideas to your students? How would you present these ideas to parents? How might you help develop an in-school suspension program in your school?

CHAPTER 6

The Nature of and Struggle for Power

CHAPTER OBJECTIVES

By the end of this chapter the reader should be able to:

◇ Describe the nature of the power differentials present in public schools
◇ Demonstrate the difference in language that defines authoritarian, permissive, and democratic power relationships
◇ Comprehend the forces that can lead to power struggles
◇ Apply communication strategies, classroom arrangements, and curriculum design that can diffuse power struggles

Scenario

The seventh-grade math lesson was moving along at a quick pace. The teacher was explaining a complicated process by writing sample problems on the chalkboard, calling on students to give answers, and erasing the solved problems to put new problems up. If students offered correct answers, their responses were recorded; if they came up with incorrect responses the teacher asked someone else for the correct answer. The teacher periodically paused to ask the students if they understood, looked at them briefly, and then turned back to the board to work another problem.

After writing a fairly lengthy problem on the board and solving it, the teacher turned to the students and observed two of them in conversation. "Hey, Mary," the teacher said. "The show is up here." "Yeah," Mary responded, "and from what I can see, it only gets one star." As the class burst out laughing, the teacher called out "That is fine, Mary! We will see how the show looks after school!" "No problem," Mary said sarcastically. "Can I finish my conversation now?" "Get out!" the teacher said sternly, pointing a finger at the classroom door.

Questions

Have you ever been involved in a power struggle? What happened? What did it feel like? At the time, were you the student or the teacher? How was the power struggle resolved? If you observed a power struggle but were not a part of it, how did you feel while it was going on?

Discussion

According to Raaum (1971, p. 29), "Every unilateral move toward a predetermined end is, at base, a power play. . . . It is patently clear: If we are trying to move someone along a path toward a present goal, we are—in one way or another—utilizing POWER as our moving force." Issues of power—who should have it, who wants to have it, and who shares it—are difficult, contentious, and covert as well as overt conundrums in the world of education. The dynamics associated with who holds power and whether that power is wielded, given away, or shared provide structure for how all members of a learning community, including the school board, administrators, teachers, students, and parents, interact with each other and reach decisions separately or together. Schools have a predetermined and undeniable power configuration that determines how districtwide rules are developed, administrative policies are handed down, and classroom decisions are disseminated.

A teacher standing in front of a classroom holds power just by being in that situation. The professional training educators receive and their knowledge of learning theory, curriculum design, and educational psychology give them the license needed to assume their role of authority. I do not intend to suggest that power and its uses are inappropriate in school; however, given that power structures do exist, it is important to discuss how power can be shared to enhance the educational experience for all members of the learning community. This chapter examines power and how its uses can encourage or discourage the process of creating and sustaining a democratic classroom environment.

POWER AS THE DEFINING ELEMENT OF THE CLASSROOM

Power can be used to include or exclude and to value or devalue. Whether power is wielded, given away, or shared in a classroom makes obvious to even a casual observer whether a teacher employs behaviorist management strategies, permissive methods, or democratic management practices. In a behaviorist classroom, power resides with the teacher, who makes all decisions about what, when, and how students will do their work. Power typically is enforced through highly visible forms of rewards and punishments to ensure students will do what they are told to do.

In a classroom based on behaviorist practices, the teacher might occasionally seem to share power on a conditional basis. Students might be told that they can choose to behave or not and that they can decide to act in ways that will lead them to receive rewards or punishments. Rarely imparted in these classrooms is sufficient information to assist students in learning how to make decisions about their own behaviors that will consistently contribute to the maintenance of a mutually supportive learning environment. Students are given no real opportunity to provide input into how their classrooms will operate. By and large the teacher has determined how the class will function, what behaviors are acceptable, and who shall receive rewards or punishments. Therefore, the teacher holds all the genuine power in a behaviorist environment.

Another approach to classroom structure is permissiveness. Some teachers who use permissive strategies try to be egalitarian by giving away power. They begin by asking students to develop the rules for the classroom. This permissive approach does not foster self-discipline or model democracy. Students who do not understand the basic principles of democracy on which to base the rules can hardly be expected to develop a classroom structure that will serve their educational needs for the entire year. Relinquishing the decision-making process about classroom management to those who lack the professional training, maturity, wisdom, and insight needed does not promote democratic values or serve the educational needs of teachers or their students.

Permissive classrooms are not models of democracy, but they can be models of anarchy. Democracies are not based on a what-sort-of-rules-do-you-want approach. As with our country's democracy, classroom democracies are based on a foundation of laws that protect the rights of individuals and at the same time protect the needs of the majority. Teachers cannot relinquish their professional expertise to the whims of their inexperienced students. Students can be given some power, but they are not developmentally, morally, or intellectually prepared to have total power.

In behaviorist classrooms, then, power is tightly controlled by teachers. In permissive classrooms, power is given away rather than shared. In contrast, a principal goal of democratic classroom management is to engage in a process for developing and instituting practices that can support the equitable sharing of power. As stated earlier, the very fact that a teacher is in front of the classroom establishes a position of power. Some believe, then, that because the power structure is so clearly delineated, the act of sharing power is impossible. However, students can be empowered in any number of ways, and some methods work better than others. In Ayers's words, "people learn best when they are nurtured as well as challenged, when they are allowed to explore, experiment, and take risks. We learn when we feel good about ourselves and others, when we trust the environment and the people in our lives, when we are safe."*

Classrooms are not owned by the teachers assigned to them, but neither should they be arenas for student anarchy. The contrast to either of these approaches is the democratic classroom, in which power is shared among all members of the learning community.

HOW LANGUAGE CAN BE USED TO LIMIT OR SHARE POWER

The fundamental difference that delineates behaviorist, permissive, and democratic classrooms is the language used to support each stance. *I* is the language used by teachers in behaviorist classrooms, as in "I like the way you are sitting right now," and "I am not happy with the way you are making noise right now," and "I am not going to remind you again." The language used reflects the idea that all the decisions are based on one person's preferences and desires.

You is the language of the permissive classroom, as in "You get to decide the rules we will have here," "You need to think about your behavior," and "You can choose to do this activity or not." The language used has the effect of turning power over to students rather than sharing it with them.

We is the language of a true democratic classroom. The use of *we* is devoid of personal bias that excludes students but rather is an inclusive term that reflects the respect and trust essential to a true democratic environment. The language of *we* serves to distribute power among the community's members.

Democratic language that reflects the rights and responsibilities of citizens is the most logical framework on which to build an equitable classroom climate, in part because it teaches the expectations for behavior in our larger society. As students go about their daily interactions with teachers, they are also learning behaviors that are appropriate for adults in a democratic country. In addition, the language of citizenship expectations helps students and teachers focus on how to solve problems by working together.

This is the essence of the language of *we*. The teacher need not be adversarial, and the student need not try to wrestle power away from the professional educator. The teacher might say: "I noticed you did not hand in your homework and I am wondering if there is a way I can be of help to you. It is important that your work is handed in so it can be assessed. How can we work together to get this done?" In this example, the teacher is focused on the problem of the missing work. There are no threats of punishment, as would be the case in a behaviorist classroom, and the teacher is not ignoring the problem, which can happen in a permissive classroom. The teacher is addressing the problem and offering to work with the student to resolve the issue. The teacher is not offering solutions, trying to make the problem go away, or further exacerbating the problem by making the missing work a source of tension. Through the process of asking questions rather than giving directions the teacher is emphasizing that the student must ultimately find the solution to the problem of the missing work.

LOOKING AT THE MAIN IDEAS

Reducing Power Struggles through Language

The language of *we*

- Is inclusive
- Supports equity
- Prevents teachers from singling out a single student

The role of the democratic educator can be likened to that of a person who is standing by a path and shining a flashlight to help others find their own way. Teachers can guide, encourage, and make decisions that reflect their levels of professional expertise. The role of a teacher in a democratic classroom is to facilitate the learning process for students, whether that learning be math, language arts, or socially responsible behaviors.

POWER AND ITS RELATION TO MULTICULTURAL ISSUES

Beyond the obvious power dynamics that define the relationships among educators, parents, and families, additional layers of power reflect some of the more difficult realities of our larger society. The struggles for power that occur throughout the educational system cannot be divorced from the painfully arbitrary nature of who has and does not have a voice in our society.

> Schools are one of the arenas in which people can work to change the existing distributions of power and knowledge in our society. When school practice is conducted according to the existing conventional wisdom, minority students—especially domestic minority students— usually do not fare well. The conventional wisdom involves assumptions that are part of the cultural hegemony of established classes in society. (Erickson, 1993, p. 45)

Assumptions about power can often reflect assumptions of societal privilege. Issues of privilege associated with race, class, gender, sexual orientation, religion, and national origin must be considered in the way power is defined in the world of education.

People who grow up in and are members of majority cultures, religions, and races make conscious and unconscious assumptions about their roles in society, many of which relate to the power they personally wield based on who they are. According to Erickson (1993, p. 45),

> Hegemony refers to the ubiquitous and taken-for-granted status of a dominant culture within a culturally plural and class-stratified society such as the United States. Because of the ubiquity of the dominant culture and of the institutional arrangements that are consonant with its assumptions, it is not necessary for the dominant groups to use overt means, that is, naked force, to maintain their position of advantage. Rather as members of the society, dominant and subordinate alike, act routinely in concert with the cultural assumptions and interests of the dominant group, existing power relationships can be maintained, as it were, by an invisible hand.

People who grow up in and are members of minority cultures, religions, and races draw conclusions about their ability or inability to access and wield power based on their life experiences. The dichotomy between the perspectives of those from majority cultures and those from minority cultures results in tensions and anxieties that ripple throughout our society. It is unrealistic to imagine that this dis-cord would halt at the schoolhouse gate.

> Consistent patterns of refusal to learn in school can be seen as a form of resistance to a stigmatized ethnic or social class identity that is being assigned by the school. Students can refuse to accept that negative identity by refusing to learn. Yet the sensitivity and salience of stigmatized ethnic identity among teenagers who are members of domestic minority groups . . . is not a phenomena that derives exclusively from within a school. Students' school experiences may contribute to their need to resist accept-ance of a stigmatized identity, but the sources of such an identity lie in part outside the school in the conditions of access to the labor market and in the general assumptions of the nonstigmatized members of society regarding the members of stigmatized groups. (Erickson, 1993, p. 43)

Those who are members of majority races, religions, and nationalities have typically experienced (whether they are aware of it or not) the power of easy educational access; the power of belonging to a dominant culture; and the power of looking like, thinking like, and acting like those who are widely recognized as having the power to make decisions in our society. All of these issues play themselves out on the educational stage because most teachers look like and come from cultures similar to those who wield power in our nation.

At the same time, student populations are becoming increasingly diverse. Terms such as *majority* and *minority*, with all the historical power assumptions those words carry, no longer accurately describe the demographics of some school districts. Although the demographics of student populations are changing dramatically, the traditional power structure of schools is not changing or is changing very slowly. A demographic gulf certainly exists between teachers, who primarily represent the majority culture, and students, who increasingly represent a variety of cultures. Teachers can appear to many students from minority cultures as being an integral part of the societal structure that seems to be weighed heavily against any of them achieving parity in their lives. Consequently, issues of who has power and how power is exercised create conflict, frustration, and outright anger in our public schools.

POWER AND ITS RELATION TO SCHOOL CULTURES

Power struggles can be a result of a clash of cultures and their associated expectations. They can also occur because students want to get along in school but cannot abide by the tasks they are assigned.

> Still beyond the control of the typical teacher are the causes of behavior problems that stem from the way schools are organized. Sometimes school structure forces students to take courses that are inappropriate for them, that do not allow for their individual needs or level of achievement. This kind of structure breeds failure and threatens self-esteem. And delinquent behavior is one way of escaping that failure and threat. (Gage & Berliner, 1988, p. 518)

When young people are given no genuine authority over their daily circumstances in school, they sometimes seize power out of sheer frustration; such drastic measures are often the only means to power that the educational system allows students.

Although this resistance may be associated with minority populations, it is just as often associated with mainstream cultures. Kozol (1990, p. 119) says

> I talk with students in the high schools of the all-white suburbs west of Boston. The students here are, by and large, incredibly well-trained, skillful in math, adept with words, successful in exams, confident of their prospects, and well-padded by the social situation of their folks. It is

apparent, nonetheless, that most of these students feel inhibited, constrained, and impotent in every way that really matters to their sense of fair play.

Disempowered people resist their domination. Although educators and politicians decry resistance behaviors of public school students, the same actions are admired when demonstrated by people in difficult circumstances around the world. We applaud acts of resistance against authoritarian governments. A lone individual who placed his body in the path of a tank bound for Tienneman Square in China is an image burned into our common psyche. Even those who resist a wrong in a democratic society emerge as cultural heroes, Martin Luther King being a prime example.

This common celebration of resistance against the unfair and inequitable forces in society stands in dramatic contrast to the fear generated in educators when students attempt to resist the dominance of an inequitable authoritarian school structure. The same spirit of resistance that is admired in our cultural icons is viewed by some educators as dangerous to members of the learning community when it is directed against how schools are organized. In Kozol's (1975, p. 48) words,

> School defines the act of SAYING NO, in general, as unsound and unwholesome; but SAYING NO to school itself is treason. If moderate terror and a certain modest level of contamination are attached to any child who attempts to question the Scott Foresman Reader, Language Arts, the definition of "peninsula" and such, a far more dangerous level of contamination is attached to those who dare to undermine the larger, twelve-year interlock of school-credential and reward.

The dynamics of power and its uses and abuses can stem from the basic classroom structure of behaviorism, permissiveness, or egalitarianism. They can reflect the larger societal structure of majority–minority cultural tensions. Finally, the way schools are structured can foment or ameliorate the struggles for power in which students are so willing to engage.

POWER RELATIONS AND POWER STRUGGLES

The give and take of power sharing and its associated dynamics can lead to a sense of shared anxiety or a sense of shared enjoyment, depending on how the classroom environment is structured. When power relationships have been ill defined, as in the permissive classroom, or rigidly defined, as in the behaviorist classroom, students struggle to discover which avenues might offer them opportunities for a recognized role in the daily interactions that occur within their classrooms. If their roles are tightly controlled by teachers who use behaviorist methods or left to personal discretion under the benign neglect of a permissive teacher, struggles can result as students try to comprehend the contribution each member of the learning community is expected to make.

Teachers and students compete for power and position. Teachers often use approaches to controlling students and classrooms that are unsuitable for developing mutual respect and shared responsibility. Under these conditions, authority is questioned, and the teacher's position is vulnerable to attack. The dominant approach to classroom control and discipline is haphazard, a contest of wills that is constrained by a lack of understanding of group dynamics. (Queen, Blackwelder, & Mallen, 1997, p. 5)

When power is ill defined or tightly regimented, who is allowed to define or control the power is a logical source of conflict. In educational terms, these conflicts are called power struggles. They can occur at any time and take a variety of forms, but they all relate to the very human need to feel a sense of control over one's own life. When power is tightly controlled by the teacher, students are likely to use a variety of sanctioned or unsanctioned methods to access power. If there is no obvious access, then students will seek avenues to power that fall outside school-sanctioned behaviors and the likelihood of power struggles will increase.

Power struggle has no single definition because, depending on how the power is structured and how students choose to wrestle it from the authority figures, the struggles can take any number of forms. The one common element of power struggles, however, is fear. Power struggles are not unique to teaching, but they are perhaps most frightening to teachers because they seem to portend the end of the well-ordered classroom and the onset of chaos.

Power struggles can probably not be avoided, and there is no single solution to resolving them or any guarantee that even the most democratic of educators will not experience them from time to time in their classrooms. There are no sure preventions for conflict or quick resolutions when they happen; however, patience, good communication, and respect can go a long way toward identifying the means with which to solve the inevitable problems that arise during the average school day.

ANALYZING THE POWER STRUGGLE

It is important to first understand why power struggles occur at all. What causes teachers and students to draw their lines in the sand? Dreikurs, Grunwald, and Pepper (1971, p. 18) describe the need for power as being a mistaken goal: "When [parents and teachers] . . . try to control the child, they reach a deadlock through the child's attempt to overpower them, or at least to resist their control. The child feels accepted and worthwhile only when he can do whatever he wants, and thereby refuse to do what he is supposed to do."

People want recognition and acceptance from those around them. They seek a sense of permanent value and want acknowledgment that they matter, that they belong, and that others are taking note of them. When those needs are met because everyone is behaving appropriately and receiving the social rewards for doing so, all is well. In the classroom, this would mean that all the students are calm, polite, and on task.

Most teachers dream of classes with only such students. But life can deal harshly with young people, just as it does with adults. Children do not have to live long in difficult circumstances before they discover that to receive social recognition from those around them, they sometimes must act in ways that are dangerous and threatening to others. When they enter school, they bring their understanding of how to receive social recognition with them, an understanding that is often diametrically opposed to the climate educators are trying to promote. The clash is inevitable, and the term we give to this clash is *power struggle.*

Power struggles occur in school when students attempt to take control of the classroom and teachers experience the sense of standing on quicksand and sinking rapidly. At such times, teachers often wish for some quick fixes to power struggles: fast and sure strategies that are guaranteed to solve any conflict in a short amount of time. Although such strategies are desirable, the works-everytime-sure-cure solution to any power struggle is a fantasy.

Human relationships are complex and multidimensional, particularly when the dynamics of power are included in the mix.

> Dreikurs, Grunwald, and Pepper (1971, p. 187) report a study showing that teachers want immediate solutions to discipline problems in their classrooms. Their requests for help often take the form, "What can I do to make the kids pay attention . . . so that I can teach?" However, teachers must realize that only a part of student misbehavior is wholly spontaneous and unanticipated. The quality of teacher-student relationships, the clarity and reasonableness of the teacher's expectations, the consistency of the teacher's behavior, and the general level of motivation are among the factors that condition student behavior, including misbehavior. (Hoover & Kindsvatter, 1997, p. 10)

POWER AND EQUITY

Inconsistencies often occur in the ways various students are treated by the same teacher. Personal bias and values can often be the determining factors in how a teacher responds to student behaviors. Blatant inequities can lead to struggles over power in a classroom.

Oregon is one of the few states in our nation that requires a course on civil rights and discrimination for teacher licensure. Those who wish to be licensed in that state are asked to complete a self-check designed to assist in the creation of an inclusive classroom climate. The self-check includes the following items (Teacher Standards and Practices Commission, 1996, p. 12):

- **"Do you make seat assignments, work assignments, line assignments, or play-group assignments by race, sex, age, national origin, disability, language spoken, marital status, or religion which isolate or negatively affect students?"**   For instance, asking students to line up according to height or gender could discriminate against students on the basis of who they are. To equitably share power, students cannot be relegated to positions that relate to who they are; rather, decision making can focus on ways to effectively maintain a safe and healthy community.

- **"Do you use male pronouns to the exclusion of female pronouns or man to the exclusion of woman in your language?"** Gender issues are also important when we begin to assess how often we call on which students and the quality of our responses to their questions or comments. To equitably share power, teachers must think in terms of inclusionary practices and inclusionary language.
- **"Do you maintain eye contact, smile, or stand close to some groups of students more than others because of sex, age, race, national origin, disability, marital status, religion or language spoken?"** Power dynamics, equitable or inequitable, can often be established through body language. If teachers keep a greater distance from students who are from minority cultures, if they ask students who speak English as a second language to continually repeat what they have said when they do not ask the same of other students, and if they do not display an equally warm greeting for all students, the power dynamics in the classroom can be exclusionary for students who represent cultures that are not the same as their teacher's.
- **"Do you use the same kind of disciplinary measures regardless of the student's race, age, sex, or national origin?"** Expectations for appropriate behavior should be equally high for all groups. Individual students may need different information to help them correct some inappropriate action (addressed in chapter 5), but who a student is should not be the determining factor for the responses that occur when problems arise.
- **"Are your classroom displays integrated with different kinds of people in different roles based on these categories?"** Equal educational opportunities are protected through a variety of deliberate practices. Teachers have available many practical ideas that can be feasibly implemented to ensure equity. (Teacher Standards and Practices Commission, 1996)

> The children become aware of their power as a group, are intolerant of strong assertions of teacher authority, and resist the status of dependency presupposed by such assertions. In ethnographic accounts of school children who do not fear or value the structural implications of school, one hears repeatedly that the children feel they are put down or treated like babies at school (Clark 1976, p. 256; Gallimore, Boggs, and Jordan 1974; Tripp 1986, p. 141; Williams 1981, p. 217) and that the road to sustaining interaction with the children involves some form of power sharing. (D'Amato, 1993, p. 197)

THE ROLE OF PERMANENT VALUE IN DIFFUSING THE STRUGGLE FOR POWER

The decisions educators make concerning the particulars of how their classroom climates will be established are critically important to whether students will see themselves as permanently valued members of the classroom or as perpetually facing the possibility of exclusion. If the language teachers use for their rules reflects a punitive stance, students know they are in the presence of adults who may not have their best interests at heart. If the language of the rules reflects acceptance for all the needs and interests represented in the classroom, students know that their educators are willing to help them over the rough spots and work with them to resolve problems.

A sense of being permanently valued, as opposed to conditionally appreciated, is also reflected in the differences between behaviorist and democratic classroom policies. In a behaviorist classroom, students are valued only if they willingly comply with the directives of their teachers. In a democratic classroom that supports permanent value, students know that they can make mistakes and still have a chance to fix the problems with the help of their teachers.

When permanent value is not given, students can feel outraged at a system that seems rigged against their chances for success. That sense of outrage spills over into unfinished work, insults hurled at peers and educators, and a continual sense that teachers and students are battling each other for control. According to Gage and Berliner (1998, p. 518),

> Schools that are impersonal and overcrowded, and have weak administrative leadership, low expectations concerning student achievement, little emphasis on basic skills, large classes that prevent teachers from helping or even identifying students who need special attention, poor communication between school and home—schools that operate under these conditions contribute to the crime, delinquency, and problem behavior that exist in them.

If everywhere in society students receive messages that they have no voice, no access to power, and no prospects, then resistance to all the institutions of that society can seem a very logical response.

LOOKING AT THE MAIN IDEAS

Permanent Value in the Classroom Can Be Ensured by

- Avoiding accusations
- Focusing on correcting behaviors rather than on individuals
- Ensuring that every student will have an equal opportunity to succeed

The art of avoiding power struggles, then, begins with educators who not only recognize but manifest in their actions and words a true respect for the permanent value of their students. Citizenship is a permanent value that teachers cannot take away, although personal freedoms may be limited by circumstances and common need. Accordingly, teachers cannot grant permanent value to the citizens who enter their classrooms, but rather they can recognize that permanent value exists and then make decisions that protect it.

PREVENTIVE MEASURES FOR AVOIDING CONFLICTS

Democratic classroom management practices can help to resolve conflicts peacefully between educators and their students. These practices include such basic strategies as giving students clear instructions for tasks, developing an engaging curriculum appropriate for a wide variety of learning styles and needs, creating a welcoming classroom environment, basing assessment on students' learning rather than on attitudes or behaviors, and using cogent communication techniques.

Teachers often speak of how important it is to have a bag of tricks for managing classrooms. The term *bag of tricks* may trivialize the message, but being able to draw on a variety of disciplines such as educational psychology, learning theory, and motivational strategies can help to reduce the likelihood of a power struggle. Mediation and peaceful conflict resolution strategies are also helpful when it comes to alleviating tensions that might arise. The professional knowledge particular to education serves teachers well when they work to resolve conflict and maintain a peaceful learning environment.

Preventing Power Struggles through Good Communication Strategies

No matter how diligent teachers are in their efforts to ensure equity and fairness, power struggles still occur. Despite all attempts by educators to create welcoming and supportive classrooms, students may feel frustrated, insecure, ill informed, out of control, or angry and exhibit those feelings uninhibitedly. Teachers often become targets for this frustration simply because they are conveniently available. The anger evident in students usually has nothing to do with the teacher; however, if teachers respond to the anger by trying to squelch it, they can often find themselves in the line of fire.

Imagine that you are sitting at home at the end of a very long day. You are reading a good book, listening to quiet background music, and doing your best to relax and unwind. Suddenly the door bursts open and the person who shares your living space is standing in the doorway. This person is obviously upset; before you can say anything, the other person hurls a backpack across the room, kicks over a magazine rack, and slams the door.

Without skipping a beat, you stand up and say "I want that backpack picked up this instant! Get those magazines off the floor! And then show me that you know how to shut a door properly!" The response may strike the reader as laughable. The idea of treating an adult in such a way is funny in large part because of the response such commands would engender in the person who is already so upset. Very likely the response would be far from peaceful, and our survival instinct keeps us from allowing ourselves to become the target of the person's anger. Yet this is exactly the way many teachers respond to similar behaviors in students; as a result, teachers position themselves strategically to be the targets of anger and can quickly find themselves engaged in a power struggle.

It seems obvious that adults who live together would respond quite differently to each other's angry outbursts. Depending on the nature of the outburst and the attitudes of those involved, an initial comment might be, "It looks like you had a tough day." That simple sentence tells the other person that the speaker understands. It also opens the door for the other person to begin to talk about the problem. The backpack will get picked up and the magazine rack will be righted, but that is not the most pressing issue to be addressed between adults who want to share power. It is more important that the anger be dissipated through empathetic communication strategies than that the magazine rack be repositioned.

The scenario that opened this chapter is a common example of how the dynamics of power can lead to struggles in the classroom. The teacher presenting the math lesson is in control not only of the lesson but also of how the information is being presented and the opportunities students have to comprehend the math concepts they are responsible for learning. The problems are rapidly written on the board, solved, and erased, and little process time is provided. This may well be an effective learning situation for students who have high mathematics abilities or who are auditory learners. Students who have intelligences in other areas such as linguistics, who learn better through tactile experiences, who do not speak English as a primary language, or who have auditory processing problems may be unable to comprehend the information in the lesson. They have been excluded from their opportunity to access the content and are probably feeling frustrated and disempowered. As a result, the power distribution in the classroom has shifted in favor of those who can learn the way the teacher is teaching.

The student who was talking in the opening scenario, Mary, might have been unable to follow the progression of information for any number of reasons. Once the student was effectively excluded from the lesson, talking to another student probably seemed like a reasonable way to express the frustration she was feeling. And by turning her attention elsewhere, she was able to assume some measure of power by taking control of the situation in a manner that suited her. Through her actions, she removed herself from the learning process and took with her the student sitting next to her and then the entire class.

When the teacher singled Mary out in front of the class, the student was provided with a clear target for the anger she was feeling. Her response to the teacher immediately won her at least temporary admiration from students who were having a similarly difficult time following the lesson. The teacher may have "won" the encounter, but students will not soon forget the loss of professional aplomb. The next time the lesson does not catch the interest of the students, they will have a good idea of how to make the class more entertaining.

This is not to imply that students usually misbehave out of malicious intent. The more likely scenario is that power struggles occur when students are feeling a sense of disempowerment. When teachers take these struggles personally and become confrontational, they allow the students to focus what might previously have been a general sense of unease into clear anger. In other words, teachers who do not understand the dynamics of a power struggle can unwittingly make themselves the target of a student's anger. Gathercoal (1994, p. 109), says that "the key to avoiding a power struggle is knowing when, where, why, and how to back off."

On the other hand, teachers who use their professional knowledge of learning theory and motivation understand the need to present information in a variety of ways to provide all learners with an opportunity to be successful. When students express frustration, teachers can explore ways to restate the information or they can present it in another way. "Teachers may be surprised to read that nobody has to fight with a child. Many believe just the opposite, that one has to assert one's authority. Few teachers realize that they do not lose status if they openly admit their defeat" (Dreikurs, Grunwald, & Pepper, 1971, p. 197). But when egos get in the way, frustrations become power struggles and nobody wins.

The Fine Art of Backing Off

According to Dreikurs, Grunwald, & Pepper (1971, p. 197),

> The first obstacle toward a solution of a conflict is the widespread assumption that one has to subdue the defiant child and make him respect adult demands. The second stumbling block is the teacher's personal involvement in a power conflict. One cannot extricate oneself if one has a feeling of inadequacy and is concerned with one's own prestige. No conflict can be resolved as long as one is afraid of being humiliated, taken advantage of, and personally defeated.

People who are new to any professional role that places them in a responsible position can feel a sense of panic over a power struggle. They fear that rebellion, if not immediately put down, will spread and they will soon have lost any control. The typical response, then, is to engage in the struggle and attempt to obtain dominance through sheer force of will. Such strategies do not work or help people feel successful in their professional roles. They must continually fear the next challenge to their power and whether they will have the strength and will to once again force another person to acquiesce. Their average workday is characterized by exhaustion and stress as a result of the fear and uncertainty that haunt them.

New teachers often struggle with students who want to wield power. It does not really matter what the student is refusing to do, because the fear that act generates in new teachers can make them quickly lose their tempers. Even worse, teachers may not see past their own panic to recognize the fear and panic that often motivates students' actions. The idea of pausing, composing themselves, and patiently asking students about the problem seems to be an invitation for classroomwide chaos. In fact, such actions have been shown to result in a peaceful and beneficial end to whatever problem was occurring. Power struggles can be resolved in ways that are mutually beneficial when educators understand that backing off is not the same as backing down. Just as an individual may choose which battles to fight, it is equally wise for an individual to determine the best time to take a stand. The best time may not always be when the problem happens.

◈ Looking at the Main Ideas

Backing Off Models Professional Demeanor by

- Giving students the gift of time
- Encouraging everyone to calm down before mediating a problem
- Presenting a calm adult role model rather than an adult who is not in control of personal emotions

A troubled student is not helped by yelling, threatening, coercing, or cajoling. Dialogue about the problem and ideas about how to resolve it peacefully are needed. That sort of reasoned exchange may not be possible when tempers flare and perspectives are lost. Taking a mutual time-out to calm down, breathe, and consider options helps teachers maintain their professional demeanor when they sit down to work through a problem with students. Sometimes students just need respect, understanding, and, most important, the gift of time. Teachers who take the time to calm down and consider their options are also giving their students some time to recover their dignity. The simple act of giving both parties some time goes a long way toward building trust in the classroom.

As in the opening scenario, teachers sometimes use sarcastic remarks to embarrass a student who is off task. The comment may get a laugh, but the student who is the target of such a remark feels hurt and ostracized. Sometimes quick, sarcastic comments lead to an escalation of the problem (as in the opening scenario) or bring a potential confrontation to a quick end because the student is too hurt, stunned, or embarrassed to respond. The damage done to the professional relationship between the teacher and the student will take a long time to repair, if it ever can be.

Another student response that can precipitate a power struggle is the phrase "This is stupid." The response is usually part of the following scenario. A student is not doing the in-class assignment or perhaps has not completed a homework assignment. The teacher asks what the problem is and the student says "This is stupid." Although adults often characterize anything that frustrates them as stupid—stupid golf clubs, stupid computer, stupid car—teachers nevertheless tend to take it personally when students use these words to describe an assignment. Teachers sometimes use sarcasm or threats to get control of the potential power struggle, but other, more professionally satisfying, strategies can be employed at such times. For instance, teachers can begin by asking students what is going on and whether they understand what they should be working on. This approach immediately focuses both teacher and students on the work and not on the behavior. When students are off task and describe the work as stupid, boring, or dumb, teachers have only been given a smoke screen that needs to be cleared away before they can understand the real problem. The challenge is now to ask questions that will reveal what is really going on.

Asking questions requires some response from students. The questions teachers ask can help involve students as partners in resolving the problem. If teachers instead choose to lecture students about their behaviors, they are missing their chance to discover the true nature of where the students' learning is breaking down. As teachers lecture them, students can sit passively by, listening or not, but there is no real communication between the student and teacher.

Questioning students, on the other hand, typically yields some response. A teacher might respond to the comment that the work is stupid with the following: "You seem to be pretty frustrated. I am wondering if I can help you get started with this." If the student is still reticent, a teacher can ask what the student needs to know about the first math problem or for some ideas the student might have about the writing assignment. If this does not seem to lead anywhere, a teacher might ask if something is wrong or if the student is having a tough day. If the student does not respond, the teacher can say: "We really need to solve this problem, but this does not seem like a good time. Why not take some time to sit here, and I will come back to you as soon as I can."

The teacher can give the student the time needed to recover. The issue of the work that needs to be completed can be addressed after the student is feeling safe and more stable emotionally. If students are bullied or threatened into doing work when they feel emotionally troubled, the activity will probably not make a lasting impression on them. A safe and productive learning environment is one in which students feel supported on their toughest days.

If the student begins to engage in the task, the teacher should compliment the student's cooperative attitude and offer to check back in a few minutes. The problem will probably not take more than one or two minutes to resolve; if the problem is more complex, the teacher can arrange with the student a mutually convenient time to meet and work together to solve the problem.

Some teachers dislike such strategies because they are concerned that the rest of the class will get off task during the brief conference. To avoid this problem, teachers can discuss with students at the beginning of the school year what the expectations might be when one student needs a private conference. Teachers can tell students that the most important goal is to respect and listen to each other; they can also convey to students what they should do while such a private conference is going on.

When asking questions, it is a good idea for teachers to lower themselves to the student's eye level. Assuming that posture accomplishes two things: (1) it establishes equitable communication, whereas standing over a student can convey a message of power, and (2) it makes establishing eye contact much easier. Although eye contact is not culturally appropriate for every student, establishing eye contact can convey a message of caring and help to ensure privacy. In this position a teacher can ask some quick questions and show genuine interest in the student's situation.

When asking questions, it is important to remember that the least useful question is why. Asking a student why the assignment is stupid will not yield the information necessary to resolve the problem. The student will likely shrug and say something like "I don't know. It just is." Asking why is pointless if the student is having trouble understanding what needs to be done. Asking why does not tell the teacher if the student is embarrassed, frustrated, or bored. These problems can only be resolved when the teacher asks specific questions aimed at ascertaining the nature of the problem.

In a situation like this, teachers find that potential power struggles can be diffused if they focus their problem solving on the assignment, rather than the student's behavior. The teacher can begin by saying, "You sound pretty frustrated. Tell me what is confusing to you. I will see if I can help." If the student is still reticent, the teacher can suggest looking at the first step and then going through it together. By doing so, the teacher demonstrates patience and a willingness to help the student figure out what needs to be done; however, the teacher should avoid doing the work for the student. Because the student needs to learn the information, it is the student's responsibility to engage with the teacher to understand the task.

Stopping by a student's desk to ask a quick question and help the student refocus may take only a minute or two, but resolving a problem takes more time. Teachers can choose to spend the time in a power struggle or they can provide a professional model of conflict resolution. To maintain a professional posture, it is essential for educators to strive for the latter.

A productive approach to conflict resolution is to find ways to personally connect with students, which is not as difficult as it may seem. According to Jones and Jones (1995, p. 69), "We can express our interest in and concern for students by (1) monitoring the quality of our relationships with students, with a focus on maintaining a high rate of positive statements; (2) creating opportunities for personal discussions with them; and (3) demonstrating our interest in activities that are important to them."

These three items can be addressed through interactions even before a class starts for the day. As students enter the classroom, the teacher can greet them with a smile and ask how they are doing. Some teachers try to use every minute to organize paperwork and make sure necessary materials are collected, organized, and ready for the next lesson. Equally as important as organization, though, is the one-on-one human contact that demonstrates caring and can help to build positive relationships with students. When the first words students hear a teacher say are "Today we will be starting with chapter 3 in your textbooks. I hope you all remembered to bring your books with you," no sense of welcome has been conveyed to them. Teachers usually display these behaviors not because of a lack of caring but because of the press of time and a considerable workload. However, a teacher's job becomes more difficult and stressful when students perceive the environment to be difficult and stressful and respond accordingly. A few positive exchanges with students as they enter the classroom can prevent many of these potential problems.

THE RELATION OF POWER STRUGGLES
TO THE PHYSICAL ENVIRONMENT

Seating Arrangements

As mentioned earlier, the first time students enter a classroom, they get a sense of whether their teacher is working for their success. The arrangement of the desks, the displays on the bulletin boards, the language of the class rules, and how the syllabus establishes expectations all reflect the basic beliefs about students that govern the teacher's decisions.

Although the placement of desks might not initially seem to be linked to power struggles, the ease with which every member of the learning community can move about in the classroom affects whether students feel welcomed. When desks are arranged in rows, communication among peers typically is discouraged. Students are often made to feel they are in competition with their peers and that the power structure of the classroom is working to build a sense of disassociation among its members.

This common classroom arrangement is particularly troublesome to many Native American students, whose cultures value community and cooperation. Native American students, who are representatives of various tribes, sometimes express anger toward school system structures that are diametrically opposed to their cultural values. These students express a sense of feeling devalued because public schools force them into behaviors that are an anathema to their tribal and family values.

On a pragmatic level, seating students in rows can often precipitate a power struggle simply because the students seated farthest away from the teacher are most likely to talk among themselves and be off task. Their location at once seems to give them license to act in ways that might disrupt the classroom and makes it difficult for a teacher to effectively address problems except by giving directives from across the room.

Teachers who arrange the desks in rows often do so because it is the arrangement with which they are most familiar. Problems occur when they find themselves in the front of the room trying to quiet students sitting in the back. Teachers may order offending students to move to the front of the room, and students may decide to comply; however, in the course of doing so, they often noisily pack up their things, lift themselves slowly out of their seats, and stop to speak with a few different students on their way to the front.

These acts of resistance all fit within the definition of *power struggle*. They consume precious instructional time and may make teachers frustrated and angry to the point of losing their tempers. When teachers arrange their classrooms so that there is no easy way to move closer to students when necessary, then corrective messages about behavior must be done publicly.

Teachers who choose to address the problem in front of the whole class leave their students with few options for resolving problems appropriately. Students might quietly comply with the edict being handed down from the front of the room but later face the negative fallout generated among their peers. When students are publicly singled out in such a manner, they often engage in defiant behaviors just to save face with their friends.

Students may choose to openly defy directives and suffer the punishment or engage in the power struggle (they seem to comply, but every action reflects the reality that they still hold their measure of power in the classroom). Teachers, concerned about the economy of time and the desire to show who is in control of the classroom, may too quickly respond to behavioral problems with the least effective choice—public confrontation. The possibility of employing some preventive, intermediate steps is eliminated, at least in part, because of the physical arrangement of the classroom. When the physical arrangement permits teachers to move to where a problem is occurring, they can often curb the behavior just by establishing proximity. If proximity alone is not effective, teachers can pause for a moment to quietly ask students whether everything is all right, which is often sufficient to peacefully resolve a minor disturbance. Classrooms that are arranged to allow for easy movement help teachers dramatically reduce the time spent on conflicts. More importantly, the tension and harm to the student–teacher relationship can be avoided.

Bulletin Boards

Bulletin board displays that reflect the entire school community, including all its diverse members, communicate messages of welcome and inclusion. If students know they are valued and are equally represented members of the community, they are far less likely to disturb a classroom in their quest for recognition.

At the secondary level, bulletin boards are typically left unattended or are reserved for notices at the beginning of the year. Although teachers need not spend a lot of time preparing attractive bulletin boards, creating a visually appealing classroom is an important way to welcome students. Students who are visual learners feel more comfortable in a room that uses bulletin boards as a teaching tool and might be willing to help the teacher plan future displays.

REDUCING POWER STRUGGLES WITH INCLUSIVE CURRICULUM PRACTICES

The exciting challenge before professional educators lies in discovering which educational practices will best suit the various learning needs in a classroom. When students are actively engaged in their learning, they are far less likely to seek amusement as a replacement for boredom or revenge as a replacement for frustration.

> Teachers also play an important role in helping students meet their needs for affiliation, power, and approval. What is important here is matching the teaching environment to the students' motive patterns. For one student you might increase social reinforcement; for another, you might require group work; for still another, you might talk about tendencies for overdependence. We know that factors in the learning environment influence motivation and behavior. At present, it is mainly through "intuition" that a teacher can try to use this kind of knowledge to make learning more efficient and effective. (Gage & Berliner, 1988, p. 359)

A curriculum that stimulates and motivates young people is far easier to carry out successfully than one that bores or frustrates them. An important first step in this process is to begin the year with preassessments that not only ascertain what students know about the subject matter but also provide insight into their interests and learning styles. The information rendered by such pretests is an important asset to teachers who plan to design curriculum that will invite and engage rather than frustrate and produce tedium.

Boredom or frustration encountered on a daily basis can lead to power struggles as the students seek some end to the real or perceived curricular tyrannies they are being required to endure. According to Kohn (1996, p. 19),

> The curricular problems connected to troublesome behavior often go well beyond the difficulty level of assignments. Let's be honest: students frequently perceive the tasks they are given as not worth doing—and sometimes for good reason. Worksheets and textbooks and lectures are often hard to justify pedagogically. Even an assignment that could in principle be worthwhile may fail to engage students because its meaning and relevance were never explained, or because students had nothing to say about how it was to be done.

As teachers begin to explore the various aspects of their profession, they often find that their greatest management difficulties center on how to help students start on a task, stay on a task, and complete a task. Preservice and many new teachers tend to focus on getting students to do the work without considering why students might wish to do the opposite. Such teachers are in the process of integrating their knowledge of learning theory and motivation with strategies for classroom management. Unfortunately, before they discover the powerful connection between a motivating curriculum and the reduction of behavioral problems, they see every student's challenge to some required class assignment as a potential power struggle.

Curriculum that draws on the talents and needs of students can provide young people with a powerful opportunity to be authentically engaged in the decisions about how they will learn rather than what they will learn. The trained professional educator determines what content is appropriate for the developmental levels of his or her students and ensures that the curriculum is designed to meet state and district expectations. However, students can help to structure how information might be accessed and the vehicles through which they can demonstrate their learning.

An important legal exception to the assumption that teachers alone determine what will be learned occurs when the curriculum content is diametrically opposed to the family values of students. If the families of students, or the students themselves, decide a topic scheduled for class discussion falls outside their family value system, they have the right to successfully challenge the teacher's plans. A common example of this legal exception is the study of evolution. Some students will not participate in course work related to evolution, and trying to force them to participate can create power struggles among all the stakeholders in the situation, including families. Legally, parents or guardians have the right to cast the final vote on whether a student will engage in any unit of study. Teachers can reduce the chance of power clashes by understanding and working with this parental right in mind.

Some teachers fear that if they honor the rights students have to not learn about a subject chaos will ensue. However, such encounters are rare; when they do occur, dialogue and negotiation can resolve the situation peacefully. For instance, some students' religious beliefs may conflict with the assigned readings in an English literature class. Alternative reading assignments can be developed by working with students and their families. Teachers need to be aware of what skills they want to assess; for example, if the goal is to assess reading comprehension, it does not matter what material students are reading.

The design of the curriculum and the course syllabi used, depending on the grade level, can either contribute to the possibility of power struggles or diffuse potential problems. The more power is shared with students in the basic class structure, the less students will be tempted to try to wrestle power from the teacher. Curricula and syllabi that include students in the decisions to be made and the ideas to be shared send a message of mutual empowerment that can prevent power struggles. Clearly academic standards must be maintained, but within the framework of those standards, students can have some authentic choices in terms of how to demonstrate understanding of subject matter.

For instance, if students are studying an area of social studies, they might be able to demonstrate their levels of subject matter mastery by selecting one of several project options. This inclusive strategy appeals to visual learners, who might want to make a poster or some other display, to kinesthetic learners, who might want to act out a play about the topic, and to students with artistic ability, who might want to create a piece of artwork to demonstrate what they have learned.

LOOKING AT THE MAIN IDEAS

Curriculum Can Reduce Power Struggles When

- Lessons are designed to address a variety of learning styles
- Peer social interaction is naturally a part of the learning process
- Special needs and cultural values are considered in the curriculum design
- Assessment practices are equitable

Teachers must assess such projects based on objective standards, such as the accuracy of the information presented. Basic criteria for such projects should be developed with students before they begin the activity, so that they understand the criteria they must meet to demonstrate subject mastery. It is important for teachers to grade only on the objective criteria established by them or as the result of input from all members of the class. These criteria cannot reflect the economic levels of the students; in other words, grades cannot depend on how attractive the project is—especially if the student worked on the project at home. Students' equity is not protected if their grades are tied to the quality of art supplies their families can afford. If assessment criteria are equitable and students have opportunities to demonstrate subject area mastery in ways that reflect their preferred learning modalities, they will be more engaged in the work.

Assessing learning styles can yield important information that can be applied to the types of projects and activities assigned and also to determine the best strategies for direct instruction. Teachers tend to teach in ways that fit their own preferred learning modalities, regardless of whether those strategies are compatible with the preferred learning modalities of their students. For instance, teachers may be random, or right-brain, thinkers. They may be spontaneous and creative, delivering instruction inspired by a sense of whimsy and surprise. Many of their students, on the other hand, may be sequential thinkers who want information presented in ways that can be understood in a step-by-step fashion and recorded in notes that are easily outlined. Even if mutual respect exists between teachers and their students, they will both experience a sense of frustration in this situation. The students may be confused and ask questions that the teachers is sure have been previously addressed.

Learning style surveys completed by both teachers and students can quickly reveal where communication is breaking down and how to fix it. Teachers may have to adapt or change some of their teaching strategies. Although teachers are free to choose their approaches to subject matter, they might want to incorporate the use of transparencies, giving hard copies to the students, and use sequential order to direct the flow of their instruction. As a result, teachers will ramble less, students will feel more secure, and everyone's frustration levels will decrease dramatically.

Cultural differences and learning styles are often inseparable. To maintain an equitable learning environment, addressing a broad range of needs through a variety of curriculum strategies becomes even more important. In Purkey and Novak's (1984) book *Inviting School Success* the authors describe an invitational climate as being one in which "students are taught that each person has relatively untapped capacities for learning, and that this learning is something that happens inside themselves; it is not something that happens outside. Students participate in deciding what they will study, how much they will learn, how fast they will learn, and how they will evaluate their own individual progress" (p. 97). The authors do not suggest that addressing learning styles and individual needs means teachers must relinquish their professional responsibilities to direct curriculum. As with management, all members of the community share a mutual responsibility for learning.

SUMMARY

Let us go back once more to the scenario that began this chapter. What elements led to the power struggle? In the scenario the teacher was writing quickly on the board, presenting and solving problems, and only briefly checking to see if students were following along. If we were to rewind that scene and start again, the teacher might have used an overhead projector. That way the teacher would be facing the students and be better able to monitor their behaviors and levels of understanding. The teacher could have written the problems on a transparency and then discussed the strategies for finding the solutions with the entire group.

The teacher might have put problems on an overhead transparency, asked students to work together with partners to solve them, and then had everyone share answers with the rest of the class. Students would thus have had some opportunity for social interaction, and students who were not following the information would have had an opportunity for peer tutoring.

Another strategy is to put a question or problem on an overhead transparency and then walk to the back of the room to discuss the possible solutions with the class. Walking to the back of the room helps a teacher to monitor the class more effectively, shifts the focus of the discussion away from a stagnant view of the front of the room, and allows the teacher to make sure that the transparency on the overhead projector is clear and readable.

When the teacher in the opening scenario turned around and saw Mary engaged in a side conversation, one way to avoid the ensuing power struggle might have been to ask students to take a minute to make sure they could hear the information and ask themselves if they were helping themselves and others to learn. This message not only helps students to recall the established expectations for classroom behavior but also conveys to students the moral message of considering the welfare of others and themselves. Most important, such a strategy avoids singling out one student and creating the unpleasant situation that followed in the chapter-opening scenario.

Finally, if the teacher challenged Mary in front of the group and received Mary's sarcastic response, it would have been appropriate to say something like "Mary, let's take a minute to talk about this later." The use of this strategy is an example of backing off, not backing down. It allows the teacher to maintain a professional demeanor because the response models respect rather than inappropriate use of power.

Power struggles are scary, and the possibility of losing control haunts many teachers. The most challenging part of teaching is being able to remain above the fray, model patience and tolerance, and use a variety of strategies to resolve conflicts in ways that maintain everyone's dignity.

APPLYING THE CONCEPTS

Earlier in this chapter you were asked to recall a power struggle in which you were engaged or one that you witnessed. What strategies did you learn in this chapter that might have prevented or diffused that struggle? Please reflect on which strategies you will use in the classroom to diminish the potential for future power struggles.

CHAPTER 7

Those We See and Those We Do Not See:
Understanding the Issues of Highly Visible Students and Invisible Students

CHAPTER OBJECTIVES

By the end of this chapter the reader should be able to:

◇ Demonstrate an understanding of the legal issues integral to a discussion of high visibility and invisibility
◇ Articulate the difference between management practices that promote high visibility and management practices that protect confidentiality
◇ Discuss the role culture plays in the high visibility and invisibility of students
◇ Apply strategies to promote equal standing among all students in a classroom

Scenario

Nadia was preparing to hand back the tests students had taken the day before and made a quick decision to turn this into an opportunity to motivate her students. T.J., a particularly quiet student, had done an excellent job on the test. Nadia decided to hand all the papers back with no comment but to save T.J.'s until the very last. She smiled to herself as, out of the corner of her eye, she watched T.J. grow more and more nervous waiting for the tests to all be returned. "This will be such a pleasant surprise for T.J.," Nadia thought to herself. Finally, when all the other papers had been distributed, Nadia walked over to T.J.'s desk. "Class, I think we can all share in a special moment for T.J.! This is the only A+ earned on this test. T.J. has worked very hard and it really showed. Congratulations, T.J.!"

As the teacher placed the test in T.J.'s hands she smiled, but T.J.'s head was down. The teacher was disappointed that her smile was not returned. Feeling confused and a little hurt, she turned to walk back to the front of the room. Suddenly T.J. felt a poke on the shoulder and heard a taunting voice: "Show off!"

Questions

What do you think happened in this scenario? What would you have done differently if you were the teacher? Why? Take a minute to consider these questions before reading on.

Discussion

Among the many personalities, proclivities, and psyches represented in classrooms, two particular kinds of students are inevitably found there: the highly visible student and the student who seems almost invisible. Highly visible students and invisible students are so recognized partly because of their own actions and partly because of the way teachers respond to them. The former tend to get far more attention than the latter. Nevertheless, each type of student brings to the classroom an equal weight of associated legal, pedagogical, and psychological issues. Most teachers eventually learn that highly visible students and invisible students can be almost anyone, depending on the students' current life situations.

A PARADOX

There is a noticeable paradox pertaining to issues of high visibility and invisibility. Teachers often say they dislike any form of public correction or praise, and yet many teachers admit that they use these strategies to control students.

If a teacher were having management problems and the principal chose to publicly discuss those problems at a staff meeting, the teacher would probably react with hostility and very likely seek legal redress against the actions of the administrator. And yet their students, who may be experiencing a variety of personal difficulties that contribute to behavioral problems, are often made to endure the very treatment their teachers would not tolerate.

Public praise can be equally difficult for teachers. Teachers recognized as exemplary models may be isolated from their peers because of public praise. Thus, this chapter begins with a version of the golden rule: being singled out is not comfortable for adults, and therefore it does not enhance an educator's professionalism to use such strategies with students.

LEGAL CONCERNS OF HIGH VISIBILITY AND INVISIBILITY

Among the Fourteenth Amendment protections afforded to individuals is the right to equal protection under the law. Equal protection extends to a number of educational issues, including exercising care that students are not made highly visible or invisible because of who they are.

> From an educational standpoint, the Equal Protection Clause represents the legal basis for prohibiting unreasonable classifications. Although some type of classification is often necessary in laws, rules, or policies, arbitrariness may not play a part. . . . The principal idea inherent in equal protection, as in due process, is the concept of fairness. And as is the case with due process, whether or not equal protection has been granted or denied depends upon a balancing of several elements. These include sociological and psychological factors, sound educational policy, the benefit of a larger good to society as a result of the classification, contemporary customs and mores, and the protection of the individual's rights in the light of these considerations. (LaMorte, 1996, p. 8)

Equal protection covers what have come to be called the seven protected classes. These are broad labels that encompass essential elements of any person's life, so that none of us can be discriminated against on the basis of our race, religion, national origin, sex, marital status (which includes pregnancy), disability, or age. We all have a race, a national origin, and a religion (or some belief about the way to live our lives and the role a creator may or may not play in that process). We are male or female; we are single, married, divorced, separated, or partnered; some of us are pregnant; we are all variously abled or disabled; and we all have an age. In some parts of the country, but not nationally, sexual orientation has been recognized as an eighth protected class. Again, we all have a sexual orientation. The classes are not *us, them, those, we,* or *other* labels. The seven protected classes protect us from discrimination based on all the aspects of who we are.

LOOKING AT THE MAIN IDEAS

The Seven Protected Classes

The seven protected classes describe all the ways in which we are protected from discrimination. We are all protected on the basis of

1. Religion
2. Race
3. National origin
4. Disability
5. Age
6. Marital status
7. Sex

And in some states

8. Sexual orientation

Laws that protect students from discrimination on the basis of who they are must be viewed in combination with laws that compel students into the public education system. As stated in an earlier chapter, when students are required to attend school, they have the right to expect equal treatment. In terms of visibility, equal treatment means that students should never experience public praise, public reprimand, or any public comments associated with who they are. No student should experience discriminatory actions, not the student who is in the ninth month of pregnancy, or the student who is emotionally disabled, or the student who is remarkably gifted, or the student who is of a race or national origin other than the majority of students in a school, or the student who has experienced a rapid growth spurt, or the student whose height is noticeably less than that of the other students, or the student who speaks a primary language other than English, or any other permutation of this paradigm one can imagine. The actions and words of their educators should do nothing to make students highly visible or invisible based on who they are.

HIGHLY VISIBLE STUDENTS

Management Practices That Contribute to High Visibility

The focus of this chapter is the connection between the protected classes and how teachers manage their classrooms. In some cases, teachers' actions can exacerbate high visibility or encourage invisibility. In both instances, legal considerations are associated with management practices, particularly when those practices violate the privacy rights of students. The federal Family Education Rights and Privacy Act (FERPA) makes clear the requirement that educators protect the privacy of all student records, including behavioral records:

> FERPA regulates access to, and disclosure of, student data in "educational records" of schools that receive federal aid. . . . FERPA's principal thrust is to assure record access by . . . students and their guardians and to prevent disclosure from those records of "personally identifying information" to unprivileged parties without the written consent of affected students and their guardians. (Valente, 1998, p. 185)

One cultural myth—evident in many public schools—promotes the idea that student behaviors can best be managed by making them highly visible. Names written on chalkboards as congratulatory messages for good behavior or warnings associated with bad behavior, behavior charts mounted on the walls, stars or "self-manager" buttons that are prominently displayed on the clothing of students, stickers on papers or school lockers, stamps on hands, and tickets handed out for good or bad behaviors are all examples of managing student behaviors through the use of public praise or correction. In schools all over the country, attempts to manage student behaviors have become inseparable from violations of the right to privacy.

Even teachers who use such management strategies admit that the same students are singled out, particularly for inappropriate behaviors, day after day. Students who are consistently made highly visible in this manner can quickly become pariahs among their peers. Students of any age understand that it is better not to associate with someone who is always in trouble, unless, of course, they are choosing to go down the same path.

Making public displays of students to resolve behavior problems is always a questionable practice, and the strategies teachers select for resolving problems should at least consider the private difficulties with which a student might be struggling. Students' private issues are often directly associated with the students' protected classes or the personal situation from which the student comes.

When educators single students out to be the focus of public behavioral corrections, they convey a message to all their students that the classroom is not a safe place for learning. Students who are humiliated in front of their classmates in an attempt to correct their behaviors are likely to view education with hostility and anger, but they are not at all likely to become model students. Even worse, the lesson learned by the other students in the class is that they can expect to be similarly embarrassed when they have bad days. No student feels a sense of safety in such classrooms.

High Visibility Is Sometimes a Result of Student Actions

Students can be made highly visible by teachers or themselves. Robert J. Ackerman (1983, p. 103) describes just one of the many reasons for the sort of disruptive behaviors that result in high visibility:

> [There] are children of alcoholics who, like other children, try to compensate for being ignored at home by demanding excessive attention in school. Such children may be said to be "acting out." The attention these children get from teachers usually consists of various types of punishments. However, teachers should be alert to recognize possible underlying environmental causes of attention seeking behavior. Being the "class clown" may be one method of trying to establish valued relationships with peers when one is starved for attention at home. A poor academic performer may find that by entertaining others, he or she attains some value to others in being at school. It becomes easier for such a person to stay in school. It is their way of coping with a poor school situation.

Chapter 5 discussed the behaviors students might exhibit to become highly visible. The efforts a teacher extends to ensure confidentiality for these students can seem endless—and at times profitless. Students may still choose to be disruptive because they see themselves as victims of so many circumstances beyond their control. According to Brantlinger (1991, p. 40),

> Conflicts with teachers were the second most frequently mentioned school offense for low-income students. The tendency to react impulsively or overreact to incidents with school mates is also present in their descriptions of relationships with teachers. [One student] admitted, "Teachers say something I don't like and I get loud with them." [Another student] had "got in trouble for backsassing the teachers." [A third student] had "yelled at teachers." Many feel that teachers do not like them and categorize their relationships as adversarial.

However, working to protect the rights of students is not futile. The professional integrity of educators, particularly public school educators, is inextricably linked to ensuring the constitutional rights of young people. A student acting out of fear, frustration, anger, or ineptitude who damages a classroom's learning climate in the process still deserves due process and protections of privacy.

There will always be highly visible students. Despite the best efforts of teachers, some students feel the need to disrupt and others naturally assume the mantle of leadership. Professional educators must respond to such situations as discreetly as possible. However, as indicated earlier, sometimes teachers' actions and decisions can make students highly visible. As in the opening scenario of this chapter, high visibility can be a result of attempts to praise or correct a student.

Praising Students Publicly

Teachers commonly use public praise to motivate students who are receiving it and students who would like to receive it. Teachers often believe that public praise helps all students to see that working hard and doing well in school may be rewarded. As well meaning as these intentions may be, a number of concerns are associated with the practice of public praise: [The] "common defense of praise seems to imply that the only reason a child would ever demonstrate kindness is to be rewarded with the approval of an adult. To talk about the need to 'reinforce' a behavior suggests that the behavior would disappear in the absence of that reinforcement. . . . Lots of educators seem to believe it's true specifically of helpful acts" (Kohn, 1996, p. 3).

Public praise can cause a loss of trust between teacher and student. Students may have many legitimate and developmental reasons for not welcoming public recognition for doing well in school. They want to be liked by their peers and to not be different. Being publicly recognized for doing well and getting good grades can result in students being labeled by their peers as nerds and teacher's pets, neither of which will help students achieve the social acceptance that is such a driving force in their lives.

Some schools adopt various forms of public recognition for their students who achieve good grades, maintain good attendance, or are just pleasant to have around. One student discussed his middle school's new program to publicly praise its students. The school had installed plastic windows with 12 grid squares on each student's locker. When students received good grades, came to school on time, came to school regularly, were polite, acted responsibly, and otherwise behaved in some way that the school wished to recognize, school personnel would add stickers representing that area of success to the students' plastic window grids.

The practice was problematic from the beginning. Although the educators in the school had tried to make the categories for recognition as wide ranging as possible, inevitably some students' grids filled quickly and some students' grids were empty well into the school year. Eventually the hard feelings generated by the sticker system led to the school's decision to abandon the practice. The student who related this tale could not wait for it to stop. His grid was one of those that had been filled very quickly.

As with most young people, the student found public recognition for his achievements difficult when his peers alienated him because of the praise. It was easier to experience no recognition than to have his peers dislike and distrust him. According to Dacey and Kenny (1994, p. 258),

> An ongoing debate in adolescent psychology is whether peers have a
> negative influence by pressuring adolescents to behave in undesirable

ways. A substantial body of evidence suggests that peers sometimes do influence adolescents in negative ways. . . . Other evidence suggests that the peer group fulfills important functions, and that adolescents who are not members of a peer group are at risk for academic failure and emotional disturbance. While these two lines of evidence appear contradictory, a number of explanations have been offered to reconcile these findings. One explanation is that close friendships are necessary and important, but that the larger crowd influences are often negative (Cohen, 1983).

The need for peer acceptance can even lead some students to act in ways to avoid receiving public recognition for being smart. Students know how to get *A*s, but they also know how to get *B*s and *C*s, and, by doing so, they may well see themselves as being more socially acceptable to their peers. Students who have worked hard and achieved well should receive recognition, but educators must carefully consider how that recognition is bestowed. Quiet compliments to students who have done good work can be far more motivating than public praise, which can isolate them from their peers.

Issues of equity are integral to discussions of public praise. Students who come from two-parent homes, economically stable homes, and families with adults who are supportive of their interests and protective of their welfare typically receive public praise for good behavior. Students who come from situations that are less supportive do not usually receive this sort of public praise. Far from leveling the playing field, such actions by educators only widen the differences between the advantaged and the disadvantaged.

The Conflict between Public Praise and the Cultural Heritage of Students

Some cultures view public praise as one defining characteristic of a competitive society. Robert A. Roessel Jr. (1969, p. 305) speaks to the issues of competition and how it is viewed by some Native American tribes:

> Our society places great importance on competition. In fact, many Americans believe that competition is an essential cultural trait found throughout the world. Such is not the case. Many of our Southwestern tribes place no importance on competition, but rather place a supreme value on cooperation.
>
> Most teachers have used or at least are familiar with the use of gold and silver stars placed on a chart to reward children who have turned in a perfect paper. In non-Indian schools this device has been in successful use and the author constructed such a chart for use with his classroom of Navaho children. During the first several weeks a pattern became very apparent—no child ever got two gold stars. After a Navaho student once received the recognition of a gold star he never again turned in a perfect paper. This proved very frustrating and the author felt that these Indian children just didn't care and that perhaps they were "uneducable."

> One day an adult Navaho friend came into the classroom and looked at the chart and laughed. The problem was explained to him and he laughed once again. The Navaho friend stated that many Navaho children are taught to cooperate—not to compete. They find their security in being a member of the group and not in being singled out and placed in a position above the group.

For these students, being placed in competitive relationships with their peers was the same as being placed in conflict with their fundamental beliefs of how people should interact together. As Roessel indicates, the students could only resolve the conflict by favoring their tribal culture over the imposed competitive structure of the teacher.

In addition to being culturally disharmonic, public praise can place students from diverse backgrounds into contention with their peers if they seem to be adopting the traits of the cultural majority.

> [Teacher attention] . . . sometimes has a negative impact when it comes to behavior. For example, certain cultures distrust the "white, middle-class" education system because their values conflict with many of those held by the school and the community. Therefore, many students from these groups resent teacher praise. These students are concerned that, if their behavior is approved by the "establishment," they will run the risk of becoming "white" and lose the respect of their cultural group. As a result, youngsters in this category rely on their peers for validation of appropriate behavior. Thus teachers need to give positive attention in the form of private conversations, rather than public proclamations. (Johns & Espanoza, 1996, p. 21)

Catch Them Being Good . . . or at Least Acting Differently from Their Peers

Public praise and cultural expectations can also impact issues of gender equity in the classroom. One common management strategy found extensively at the elementary levels but also at other levels is the Skinnerian practice of catching students being good. Teachers look for students who are following directions, working quietly, listening attentively, or doing what the teacher expects. The teacher will catch the student being good by saying something like "I appreciate the way Alexandra is being so polite and quiet right now."

The teacher uses this strategy to accomplish a couple of things. One is to call attention to an example of that teacher's expectation for what students should be doing. The other purpose is to settle down any disruptive behaviors that might be occurring around the exemplary student. The reasoning behind this strategy is that other students will want the same verbal recognition and will stop their disruptive behaviors in hopes of being similarly singled out.

The practice certainly makes some students highly visible. More often than not, those singled out as the objects of this control mechanism are female, particularly in the early grades. Primary grade teachers, who are predominantly female, see the behaviors of female students as close approximations of the classroom expectations. A teacher of young children related the following story: "I remember when I was first learning how to manage students, I tried this same strategy. I was teaching young children at the time in a small classroom that did not allow for very much free movement. One day I was leading the students in a very small circle dance and, at the end of the dance, most of my students decided it would be fun to fall on the floor on top of one another. I quickly looked around the room, and sitting quietly out of harm's way was Meredith. I said, 'I really like the way Meredith is sitting so quietly right now, waiting for the next activity.' The sentence was barely out of my mouth before all the other students were sitting equally quietly in anticipation that they too would receive the same verbal praise from me."

The teacher went on to say, "As effective as this seemed, what troubled me then and continues to trouble me about the practice is that Meredith was shy and female. In one sentence, I had encouraged her shy behavior by praising it." The problem with this strategy is that teachers may well be praising behaviors, such as passivity and acquiescence, that are stereotypical of a gender. These are the very behaviors that females of every age are working to overcome to achieve equity in academics and the workplace.

Teachers who use the practice of catching students being good tend to single out female students far more often than male students. White students and students from middle-class backgrounds are also commonly held up as examples of good behavior much more often than students of color or students from poverty.

A 1997 survey underscores the problems inherent in this practice:

> Girls (79%) are more likely than boys (73%) to feel that they "often" receive enough attention from their teachers. One in three girls and boys (30% and 31%, respectively) "very often" receive enough attention from their teachers in class; half (48%) of all girls and two in five (42%) boys "sometimes" do. When sex and race are looked at together, the disparity in attention received increases. White girls (80%) are most likely to feel they "often" receive enough attention, minority boys (67%) are least likely to feel this way, and white boys and minority girls (73% and 74% respectively) fall in between. ("Examining Gender Issues," 1997, p. 136)

An integral part of equal educational opportunity is every student's right to expect time and attention from their educators.

Memories of Public Punishment

Although public praise can be difficult for some students, being singled out for public embarrassment or humiliation is far more common. Primary resources for insight into how public correction can impact students are people's memories. Adults, when recalling their days in school, often tell stories of discipline they experienced or witnessed. They tend to recount their stories of these experiences in terms that are vivid and fresh, prefacing their stories by saying "I still remember it as if it were yesterday." They describe these memories as some of the most vivid they have of their school days. The memories of the hurt experienced can be so vivid that some adults' eyes well up with tears when they describe the emotional pain of enduring the public humiliation they suffered at the hands of a teacher.

These stories are powerful and credible, in large part because they are so common. Ask adults to recall a memory of a disciplinary incident from their own education, and they may relate experiences that border on cruelty. Adults recall times they were locked in closets, had their sweaters or jackets used as restraints to keep them in their chairs, or had to sit out in the hall where everyone else could see them.

One adult recalled that her third-grade teacher announced on the first day of class that she was a witch who would "get" her students if they were not good. Later, if students began talking out of turn or acting inappropriately, the teacher walked over to them and plucked a hair from their heads. The hairs were stored in a jar in the teacher's cupboard. The teacher never explicitly stated the purpose for this practice, but the implication was clear.

Adults remember their names being written on the blackboard, being forced to wear gum on their noses, and enduring other forms of public punishment that left them feeling humiliated and disgraced in the eyes of their peers. None of them seem to think that the practice helped them become better, more responsible people.

Although these stories are upsetting, the people who recount them see the incidents as isolated memories. However, some students are subjected to public embarrassment day after day in their public school classrooms. It is little wonder that these students choose to leave school as soon as they can rather than continuing to tolerate the social pain being inflicted on them.

◈ LOOKING AT THE MAIN IDEAS

Students Are Not Helped to Feel Safe in the Classroom if

- They are singled out as examples of good behavior
- They are singled out as examples of bad behavior
- They are singled out in any way that serves the purposes of the teacher but not those of the young people in the classroom

Public humiliation and embarrassment teach many lessons, but those lessons have nothing to do with helping individuals to become appropriate and responsible adults. The lessons actually being taught are that the next inappropriate act by students must be more covert. The language used by teachers even encourages this thinking: "If I catch you doing such and such again. . . ." The issue should not be what students are caught or not caught doing but rather how the correction helps students learn to manage their own behaviors and to make decisions that will benefit themselves and the rest of the learning community.

Teachers who decide to publicly praise or correct their students risk losing whatever general goodwill they are attempting to foster in their classrooms. The rationale teachers use for public corrections is the flip side of the justifications given for the use of public praise: Students who are singled out for public correction will be so embarrassed that they will never repeat the deviant act again. At the same time, other students in the classroom get the message that they will face similar humiliation if they choose to act in the same way or otherwise misbehave.

Using High Visibility to Correct Behaviors

Some behavioral models for classroom discipline rely on public embarrassment as the primary means of controlling behaviors. Canter and Canter (1979) promoted what has become the most widely practiced use of high visibility. Their idea of using publicly displayed names and check marks on the blackboard to represent warnings and consequences has resulted in some revealing stories that expose the reasons why a strategy that might at first seem reasonable can in fact be emotionally devastating. For example, a high school student, after receiving her first check mark, stood up and said, "I know where this is going." She marched to the chalkboard, added two more check marks after her name, and left the room. A school psychologist in Minnesota walked into a classroom where one student's name on the board was followed by 31 check marks. A middle school student in New York came home after the first week of school and said that his teacher had a really "neat" system for discipline. He reported that his teacher wrote names on the board as a warning; if behaviors did not stop with the warnings, the teacher put check marks after the names to represent consequences. What the student liked about the system was that, according to him, all the students in class got to misbehave once, have their names written on the board, and then settle down, so no one faced consequences.

When teachers talk about students whose names are written on the board day after day, they often remark that they do not see any change in the students' behavior from one day to the next. The same behaviors appear continually, as do the names of the students. Teachers report that although the system of names and check marks on the blackboard seems to work at first, it quickly loses its effectiveness. Students do not seem to fear getting check marks and may even view them as status symbols. If the check marks earned equate to removal from the classroom, some students actually compete to see who will "get" to leave first.

Even Canter and Canter (1992) have now backed away from the idea of making such a behavioral record public. Instead, they now advocate that such records be maintained by privately recording them on clipboards. However, although this change might ostensibly preserve confidentiality, it does nothing to help a teacher respond individually to the needs presented in the classroom.

The Conflict between Addressing Individual Needs and Correcting Behaviors through High Visibility

Sometimes students become members of an "involuntary minority" (Ogbu, 1993). The luck of the compulsory education draw does not often result in equitable demographic representation. Students of minority cultures can find themselves becoming highly visible just by walking in the doors of their public school classrooms. Regardless of the educator's intentions, the students' behaviors are often corrected simply because they are highly visible and their actions are more quickly noticed by their teachers.

Sometimes students from minority populations receive more corrections than others because of a teacher's personal bias. John Ogbu (1993, p. 105) discussed the impact of being a member of a minority group in a majority school culture:

> The real issue in the school adjustment and academic performance of minority children is not whether the children possess a different language or dialect, a different style, or a different style of socialization or upbringing. Rather the real issues are threefold: first, whether the children come from a segment of society where people have traditionally experienced unequal opportunity to use their education or school credentials in a socially and economically meaningful and rewarding manner; second, whether or not the relationship between the minorities and the dominant-group members who control the public schools has encouraged the minorities to perceive and define school learning as an instrument for replacing their cultural identity with the cultural identity of their "oppressors" without full reward or assimilation; and, third, whether or not the relationship between the minorities and the schools generates the trust that encourages the minorities to accept school rules and practices that enhance academic success.

According to Ogbu (1993, p. 106),

> Involuntary minorities have persistent high rates of school failure and social adjustment problems because they have greater difficulty crossing cultural boundaries due to an oppositional cultural frame of reference and oppositional identity. . . . Their distrust of white people and skepticism make it harder for them to accept and follow school rules and standard practices that enhance academic success.

Minority students enter their classrooms already in a state of high visibility before they do anything, and they might well bring with them a sense of distrust for their teachers before any words are spoken. This mix of high visibility and distrust lies at the heart of much of the contention and frustration that educators and students are feeling today.

INVISIBLE STUDENTS

Along with highly visible students, many classrooms also have invisible students who seem to fade into the background. Like highly visible students, students can become invisible by their own actions or those of their educators. Some students become invisible because they are barely noticed by their teachers, even when they are in class every day. Other students are quiet and withdrawn, deliberately making use of their own strategies so as not to draw attention to themselves. The most common characteristic of invisible students is that they seem to pass through their school experience as if they were apparitions.

There are no simple issues in education. Every educational concern has the potential for being viewed through a number of professional, personal, and cultural lenses. Just as with high visibility, invisibility can reflect issues associated with law, pedagogy, and psychology.

Legal Issues of Invisibility

In terms of law, equal protection is as much a rationale for not allowing students to fall through the cracks as it is for not turning a spotlight on them. Students who are members of minority groups may be visible because of the color of their skin, their dress, or their language, but if they are not valued for who they are they can develop a sense of invisibility. Nieto (1995, p. 395) says that

> Feelings of marginalization among Latino students have been a chief consequence of the negative perceptions of teachers and others concerning them and their academic abilities. For example, Zanger found that Latino students in one high school in Boston felt excluded, invisible, and subordinate to other students. She also found that some teachers were just as contemptuous of Latinos as the most racist students.
>
> An ethnographic study of high school dropouts who had returned to attend an alternative high school program in New York City examined the reasons these young people gave for dropping out (Saravie-Shore, 1992). Criticisms of their former school experiences included teacher favoritism toward better students, and the lack of respect, care, and concern of teachers for them.

Students can find themselves alone and feeling isolated because the protected classes that define us all give them minority status. Students can develop a sense of not fitting in or can be overtly ignored based on their national origins, languages, religions, genders, races, ages, marital status (including parental status), disabilities, or sexual orientations: "Loneliness is the deep, deserted feeling that a person experiences when he or she feels different, alone, and separate. It is an inability to be in touch with one's self—a feeling of disconnectedness. Sometimes, the deeper the loneliness, the more intense the sadness, unhappiness, and desire to find some connection with life or with oneself."*

*C. Igoa, The Inner World of the Immigrant Child. (1995, p.54). Lawrence Erlbaum Associates, Inc. Reprinted by permission

Disabilities That Can Lead to Invisibility

Just as some students become highly visible because of a disability, others choose to become invisible in classrooms because of their physical, learning, or emotional disabilities. Students with learning disabilities that prevent them from processing auditory or visual information at the same rate as their peers often find ways to become invisible rather than risk being called on by their teachers. One common practice is to avoid eye contact with teachers in the hopes students will not be called on to participate in class or to read aloud. Another is to answer questions with "I don't know," because the teacher will likely move on to another student. In the minds of students with learning disabilities, embarrassment associated with not knowing answers is easier to handle than the humiliation of having to publicly acknowledge an inability to read the chalkboard or their textbooks.

Unless teachers make an effort to discover why students are reluctant to participate in class, they may never understand the true nature of their students' problems. Faculty in higher education often work with adults whose learning disabilities have just been diagnosed. Adults whose disabilities are identified later in life commonly speak of how difficult school was for them. They recall experiences of being ignored and feeling stupid. Once their disabilities are correctly diagnosed, they understand that they can function as equals in their learning communities with appropriate adaptations. But shaking off the assumed status of invisibility is difficult for them because of the many years they played that role.

Emotional Causes of Invisibility

Sometimes the invisibility of students is not associated with a learning disability but an emotional difficulty. In some cases, their emotional disability is a direct result of abusive home situations. For instance, children who are sexually abused at home may choose to assume the role of invisible students in school. Because their self-esteem is low and they are young victims of abusive adults it is easier for them to fade into the walls than risk being noticed by the adults in their school settings. If the abuse continues into adolescence, the damage to the emotional state of the victim has long-lasting effects on all the individual's future relationships. In the case of female victims,

> The most common type of serious sexual abuse is incest between father and daughter (Alexander & Kempe, 1984) or stepfather and stepdaughter. This type of relationship may last for several years. The daughter is often manipulated into believing it is all her fault, and that if she says anything to anyone, she will be seen as a bad person, one who may even be arrested and jailed. The outcome is often another adolescent statistic: a runaway or even a prostitute. (Daceyo & Kenny, 1994, p. 294)

Physical Illness and Invisibility

Some illnesses can encourage students to seek invisibility rather than run the risk of being scorned or shunned by their peers. This is particularly true when the illness that afflicts students is HIV or AIDS. Apprehension about the disease is warranted, particularly given the statistical evidence that the disease is spreading internationally at a greater rate than previously believed. However, that apprehension is unfairly extended to the young people who may be its victims. Individuals can make personal decisions about their lifestyles to help stem the spread of the disease, but creating outcasts of the infected population ignores the evidence of how the disease is actually spread.

People still fear individuals who are infected. As a result, students who have been diagnosed with HIV or AIDS may choose to be invisible as long as possible because they are afraid their peers will avoid all contact with them. The law protects their privacy in this area; teachers are unlikely to know which students are infected with HIV or AIDS unless the students or their parents have chosen to share that information.

The social implications of having their infection publicly recognized may lead students to maintain their invisibility for as long as possible. Silin says that

> The distinction between socially sanctioned blame and meaningful personal responsibility may be especially hard to maintain in a society that has used blame as an indicator of social worth. . . . In the contemporary world, blame is not only defined in theological or secular terms as the result of moral wrongdoing. A subtler but even more damaging form of blame is aroused by psychological interpretations, indicating that character flaws may not only be expressed in specific diseases but may actually cause them.*

Given the common misperceptions about HIV and AIDS infection and its perceived link to moral behaviors, it is little wonder that students infected with the virus may prefer anonymity. When teachers consider how their classrooms can be made safe for all learners, they must include children who are diagnosed with any disease.

Invisibility and Societal Expectations

Some students become invisible because of who they are, the families from which they come, or the cultural expectations placed on them. The cultural expectations can derive as much from the educators who work with these students as from the students' personal situations. For instance, cultural expectations of educators can relegate female students to a role of invisibility.

Gender inequities in classrooms have been well documented in a number of studies. Teacher educators, field supervisors, and school administrators have all seen teachers call on more male students than female students. When these

---

*Excerpts reprinted by permission of the publisher from Silin, Jonathan J., *Sex, Death and the Education of Children: Our Passion for Ignorance in the Age of AIDS* (New York: Teachers College Press, © 1995 by Teachers College, Columbia University. All rights reserved.) pg. 16.

observations are brought to the attention of teachers, they often react with surprise because their own perception and intent are to acknowledge students equally.

Although teachers may wish to be equitable in their practice, other forces subtly influence how classroom interactions are managed. One common perception is that male students are more energetic and more easily distracted than female students. As a result, teachers call on male students first because they fear male students will not wait patiently to be called on but will quickly become disruptive. Conversely, and similarly misrepresentative, female students are thought to be more passive and willing to wait for recognition.

Some effective strategies are available to help teachers to equalize classroom discussions. One idea is to develop some system for calling on students in a random fashion, such as by using index cards or sticks with one student's name per card or stick. Teachers can simply pull a stick or call a name off a card when asking for answers to questions or checking for understanding. Such systems need not be used all the time, but their occasional use during the course of a school day will help to ensure gender equality.

Another strategy for encouraging students who might otherwise be invisible to participate equally is the use of wait time (i.e., asking a question and then waiting before calling on students). "When [M.] Rowe trained teachers to increase their wait time to 3–5 seconds . . . students responded positively. Specifically, they (1) gave more detailed and thoughtful answers, (2) displayed increased self-confidence, (3) generated more questions themselves, and (4) interacted more with other students in class discussions (Rinne, 1997, p. 184). The use of wait time is considered to be an effective way to increase female participation in class.

If teachers use wait time, they might also want to explore use of a second wait time. This practice involves listening to a student's comments, acknowledging the comments through body language, and then waiting silently for the next comment. This practice tends to encourage genuine exchanges among students rather than the ping-pong discussions that typically occur in the classroom, characterized by a student's comment, followed by a teacher's comment, followed by a comment of another student, bouncing back to the teacher, and so on.

LOOKING AT THE MAIN IDEAS

Practices That Equalize Male and Female Students

- A systematic approach to calling on students that ensures proportional numbers of male and female responses to questions
- Wait time to give everyone time to formulate answers to questions
- Stated academic and behavioral expectations that are the same for all students

The need to equalize classroom discussions may seem trivial, but it is directly linked to the expectations we, as a society, have for the success of all students. According to Research for Action, Inc. (1996, p. 3),

Finding what works for girls requires broadening the scope of inquiry to include such factors as school reform and home and peer cultures. First, we must grapple with outcomes: What do we want for girls? Our reading of the literature on adolescent girls in tandem with our research in middle schools suggests this answer: Girls should be recognized by adults and taught to recognize themselves as complex individuals with an emerging vision, an ability to think critically, a sense of entitlement of giving voice and being heard, and a range of choices about who they are and want to become.

Choosing Invisibility: Being in the Closet

Sometimes students choose to be invisible because of their minority sexual identity. Peer pressures to conform are so great and the penalties for being different are so profound, particularly in adolescence, that it is easier for some students to be "in the closet." In Silin's words

> The closet defining my life as a gay adolescent tells of my desire for other men. . . . My family closets speak to the impermanence of life as well as to the possibility of communication between generations. In this sense they are not so different from the closets of my youth in which I sought to hide my gayness, to make it go away, while simultaneously communicating to others who would be sympathetic. The closet sounds a death knell to a public identity even as it promotes a secretive form of community life.*

Sexual development is an ongoing process, and students discover their sexual orientations over a span of years. Revealing one's minority sexual identity does not happen once; rather, the choice to "come out" happens or does not happen each time a new personal contact is made.

The process of coming out becomes more difficult when the cultural norms established by educators all reflect heterosexual absolutes. When all the bulletin boards, literature, history, biology, and other aspects of curriculum and the classroom setting reflect the expectation that the world is heterosexual, students who are discovering they are gay, lesbian, or bisexual may find it safer to hide their true identities to fit into the mainstream.

> Every member of the community has a right to play his or her role without fear of harassment by peers: it is the school's obligation to take pro-active measures to ensure this right. . . . Clear harassment policies, which include sexual orientation as a protected category, must be developed and then publicized to the entire school community, so that the consequence of and procedures for dealing with such behavior are clear to all. (GLSTN, 1997, p. 1)

Teachers can comfortably and safely remain neutral on this subject to protect their students' sense of safety in the classroom. Regardless of a teacher's personal views, the compelling professional expectation is a consistent attitude of tolerance

---

*Excerpts reprinted by permission of the publisher from Silin, Jonathan J., *Sex, Death and the Education of Children: Our Passion for Ignorance in the Age of AIDS* (New York: Teachers College Press, © 1995 by Teachers College, Columbia University. All rights reserved.) pg. 181.

toward all students. The high suicide and dropout rates of young people with minority sexual identities show the need for tolerance and neutrality in educators' attitudes. The alternative can be devastating emotionally to young people.

Students may wish to be invisible or in the closet, but teachers cannot engage in acts that force them there.

Snide remarks about lifestyles, careless jokes in class, comments to male students such as "you run like a girl," or to female students such as "aren't you strong for a girl!" can be frightening to students with minority sexual identities. All students should receive a consistent message of acceptance. Students know they may not be the same as other students in their classrooms; however, educators should not impose on students the perspective that because they are different from the majority they are also somehow undesirable.

EFFECTIVE STRATEGIES FOR BALANCING HIGHLY VISIBLE STUDENTS WITH INVISIBLE STUDENTS

The balancing act involved in managing classrooms that address individual needs, maintain confidentiality, recognize and tolerate all students, and still attain learning goals is a challenging feat of professional artistry. Although there are no easy solutions, educators have a professional responsibility to give it their best effort.

Educators can help highly visible students work effectively with others to learn that sharing the spotlight does not eliminate their impact. At the same time, invisible students must be invited into the spotlight ever so gently and only at a pace comfortable for them. An invitational curriculum that offers open-ended opportunities can effectively accomplish both goals over time. Choices about how to demonstrate subject area mastery enable all students to find their comfort zones. Highly visible students can assume leadership roles, demonstrate skills, or take part in skits. Invisible students can play supportive roles in groups until they feel safe and confident enough to emerge out of their protective shells.

Even the most open-ended of curriculums will probably accomplish only some of these goals. The life circumstances that lead any student to assume the role of high visibility or invisibility cannot always be ameliorated by creative lesson plan design. However, the effort is always a worthy one.

MANAGING STUDENTS WITH SEVERE EMOTIONAL DISTURBANCES

The need to equalize the classroom environment is particularly critical when the visibility or invisibility of the student is linked to a special need or disability. Of particular concern are students who have been identified as having a severe emotional disturbance, because their behaviors may not only make them highly visible but at times dangerous to their classmates. Given the requirement to serve the needs of severely emotionally disturbed students by keeping them within the school environment and the equally compelling need to effectively educate all young people, educators are constantly seeking management strategies that will help them meet the needs of their students equitably.

Educators must be particularly cautious when responding to overt challenges made by students, because the underlying causes for such confrontations may lie in a diagnosed or undiagnosed emotional disability. Classrooms led by teachers who create situations of high visibility often leave emotionally troubled students feeling out of place. Although these students present significant challenges to teachers, they have a right to be treated in ways that protect their opportunities to be successful. They have a right to feel that their classrooms are safe and welcoming places led by educators who genuinely care about their learning.

There are many ways to respond to even the most extreme behaviors to help resolve problems while preserving a personal sense of dignity and value. Setting clear limits, maintaining high expectations, helping students to set and achieve their own behavioral goals, working with students to solve problems in peaceful ways, and consistently modeling patience are all powerful management tools that are particularly effective with troubled students. In order not to exacerbate a student's high visibility, teachers can address behavioral issues during quiet moments in the corner of a room, in one-on-one conferences outside the door of the classroom, or as whispered conversations with students while they sit at their desks.

One teacher related the practice of taking disruptive students into the hall for quick conferences to discuss whatever problem might be occurring. If she needed to speak privately with students, she would invite them into the hall with her for brief discussions. The students would stand against the wall and, while facing them, the teacher still had an unimpeded view into the classroom. The students were already highly visible because of whatever disruption had just occurred, but the teacher's actions did nothing to further exacerbate the situation.

However, the teacher was still concerned about maintaining privacy, especially when she and the students reentered the classroom. She found that the other students in the class stopped working and stared at the students with whom she had just been speaking. To resolve the potential complication, the teacher called a class meeting. During the meeting, she asked students how they would want other students to react if they had to speak with the teacher in the hall. The students agreed that when they reentered the classroom, they would not want to be the subject of staring eyes. One student said that it was okay to take a quick look, just to see who was walking in, but staring was not okay. The students agreed to respect each other's privacy by not gaping. Whatever the reason a student was in a conference with the teacher, the potential for high visibility was lessened by engaging the entire class in a conversation about fairness and mutual respect.

SUMMARY

After examining the educational concerns associated with high visibility and invisibility, let us revisit the scenario at the beginning of this chapter and see the differences that result from a few modifications. The teacher is distributing the tests students took the day before. T.J. has worked hard, and the results are evident in the work the teacher is about to hand back. Making sure all the grades are recorded on the backs of the papers to protect students' privacy, the teacher quietly passes the tests out with no comments. Then, to the whole class, the teacher says: "I know many of you worked very hard on this test. If you have concerns about your grade or want to check some of the information with me, please see me so we can do that. I have written some comments for you in the margins of your papers and will be happy to help you with any questions you might have. I also want to say that many of you did very well. I really see a lot of growth happening in this class. I am proud to be your teacher."

Later, at the end of the class, the teacher approaches T.J. and says, "I know you really worked hard on this test and you did very well. I just wanted you to know I am very impressed with all the work you did and pleased that it came out so well. I just wanted to say congratulations." T.J. smiles, mumbles a thank you, and leaves. The teacher–student bond has been strengthened by the trust developing between them and the respect for privacy demonstrated in this exchange.

All behavior problems take some time to resolve, and educators must be concerned with how their time will be used. Educators must decide if they are using their time effectively when they act in ways that create highly visible students or invisible students in their classrooms or if their time would be more effectively used by relying on appropriate professional behaviors and modeling reasoned responses to frustration and anger. The respect teachers earn when respect is given to even the most difficult students can go a long way toward establishing and maintaining a productive learning environment for everyone.

APPLYING THE CONCEPTS

Earlier you were asked how you would have handled the scenario if you were the teacher. What were some of your ideas? Were they similar to the ones suggested in the summary? Did you come up with different ideas? What else could you try that might also be effective?

CHAPTER 8

Creating a Welcoming Climate for Parents

CHAPTER OBJECTIVES

By the end of this chapter the reader should be able to:

❖ Apply practices that help teachers build working relationships with families

❖ Understand various issues of diversity that can influence families' perspectives of their children's school experiences

❖ Communicate effectively with parents who represent a diverse range of needs and interests

❖ Implement strategies that promote authentic outreach and inclusion

Scenario

It is the middle of December. In Daniel's third-grade classroom the students are preparing for their class holiday concert by painting a life-size Santa Claus, decorating a Christmas tree, and rehearsing the carols they will sing. Time has been reserved for these activities at the end of each school day for two weeks immediately before the concert. The music program, to which friends and families have been invited, will occur during the last afternoon before the elementary school closes for its winter vacation.

At 1:45 P.M. each day, as the class is completing a science activity, is finishing a writing assignment, or is engaged in its physical education class—depending on the day of the week—Daniel excuses himself from the rest of the class. He knows his mother will soon be there to take him home. Some of his classmates ask him why he has to leave every day, some tease him, and some ignore him.

On the day before the class concert, Daniel announces that he will not be back in school until after winter break. As he gets ready to leave that day, a student looks at him sadly and says, "You must have a mean Mommy. You can never have any fun."

Questions

Can you remember a time when you were a student and your parents or guardians felt at odds with the values of your school or teacher? Have you had that experience as a parent? As a teacher, have you at times felt that a student's family values were difficult to honor given your planned curriculum? Did the differences have detrimental repercussions? Did the issues of concern center on social activities, behavior, or academics? How was the problem resolved?

Discussion

Although some of Daniel's classmates pity him, in fact he goes home every day to parents and siblings who love him and care deeply about his welfare. His family belongs to the Jehovah's Witness faith. The religion his family practices commemorates the Last Supper on one night every year during springtime but otherwise recognizes no holidays, including birthdays. Their beliefs are based on a traditional interpretation of the Bible, and their common values emphasize the importance of family and community.

In most public schools, though, Jehovah's Witnesses are known as the students who "do not do Christmas." This characterization of Daniel's faith is only one example of how misinformed one culture can be about the values of another. When misinformation guides an educator's decision making, however well intentioned the decisions might be, the effects of such decisions can create an environment of discomfort and misunderstanding between teachers and the parents of their students.

Daniel's story may seem to be tenuously linked to classroom management, but it serves to represent some of the ways in which the needs, interests, and values of families can be put at odds with the public schools they support through their taxes and to which they are compelled to send their children. The ensuing tensions can make students feel that they are not equal members of their classes. Students who believe they are outside the mainstream of their classroom can easily decide that they need not demonstrate a sense of personal responsibility for following the rules. A feeling of being separated from their peers on the basis of family values occurs for any number of reasons; the conflicts among the educational system, students, and their families are not limited to religious beliefs but extend to every imaginable aspect of diversity.

ACCENTUATING DIFFERENCES CAN EXACERBATE MANAGEMENT ISSUES

Students who come from diverse backgrounds, have behavioral disorders, speak a primary language other than English, or have learning disabilities—in other words, students who are in some way different from the mainstream culture or norms of their peers—too often experience the sense that they are not receiving the same treatment or consideration as those around them. These feelings can be exacerbated in the public school classrooms to which they have been assigned.

Some students enter an environment each day filled with people who do not look, think, or act as they do. When those differences are accentuated by decisions that seem to favor one group over another, students can rightfully feel discriminated against based on who they are. The results of this disaffection can be feelings of anger, resentment, and even rebellion. To put it another way, maintaining a well-managed classroom environment can be a much easier task for educators to accomplish when all students feel they are equally valued within their school communities.

In an earlier chapter we explored how this sense of not being equally valued can result in behaviors that make students either highly visible or invisible. In this chapter we look at many of the same issues, this time examining them from the perspective of the adults, families, or guardians who have personal and financial responsibility for the students.

VIEWING STUDENTS AS PIECES OF A LARGER PICTURE

It is perhaps understandable that some educators come to view their students as being isolated individuals, particularly in the upper grades when there are fewer institutionalized opportunities for contact with families. Whether the reason for limited school contact is the result of which primary language is spoken by the family, demands of the workplace on the free time available to adults, or the age of the students, the results are that teachers can lose the sense of where students fit into their larger community. When parents have few opportunities to interact with the school community or elect not to make an effort to meet with teachers, their children are likely to be seen as separate entities rather than members of families with distinct and unique histories. Educators sometimes characterize teaching as the act of going into a classroom, closing the door, and being all alone with their students. This perspective is representative of the notion that teaching is an isolated act, detached from the realities of the outside world.

A more realistic view of education, however, is that teachers are never in sole control of their students. A classroom of 25 students also contains a minimum of 25 different family interests. Educators who look out at the faces of their students are well advised to imagine a sea of other faces surrounding each of the students. Although in reality families may be invisible during the day-to-day classroom interactions, they are always present in the way students perceive and interpret the curriculum and social activities in a school day.

THE LEGAL RIGHTS OF FAMILIES

Educators must also remember the legal implications of the interests families have in their students' education. All parents have the legal authority to demand equal educational opportunity for their children and to be treated as partners in the educational process of their students.

The constitutional right of parents regarding the upbringing of their children, together with their rights as citizens and taxpayers, gives them legal standing to resist or influence many educational decisions. They may refuse forced enrollment of their children in public schools if they provide qualified alternative nonpublic education, and they may challenge specific courses of instruction or services directed to their children in certain religion-sensitive areas. Where parents' rights or claims collide with those asserted by public school authorities or other citizen groups, the decisions on how to mediate and harmonize those competing interests fall to the courts. (Valente, 1998, p. 6)

PERSONAL HISTORIES CAN AFFECT SCHOOL ATTITUDES

Parents bring their own histories to the education of their children. If, during their own school experiences, they felt discriminated against, powerless, or disengaged, the challenge to recruit their support in the education of their students is a daunting one indeed. Many parents who did not feel comfortable in school when they were students may feel equally inadequate when trying to represent the interests of their children. According to Froyen (1993, p. 321),

> Some parents may not be convinced that the teacher is doing everything possible for their child, but they do not believe that they themselves know the first thing about how to improve the situation. Others may have some ideas about how to make things better but lack the confidence to take their case to school. In both instances, the parents may be intimidated by an ingrained submissive role as student, a lack of education, or the bureaucratic attitude that contends that, when it comes right down to it, the teacher is generally right.

LOOKING AT THE MAIN IDEAS

Parents May Be Reluctant to Become Partners for Several Reasons

- They may feel intimidated by the dominant culture and see their child's teacher more as a member of that culture than as someone with whom they can relate.
- They may be uncertain of their English language capabilities and how to effectively communicate with the teacher of their child.
- They may not have had a good experience in school themselves and are not willing to become involved again in a place that does not hold good memories for them.

Some parents' histories may include diagnosed or undiagnosed learning disabilities; their own economic deprivation; and their own cultural, racial, or sexual identity that put them outside the mainstream of their schools' dominant cultures. As a result of their own experiences, such parents probably find it difficult to identify how to be effective participants in their children's schools.

These are also the parents who are most likely to denigrate every aspect of education, least likely to value or support homework, and very likely to turn some error committed by an educator into grist for dinner table conversation. In Froyen's (1993, p. 317) words, "A teacher's authority is conferred and can be taken away by members of the community. . . . All too often the ways to adjudicate differences between home and school pit the teacher against the parent. Children can only conclude that the teacher is mistaken, for parents are generally presumed to be omnipotent."

Teachers often view parents who are not supportive of their children's schools as being difficult to work with and their children as equally challenging to reach and teach. Parents can easily be made the target of an educator's anger in a misdirected sense of frustration over the inappropriate behaviors of their students. Teachers sometimes associate the misbehaviors of students with the neighborhoods in which they live, the number of adults in the home, or the relationships between the adults in the home. One teacher was overheard to say, "What can you expect? He lives in a trailer park." According to the International Academy of Education (as cited by Redding, 1995, p. 21),

> The changing face of the family, despite its adaptability and resilience, can result in specific stresses between home and school. This can be complicated by changes in family configurations, such as the emergence of working parents, one-parent families, and families in which parents come from a cultural background which differs from that of the culturally mainstream school.

THE QUALITY OF PARENTING CANNOT BE GENERALIZED

Although it is easy to generalize about the influence of family situations on the behaviors of students, such thinking can often be remarkably misleading. Experienced classroom teachers learn not to leap to conclusions about students based on the circumstances of their families. In classrooms in any inner-city school characterized by the anguishing effects of poverty, despite the unremitting effects of deprivation, some parents are deeply concerned about the welfare of their students and are working very hard to make their lives as good as possible. Other parents may be appallingly unprepared for the responsibility of raising children.

In contrast, examine any upscale neighborhood anywhere. There will be parents found in those locations who are deeply concerned about the welfare of their students and working very hard to make their lives as good as possible. There will also be parents who are appallingly unprepared for the responsibility of raising children.

Of all the lessons learned by experienced educators, this one is perhaps the most valuable. It is far too easy to assume good or bad parenting occurs in direct relation to income, education, and opportunities. It is too tempting a trap to assign virtue or blame to families based on where they live and who they are. Such generalizations are dangerous barriers to any real communication with and understanding of the issues families bring to the educational process.

The problems families face and the successes families experience when they attempt to make appropriate decisions about child rearing are not associated with any one group. Those decision-making skills are rooted in issues that extend far beyond economics and levels of education. Hidalgo, Bright, Sau-Fong, Swap, and Epstein (1995, p. 499) say that,

> On average, more educated families are more involved in schools and with their children's formal education. As important, however, some families from all situations—regardless of the formal education or income level of the parents, and regardless of the grade level or ability of the student—use strategies to encourage and influence their children's education and development. Studies are accumulating that show that family practices concerning children's education are more important for helping students succeed in school and in general than are family structure, economic status, or characteristics such as race, parent education, family size, and age of child.

Educators are often too quick to blame parents for all the misbehaviors they see in students, and parents may be just as ready to point accusatory fingers back at teachers over exactly the same concerns. The result can be distrust, miscommunication, and students who find themselves caught in the middle.

> Parents and teachers can perceive one another as a threat. Teachers worry that parents will call their behavior management practices into question or make unreasonable demands. Parents, especially ones who themselves had unpleasant school experiences, are fearful of their children having similarly devastating experiences. Yet, despite the tension that may develop, parents and teachers need each other. And, because the teacher is the professional, it is incumbent that he or she make deliberate efforts to develop productive relationships with parents. (Kauggman, Mostert, Trent, & Hallahan, 1998, p. 134)

Whatever their personal circumstances, most parents genuinely hope their students will experience success in school. They might lack the skills to effectively participate in that process but may develop those skills with information and support. However, some practices that occur in education (as evidenced in management systems, the ways students with special needs receive services, and how families from diverse cultural backgrounds are addressed) can mitigate against, rather than work toward, fostering positive school–family relationships.

MANAGEMENT AND A BEHAVIORIST VIEW OF THE ROLE OF PARENTS

As with so many of the topics discussed in this book, how teachers bring parents into the disciplinary process likely depends on the philosophy that frames the management decisions being made. Teachers who practice behaviorist strategies often use communicating with parents as a way to threaten students. The prospect of a phone call to a parent or guardian is held over students to intimidate them into behaving. It is difficult to imagine the logic that lies behind a desire to characterize communication with parents as something students should fear. Nevertheless, such threats are not uncommon. The implication seems to be that parents are the "bad guys" and sharing information with them about misbehaviors is to be avoided at all costs.

Educators who use such strategies seem to insinuate that misbehaving students who have been punished in school will be punished even more intensely when they get home. However, parents may choose to take seriously or dismiss the concerns that led their students to be punished in school. For instance, parents who routinely chew gum may not comprehend or support the reasons why gum chewing is punished in their children's classrooms. This is not a reason to exclude parents from the problem-solving process, though. Parents should be included, but the issue is how to use parental support most effectively.

Threatening students by telling them that their parents will be informed of their misbehaviors mitigates against the ability to foster partnerships of trust and open communication. The practice may instead result in parents feeling angry at being cast into undesirable roles. This practice can also result in parents being left out of problem-solving processes related to minor concerns and not consulted until major decisions have to be made. In other words, parents are deprived of hearing about problems until their students are facing serious academic consequences or disciplinary actions. Parents typically respond to these situations by demanding to know why they were not consulted before matters escalated to the point where their students may face suspensions or expulsions.

ISSUES RELATED TO ABUSE

A curious paradox is embedded in the rationale for using the threat "I'm going to call your parents" as a means of keeping students in line. As stated earlier, such statements seem to be predicated on the assumption that students who have been reprimanded in school will also receive some form of punishment, perhaps more severe, when they get home. There is a good deal of controversy over the form that punishment might take when left to the discretion of adults who may or may not have adequate parenting skills. The potential for creating circumstances that might lead to child abuse, then, is always present in such threats.

At the heart of this threat lies a paradox that should concern every teacher and administrator. There is widespread reluctance on the part of many educators to report suspected abuse, even when there is clear evidence that it exists. The paradox is that educators cannot have it both ways. If the purpose of telling parents about their students' behaviors is to ensure students are also punished at home, then there are serious ethical and legal concerns related to intentionally overlooking evidence of abuse.

Professionals who work in various levels of law enforcement often express frustration over the subject of child abuse. Much of their frustration derives from their knowledge that teachers and administrators see the evidence of abuse on a daily basis but still do not report it. Educators may say that they do not report suspected abuse because they do not want to get involved, they fear that inappropriate corrective action will result from their report, they think nothing will happen, they worry that students might be treated even worse if such a report is filed, or they fear that they themselves might become the targets of an abusive parent's anger.

Educators, like other professionals whose jobs involve regular contact with children, are mandated reporters of abuse. The law expects an elevated level of child advocacy on the part of such professionals, and educators who fail to meet that standard may be punished. Although other professionals may come into contact with young people periodically during their workdays, educators have opportunities to observe students, from their earliest preschool experiences through adolescence, on a daily basis. They have extended opportunities to observe the symptoms of abuse firsthand.

LOOKING AT THE MAIN IDEAS

Four Classifications of Child Abuse

- Physical abuse
- Neglect
- Sexual abuse
- Mental abuse

Physical Abuse

Some forms of abuse are obvious and would be difficult to ignore. The bruises and burns that appear on the bodies of students, the reluctance to allow any physical proximity with adults, a tendency to flinch in response to quick movements made by adults, and a tendency to hit when angry are just some of the characteristics an educator might see in students who are physically abused.

Teachers have more opportunities to observe the evidence on a young child who is suffering physical abuse at home. Broken bones, black eyes, and frequent bruises may indicate that a child is engaged in a lot of activities and is reckless but they can just as easily be symptoms of abuse. Incontrovertible evidence is a handprint left on a child from a slap or a burn that has a circular shape. Most burns take the form of smudged marks because people pull away from the source of pain. A round burn indicates that a child was held in place while a hot object, often a cigarette, was deliberately placed against the child's skin.

Educators at the secondary level should take notice when students always wear long sleeves, button their shirts up to the neck, and wear long pants on even the hottest days. When physical abuse continues over a long period, abusers learn to hit so that bruises will not show and victims of abuse become better at hiding the evidence. Although most secondary teachers cannot see bruises and scars, such indicators may sometimes be obvious. Physical education teachers, for instance, should not be afraid to look at students in the locker room. Intrusive examinations are not necessary, but casual observations when students are dressing may reveal evidence of abuse that would otherwise go unnoticed.

Neglect

Neglect, like physical abuse, can be obvious. Neglected children are dirty, hungry, and tired. They may come to school without lunches (or with very small lunches) day after day. They may come to school in clothes they have worn for days and with faces that have not been washed. When teachers try to communicate concerns about neglect with the parents, the child may disappear from the classroom because the family has suddenly moved.

Frequent moves can be another characteristic of neglected children. Social workers report that neglectful parents move their families continually, sometimes as often as every two or three months. They move from county to county or even state to state to stay one step ahead of child protective services. Young people appear in a new school in the middle of the year. School records are sent for, time passes, teachers begin to pick up on the fact that something is wrong, and, before action is taken, the student moves again. To help curtail this problem, social workers suggest that the authorities be called as soon as an educator suspects a student's needs are being poorly attended to at home.

Sexual Abuse

The evidence of neglect and physical abuse can be obvious. Other forms of abuse typically are not as easily identified and may take more time to detect. *Sexual abuse* falls into this category. Although the symptoms of this form of abuse may be more subtle than others, teachers' and administrators' "sixth sense" will often detect student behaviors that may be attributable to sexual abuse. For instance, students who are sexually abused may demonstrate a knowledge of sexual activity that is far beyond what is appropriate for their age levels. They may behave in ways that are promiscuous or may act very withdrawn and quiet. The symptoms of sexual abuse can be elusive, but teachers often get the feeling that something is wrong. This gut-level intuition cannot be ignored.

Mental Abuse

Mental abuse is the term used to describe the unkind words some adults use with their children. Insults, sarcastic comments, and constant criticism can all be part of a pattern of mental abuse. Although it may not be possible to easily spot a student who is suffering from mental abuse at home, it is rare for mental abuse to exist by itself. It is usually accompanied by physical or sexual abuse.

Legal and Ethical Aspects of Reporting Abuse

Educators need to be cognizant of the legal penalties associated with the failure to report suspected abuse. In most states educators can be subjected to penalties that consist of fines and incarceration. On the other hand, there are no legal penalties for reporting suspected abuse if it has not occurred. Teachers and administrators need to avail themselves of the information available nationally and in each state on the symptoms and effects of physical, mental, and sexual abuse and neglect so that they can respond in effective and appropriate ways to intercede on the behalf of their students.

On an ethical level, professional educators are child advocates who focus on helping students succeed in school. Children who come from home environments in which all their energies are focused on survival typically do not have the mental or emotional energy to devote to learning. Children who are hungry and sleepy cannot achieve to their maximum potential. If students are going to master content, they need educators who are not only skilled at curriculum design but who are also prepared to act in the manner the law expects and professional ethics demand.

Students, at the very least, have the right to expect that the possibility of being punished at home is not a threat to be held over all their actions in school, particularly when the punishments that will be handed out can be so utterly devastating to their human potential. Teachers must report abuse. Working with parents in partnership to better manage students at home and at school makes sense. Relying on parental punishments to manage an errant student when school does not attempt to work in partnership with families to create appropriate management strategies is irresponsible.

Successful learning relies in part on classroom environments in which students feel both safe and valued. There needs to be a 180-degree shift from some traditional notions of parents' role in classroom management to an attitude of seeing education as a process that draws on all the resources available. Educators must be willing to fulfill their roles as mandated reporters who act to protect students from abusive adults while at the same time working to build bridges between themselves, their students, and the extended learning community.

PARENTS' ROLE IN COGNITIVE MANAGEMENT PRACTICES

Cognitive management strategies, on the other hand, are more likely to include the viewpoint that parents are partners; educators who use these practices are typically more willing to seek family support to better understand their students. One high school decided to change from the use of behaviorist management practices to more cognitive management practices. One of the more notable outcomes was an increase in community outreach and parent contact. One teacher walked into the principal's office and said, "I'm calling parents. I don't even know why I'm calling parents, but I'm calling parents."

Teachers who wish to institute cognitive management practices in their classrooms should consider the ways in which parents will be invited into that process at the beginning of the school year. Teachers can inform their students that if a problem needs to be resolved, all possible information and expertise will be drawn on so that the most productive resolutions can be developed. In part, such a policy means that parents will be kept well informed of their children's behaviors and will be consulted for ideas to help students recover and get back on track in school. After informing students of this approach to problem solving, teachers can share the same information with parents in a letter, phone call, or both. At the same time, educators can make community resources and information concerning appropriate parenting skills available to families.

ISSUES OF DIVERSITY: FAMILIES AND CONFLICTS WITH SCHOOLS

Casting parents into adversarial roles for the sake of controlling student behavior is only one example of how partnerships can be discouraged rather than fostered. Families are also put at odds with schools when their cultural values clash with the dominant culture of their children's classrooms. One of the more regularly seen examples of this problem is the way religious holidays are handled in our public educational system.

School activities scheduled around religious holiday celebrations often reflect the values of the majority culture, and minority cultures find themselves either ignored or, at best, given token acknowledgment. At times the cultural gap between home and school can create situations in which students become highly visible and separated from peers. A case in point was the fifth-grade student who spent the last two weeks of December sitting in the hall outside her music class while the other students in her class sang Christmas carols. The student had told the teacher that it was not appropriate for her to sing the songs because she is Jewish. The teacher placed the student in the hall in an attempt to find a compromise between the student's beliefs and the teacher's planned curriculum. The teacher did not consider that the First and Fourteenth Amendment rights of the student were being violated, the curriculum may well have violated the separation between church and state, and the daily loss of privacy that resulted from sitting in the hall emphasized to the student that her rights were not respected and that she was not a permanently valued member of her class.

Some schools fail to honor the family values of their students, such as in the example mentioned, and other schools give minority cultures only token recognition. Too often schools hold winter concerts in December that consist of several Christmas carols, a few songs about snow, and perhaps one song about Chanukah. Such examples of tokenism do little to help families feel welcome when their faith is centered on the teachings of a religion that falls outside of the mainstream culture. Such practices do not help to educate members of the majority culture about the true nature of diversity existing within their community. It is difficult to sustain a climate of educational equity and tolerance when the activities planned for a classroom isolate or minimize some members of the learning community by affording them only token recognition.

Parents who belong to minority cultures often recount their experiences of contacting their students' educators to express concerns about the proliferation of Santa Claus images, Christmas trees, and other holiday decorations in their students' classrooms during the month of December. The response they hear from educators is generally that Santa Claus is not a religious figure and so it is acceptable to use the image in public schools.

Santa Claus may have become a secular figure, but the other names for him are Father Christmas and Saint Nicholas. Furthermore, there is a clear association between Santa Claus and other symbols of Christmas, however secular, and one particular religious perspective. The association, although perhaps obscure to members of the mainstream culture, is keenly perceived by parents in whose homes these symbols would not appear.

Some families take a secular approach to the way they celebrate holidays in their homes. Although they may be Muslim, Jewish, or Buddhist, their home decorations in December may include a Christmas tree or reindeer silhouettes. Such displays are their personal choice, and educators cannot assume such family activities provide public schools with the license to display the same images in halls and classrooms.

Sometimes teachers ask members of minority religions to determine whether some classroom decoration is offensive. The problem with this approach is that neither the teachers nor the parents hold the final word on how holidays can be addressed in classrooms. These decisions are not the purview of any one individual; they have been made by our Constitution and affirmed by the Supreme Court. The U.S. Constitution states that "Congress shall make no law respecting an establishment of religion, or prohibiting the free exercise thereof."

LOOKING AT RELIGION IN THE SCHOOLS FROM A LEGAL POINT OF VIEW

The Supreme Court has revisited the issue of the separation of church and state, particularly as it applies to public schools, on numerous occasions. Though contentiously divided at times, the rulings of the Supreme Court have consistently reflected the viewpoint that schools are assuredly the place to teach about the role religion has played in history and that it currently plays in society. Public schools are not the place, however, to advocate one particular religious perspective over another.

In 1992, the Supreme Court handed down a decision in the case of *Lee v. Weisman* that religious prayer during graduation exercises is unconstitutional. In that ruling the court spoke to the broader issue of why it is imperative for a free society to protect its citizenry from the establishment of religion:

The lessons of the First Amendment are as urgent in the modern world as in the 18th Century when it was written. One timeless lesson is that if citizens are subjected to state-sponsored religious exercises, the State disavows its own duty to guard and respect that sphere of inviolable conscience and belief that is the mark of a free people. To compromise that principle today would be to deny our own tradition and forfeit our standing to urge others to secure the protections of that tradition for themselves.

Whether to advocate one religious perspective over another through classroom activities, room decorations, or singing songs cannot be determined by any parent, teacher, or administrator. The decisions have already been made. It is the professional responsibility of educators to model respect for the laws of our land, regardless of personal viewpoints. Doing otherwise may devalue some students.

THE ROLE OF COMPULSORY EDUCATION IN THE SEPARATION OF CHURCH AND STATE

Some teachers justify their decisions to use Christmas decorations in their public school classrooms by citing the fact that their community's public buildings are decorated for the holiday season and that the U.S. Congress begins its sessions with a prayer breakfast. The distinction between what might be done in other public buildings and what should be done in public schools is drawn, once again, from the fact that school attendance is compulsory. Children compelled into our public school classrooms bring with them their family values, which range from fundamentalist Christian perspectives, in which secular images associated with Christmas are found to be objectionable because such items would seem to diminish the religious significance of the holiday, to children whose families do not practice the tenets represented by the holiday, to children of Jehovah's Witnesses, whose families celebrate no holidays and commemorate only one religious event. If any of these students' classrooms reflect only one religious viewpoint, they and their families can be made to feel that holding a different set of beliefs means they will never experience a sense of being fully accepted and respected members of the learning community.

Dismissing the concerns parents might express over the values being imparted in the classroom is contrary to the spirit needed for building and sustaining partnerships. A teacher may view Santa Claus as an innocuous secular symbol not representative of any religion; however, when it comes to understanding the role of public schools in the lives of students who come from diverse cultural backgrounds, how teachers interpret the image of Santa Claus is not the defining question.

UNDERSTANDING ISSUES OF DIVERSITY
BY TAKING ANOTHER'S PERSPECTIVE

When trying to understand issues of diversity, the challenge is to view situations through the eyes of another. It may be hard to understand the discomfort felt by parents who belong to minority cultures when their children come home from school singing "White Christmas" and "Jolly Old St. Nicholas," but those feelings are genuine and worthy of a sincere attempt to demonstrate respect for cultural diversity. The U.S. Supreme Court advocates a position of "wholesome neutrality" when it comes to the presence of religion in public schools, and that phrase provides educators with all the language needed to manifest respect for every student's personal belief system.

LOOKING AT THE MAIN IDEAS

The Lemon Test

The Supreme Court developed a standard for judging the wholesome neutrality of activities in the case *Lemon v. Kurtzman* (1971). Called the Lemon Test, these guidelines can be very useful for teachers. When planning an activity at any time of the year teachers should ask themselves the following:

- Does this activity promote or prohibit religion? (It should do neither.)
- Does this activity have a legitimate secular purpose? (It should.)
- Does this activity represent extensive government entanglement? (It should not.)

The concerns described are not ameliorated by having one parent come into a classroom to do a presentation on Chanukah, or Kwanzaa, or Ramadan. Wholesome neutrality exists when the activities in a classroom in December are not significantly different from those that would occur at any other time of the year. The curriculum should consistently reflect district, grade level, and school expectations as well as the legal standards for educational equity.

THE ROLE OF RELIGION IN SCHOOLS

Religion can play a role in any standard curriculum. For instance, social studies units scheduled for December could examine cultures around the world, giving equal time to cultural celebrations occurring during that time of the year. This could provide an ideal opportunity for including parents. Rather than having one or two parents from minority cultures come into the classroom to explain what they do for their holidays, all parents should be welcomed to the classroom. Representatives from every culture could be invited to speak about their December holidays. Parents can talk about what activities occur in their homes during

December, including equal time for Christmas, Chanukah, Kwanzaa, and Ramadan, which may fall either earlier or later, and for families who engage in no holiday activities. The purpose of the presentations is not to compare holidays associated with minority cultures to Christmas or to portray some holidays or people as being exotic or quaint. All holidays included in this unit can be equally compared and contrasted so that students might develop a rich understanding of the common core values underlying the belief systems represented in our country and how our multicultural society is enriched by each of them.

CULTURAL IMPLICATIONS AS RELATED TO STUDENT BEHAVIORS

Although religion is a common example of tensions that can occur between issues of cultural diversity and public schools, other examples are just as powerful in their potential to create tensions between educators and families. Families who speak a primary language other than English, particularly recent immigrants to the United States, can experience a sense of disassociation with the public schools their children attend. Nearly every aspect of the school's culture may be strange and confusing to them.

The greater the variety of services made available to families, the greater the likelihood that cultural barriers can be overcome. What follows is a description of one parent liaison program designed to bridge the gap between non-English-speaking families and the public schools in Fairfax County, Virginia:

> The nature of specific assistance varies considerably. Some families need simple guidance with procedures such as how to enroll parents in adult English-as-a-Second-Language courses. Other households face more serious issues that jeopardize the ability to nurture growing children adequately. Because they speak English in addition to other languages, the parent liaisons can connect children and families with an ever-changing menu of external organizations and school-based collaborations—for example, job training networks, adult literacy programs, financial assistance groups, medical services, and therapists. (Halford, 1996, p. 35)

Although this may seem like an extensive range of services, helping families to more effectively connect to new and strange communities ultimately works toward helping their children succeed in school.

When schools help families who speak a primary language other than English, they also help to reduce some of the internal conflicts that can occur when children appear to be adopting a culture different from that of their families. The expectation of schools that students will speak English, however desirable that goal might be, may lead to tension within the home when students begin to move between the majority culture and their own culture in ways their parents are not able to do. According to Olneck (1995, p. 315),

The encounter between immigrant children, families, and communities and the schools is conditioned by local school cultures, by perceptions relevant actors hold of one another and themselves, by the diverse meanings immigrants and educators assign to schooling, by tacit as well as explicit pedagogical, curricular, and administrative practices, by the degree of discontinuity that obtains between immigrant and school cultures, and by the structural characteristics and cultural practices of immigrant communities. The results of that encounter may be seen in status orders within schools, in the nature of mutual interactions, in the degree of acculturation immigrants experience, in the manner in which immigrants appropriate and utilize their educational experiences, and in the ways that schooling becomes a site for the construction and experience of ethnic identity.

Recent immigrants to this country, as well as those who have been here for generations, carry values and tenets particular to their ethnic roots. At the same time, however, educators can make some universal assumptions. For instance, each culture has some expectations for how children demonstrate respect for authority figures, some common desires for learning, and some shared understanding of what it means to achieve success. Although some common cultural assumptions can be made, at the same time the particular nature of how these attitudes are enunciated probably varies as much among people of a culture as it does between different cultural groups. People might appear to be outwardly similar, but all individuals have different circumstances that color their interpretation of words such as *respect, learning,* and *success.*

No one teacher can be reasonably expected to have a grasp of every cultural nuance that students might bring with them into the classroom. Although professional development courses about various aspects of our multicultural society are necessary, no one can master all the information about this topic. Educators need not have an in-depth mastery of every cultural expectation and family value but rather a shared understanding that effective education is centered on the continual quest to understand students as individuals with particular needs, interests, and values.

MAINTAINING OPEN LINES OF COMMUNICATION

The more educators inquire into and discover about the particular and special qualities of their students, the easier it will be to sustain atmospheres of trust and respect within their schools and classrooms. The key to effective information gathering, as always, is asking questions. What do parents want educators to know about their students and their values? What questions can help educators get that information while not offending or seeming to be insensitive? It would be difficult in this space to provide a detailed explanation of each separate culture and its expectations for education. It is sufficient to say that if students do not look like, act like, think like, or express religious beliefs in the same way as their teachers, then it is the teachers who, as a matter of professional acumen, need to initiate the quest for greater cross-cultural understanding.

An opening statement can be as simple as "I really want your child to have a good year and to be successful. I am hoping we can work together to make that happen. Please talk with me about your ideas that will help us build a team to support your child's achievement." If there is no time to directly deliver this message, it can be sent home as a written invitation. Teachers can enlist help from community outreach programs to translate that message into all the languages spoken among the student population. If the community is too small or too isolated for such services, volunteers may be willing to help.

PARENTS OF STUDENTS WITH SPECIAL NEEDS

Parents of students with special needs are likely to be more actively interested in the day-to-day details of their children's education than parents of children who fall within normal ranges in terms of health and learning abilities. Some special needs of students are more obvious than others. Some are more easily diagnosed. Some generate more empathy than others.

> Students are termed "disabled" because they have real, persistent, and substantial individual differences and educational needs that regular education has been unable to accommodate. These individual differences vary widely, from medical conditions such as cerebral palsy, to dyslexia, to pervasive and chronic maladaptive patterns of behavior. Many of these same students will not be considered disabled once they leave school. Nonetheless, their specialized learning needs are intense and legitimate. The public schools face major challenges in addressing those needs effectively. (Terman, Larner, Stevenson & Behrman, 1996, p. 5)

Depending on the nature of the disability, family members may have been working to address the needs of their child for a long time, sometimes going back to birth or even before birth, depending on test results from pregnancy. Their feelings of concern and their ability to advocate for the needs of their child are often well ingrained before any formal schooling begins. Parents of children with special needs bring with them critical information about the specific disability they want the school to address. Their information, however colored with the deeply personal feelings they carry, is invaluable.

Parents from culturally diverse backgrounds may have particular needs and interests associated with their specific heritage. The same is true of parents with children who have special needs related to disabilities. The range of disabilities is as complex and diverse as all the systems of the human body. The systems can break down separately or in conjunction with one another in an incredible variety of ways. Some are linked to genetics and some to environmental causes.

As with cultural diversity, there are some similarities in the experiences of parents of children with special needs. Parents of children with special needs often feel isolated from their own peers. Their children are not invited to play with other children, their lives may be continually centered on attending to the special needs of their children, and they may experience marital tensions that result from feelings of guilt for their real or perceived role in their children's disabilities and their frustration over the notable differences that frame their daily decisions about parenting.

It is essential for educators to understand these common experiences. The events that bring form to the experience of parenting a child with special needs are not limited to the hours during which school is in session. Parenting a child with special needs is a continual series of decisions, issues, and concerns that affect everything parents do.

> Parents and schools increasingly recognize the important long-term impacts of "less apparent" disabilities. Outcomes for students with less apparent disabilities, as a group, are poor. In this issue, Wayner and Blackorby note that 30% of all students with disabilities dropped out of high school, and an additional 8% dropped out before ever reaching high school. Only 30% of students with learning disabilities participated in post-secondary education, as compared with 68% of youth in the general population. The young women with disabilities were more likely than their non disabled peers to become unmarried parents: among single women with disabilities, one in five had a child within three to five years after high school, compared with 12% of single women in the general population. (Terman, Larner, Stevenson & Behrman, 1996, p. 6)

The lives of adults change dramatically when they have a child with special needs. They quickly become advocates for their children and expect nothing less than the best professional services aligned to address their children's particular needs. The concerns they have should be taken seriously, regardless of the students' disabilities.

Parents of children with special needs often go through some common steps and missteps on the road toward discovering that their children have a problem and then the exact nature of that problem. Unfortunately, some of the common events such families experience include misdiagnosis by the medical profession, well-intended but misguided information from a social worker, and, at some point, a sense of anger or frustration directed at the educational system in general out of a belief that their children's needs are not being adequately served.

Educators sometimes view these parents as pushy or troublesome—and some parents may well be. They have learned to be advocates for their children and are often efficacious in fulfilling that role. Parents, on the other hand, can view an educator's concerns about how best to balance the special needs of one student with the general needs of the entire classroom as an indication that their children's teachers are remote and unconcerned. These oppositional views can cause communication to break down between the two groups and leave both with a sense of discomfort and distrust for each other.

A 1996 study reflected some of the tensions that can arise between parents of children with special needs and their teachers:

> A few parents felt that some teachers made assumptions about them and their parenting skills simply because their child had a disability. [One parent] saw some of these attitudes arising from a lack of understanding of some types of disabilities such as emotional disturbance. [Another parent] felt that school personnel frequently "lumped parents together"— working from inaccurate assumptions about single parents and parents who were not of European heritage. School personnel need opportunities to explore the impulse to stereotype, and encouragement and support to challenge this tendency in themselves as well as their colleagues. (Davern, 1996, p. 62)

Many educators express concern over how to effectively work with students with special needs in their classrooms while at the same time working with students who have no discernable disabilities and also have a right to time and attention from the teacher. Parents of children with special needs are not insensitive to these realities, but they also know that their children have identified needs; unless those needs are carefully addressed, their children may fail to master necessary subject matter content.

The most common complaints center on communication. Parents want their voices to be heard, and they want to be addressed in plain language. It is extremely difficult to view oneself as a partner in the educational process when it is necessary to continually interrupt the conversation to have some combination of letters explained. Although educators may speak in terms of IDEA (Individuals with Disabilities Education Act) or IEP (individualized education plan), these terms may not be familiar to parents. A level playing field means, at the very least, that everyone has the same understanding of the terminology. According to Davern (1996, p. 63), "Parents often felt excluded from the planning process when professionals used unfamiliar educational terms when discussing test results, staffing patterns, and ways of organizing and identifying services. One parent referred to this practice as 'blowing all that smoke.'"

The most direct way to address this potential roadblock to effective communication is to assemble a glossary of terms that parents receive before any meetings. When a meeting with parents does occur, the teacher should first make sure everyone understands the professional terminology that will be used and patiently explain any terms about which there may be confusion. No one knows a student the way his or her parents do, and teachers should make every attempt to treat parents as equal partners in the process of addressing children's special needs.

One educator in New York State decided to take action to facilitate positive communication between her and the parents of her students with special needs. The school year was drawing to a close, and the individualized educational plans (IEPs) for her students with special needs were due to be reviewed. The educator found a time suitable for most of the parents who would be involved in the IEP reviews and invited them to a potluck supper. When she contacted the parents about the dinner, she explained that they would be discussing the IEP process in general, reviewing the laws governing education for students with special needs, and sharing other pertinent information.

The goal was to prepare these parents to be full partners in the upcoming IEP meetings. The teacher explained that no confidential information about any particular student would be discussed, but they would review issues of common concern. She reported that parents expressed gratitude at being prepared for their IEP meetings and felt for the first time that they were able to fully participate. This relatively simple example of bridge building helped parents to feel that their voices were valued and their input was welcome. Most parents simply want to be heard. They want to know that their opinions and insights will receive attention. In Davern's (1996, p. 62) words, "Teachers can maintain their expertise as educators while fully acknowledging the information and insights held by parents. The interplay of these complementary roles can greatly enrich the outcome for students."

THE VALUE OF PARENT–SCHOOL PARTNERSHIPS

Teachers can include parents in partnership roles, regardless of parents' economic status or level of education. Some parents do not feel welcomed into the role of educational partner and attribute this sense of disengagement to the fact that they are nonnative English speakers, speakers of a dialect considered to be out of the mainstream of standard English, representatives of minority cultures, or assertive and even aggressive advocates for the welfare of their children. It is imperative that professional educators make every effort to reach out to families and acknowledge the fact that students do not exist in a vacuum; rather, students represent the family structure in which they spend the majority of their time.

Unless and until teachers make an effort to understand that reality, they cannot effectively teach every student. Accordingly, educators must continually work at informing themselves about the cultures and issues represented within their school communities to more effectively equalize the educational experience of their students.

Effective education requires a broad perspective of the lives of students. Their learning is not restricted to any classroom or school day. The world educates our young people, and educators have a wealth of available resources to reach their students. There is an increasing body of research into the positive effects that school–family partnerships can have on the educational experience of students:

> Emerging from research and new practices is the understanding that neither family nor school alone can help children solve learning and development problems. Partnerships make it more likely that ideas, energy, and resources will be targeted to improve schools, strengthen families, and increase students' chances for success. School practices should help parents understand the school and their children's opportunities and programs. Two-way communication should help schools under-

stand families' cultures, strengths, and goals. Both school and family need to exchange information about the children they share. And children need to know that their families and their teachers have similar expectations for them to work hard in the role of "student" in order to succeed in school and in society. (Hidalgo et al., 1995, p. 515)

PARTNERSHIP ROLES PARENTS CAN PLAY

In the elementary years, teachers have many more opportunities to interact with parents than at the secondary level. From kindergarten through fifth grade parents tend to be more directly involved in the education of their children. They drive their children to school, pick them up after school, bring cookies for parties, and are generally around more than they will be when their children are older. They are also perceived by their younger children to be more of an asset than a liability, an attitude that tends to change dramatically around puberty. In short, the younger the student, the greater the likelihood that teachers will have frequent contact with parents.

Some parents find time to volunteer in public schools. Extra hands are always welcome in any classroom, but parents' time in the classroom is more useful if they come with a clear sense of purpose. Educators who do some thoughtful preplanning ensure that classroom volunteers feel welcome and productive. Teachers can take time to help parents understand some of the basic tenets of the classroom, particularly the management structure. In this way parents will not find themselves in a position of unintentionally undermining what a teacher is striving to accomplish.

Parents enjoy having some specific tasks they are comfortable doing and that are genuinely helpful to the teacher rather than busy work assignments. Teachers might begin by asking parents what sort of work they would enjoy doing. Rather than suggesting specific roles to them, teachers can offer parents a variety of options from which to choose. As mentioned earlier in the section on religion, some parents may be asked to do guest presentations because they represent a culture with which the general school community is unfamiliar. Although this may seem to be a good idea, parents who feel unsure about their mastery of English or are shy may find such a situation uncomfortable. A presentation can be one option, but parents should be able to choose how to participate as volunteers in their children's schools.

LOOKING AT THE MAIN IDEAS

Parents Can Make Successful Contributions as Volunteers When

- They have a specific task to do.
- They work in a part of the school that is most comfortable for them and most in need of their assistance. This may be some other place than their children's classrooms.
- They understand the need to protect the confidentiality of the students with whom they work.

Educators should provide parent aides with written information that explains volunteer roles and expectations. Once the information has been distributed, teachers can hold a meeting for parents interested in volunteering. The meeting's primary agenda is to review the written expectations and clarify any questions that remain. Then parents can be scheduled to come into the classroom individually for a trial day. The trial day allows teachers and parents to keep their options open about the extent of commitment and involvement on everyone's part. Parent help can be useful, but not necessarily in their children's classrooms. Educators may suggest that some parents might be able to use their time more effectively if their energies are directed elsewhere in the school.

Young students occasionally misbehave when their parents are in their classrooms. The dynamics of the parent–child relationship may not be conducive to having them interact in school and at home. At the end of the trial day, educators can sit down with parents and discuss how the day has gone. If things were bumpy, the parent will probably acknowledge that. If the parent feels the day has gone well but the teacher has a different perspective, one way to approach consensus on the role the parent could play in the school is to begin the conversation by saying something like, "Well, I agree. It was great having you here. I wanted to ask you about something I noticed." This provides the teacher with an opportunity to begin discussing with the parent any concerns that arose during the day.

Parents should be welcome in schools, but serving as aides in their own children's classrooms may not be the most effective use of their time or the teacher's. Parents can also show support of their schools by providing extra help in the library or office. If the trial day has not gone well, parents may have another suggestion for ways to volunteer or they can be encouraged to select another option from the provided list.

KEEPING IN TOUCH WITH PARENTS OF SECONDARY SCHOOL STUDENTS

Maintaining contact with parents takes a little more work at the secondary level. However, at any grade level, positive interactions with parents begin by understanding that they are legally in charge of their children's education and need to be kept informed of classroom rules, practices, curriculum, and special events. Letters, phone calls, e-mail communications, and newsletters are among the many ways information can be shared.

Teachers who understand the significant role parents can play in a partnership approach to education take the time to introduce themselves to students' families as early in the school year as possible. Sending home an introductory letter that sets out a general overview of goals for the year is one way to do this. Another is to make a few phone calls each evening to let parents know what kind of a year their children are having and how the teachers hope to incorporate family partnerships into the learning process. Time should be reserved at the end of each call for parents to ask questions of the teacher. One seventh-grade teacher was responsible for teaching six periods a day, with an average of 30 students per class. He began each year by making phone calls to all the families of his students, each one taking just the few minutes needed to say hello, introduce himself, and ask if there were any questions. Although it took time, the teacher said it was worth it. If, later in the year, he had a problem with a student, he had already established a positive connection with the family. Those positive relationships forged out of a brief phone call made it much easier to resolve any problems that occurred later in the school year.

SUMMARY

Whether educators are working to resolve management problems, promote cultural equity, or help parents of students with special needs become equal partners, good communication and nonjudgmental attitudes are fundamental to the process. Most parents are doing the best they can. Just as no teacher ever sets out to be a poorly functioning professional, so no parent ever intends to be bad at child rearing. Some educators need additional training to function more effectively in their classrooms, and some parents need more information to work better with their children. Negative stereotyping of parents that discourages communication and partnerships does not help to improve the lives of children. Educators can choose to be inclusive in their attitudes toward families or exclusive and judgmental. However, only inclusive attitudes will effectively help students to succeed.

APPLYING THE CONCEPTS

Consider your opportunities to interact with parents at the grade level you are teaching or intend to teach. What strategies discussed in this chapter would be most useful to you? What other ideas do you have for building partnerships with parents? Write a brief reflective paper on how you would like to be treated as a parent and how, as a teacher, you could make sure that you will treat parents respectfully.

CHAPTER 9

Creating the Democratic Classroom:
A Holistic Perspective

CHAPTER OBJECTIVES

By the end of this chapter the reader should be able to:

◇ Understand how democratic curriculum and assessment integrate with democratic management to create a synergistic classroom environment
◇ Incorporate curriculum practices that encourage peer interaction
◇ Understand that curriculum design can be inclusive of all the diverse learning needs and styles represented in a classroom
◇ Develop a basic understanding of how to address diverse learning styles through lesson plan designs
◇ Apply democratic management and curriculum practices when functioning in the role of substitute teacher

Scenario

The sixth-grade class was divided up into eight teams, each with the assignment of working together to explore a separate aspect of their current social studies unit. The class was learning about life in modern China, and each group had selected a topic for which they would be responsible. As the groups completed their work, they were to compile a classroom portfolio containing all the information they had discovered. Accordingly, each team was required to research its topic of interest and then prepare a report, complete with news footage or photographs, news reports from magazines or newspapers, and any other resource information that would document group members' exploration into details of life in modern China, such as dress, economics, food, and religious practices.

The teacher had worked with the students to establish the learning goals and outcomes for the unit, which in addition to the content included student responsibility for setting group goals, establishing a scoring guide to assess their cooperative efforts, and creating another scoring guide to assess personal portfolios. The personal portfolios contained self-generated evidence students compiled to represent the individual learning gains each had separately achieved during the unit.

As part of the introduction to how the teams would be organized, the teacher had included a reminder that all students would have an opportunity to earn points on a daily basis for working together quietly and efficiently. The teacher said he would be watching them and awarding points when he noted good group behavior. At the end of the unit, the team with the most points would earn a popcorn party.

Questions

Can you see any contradiction emerging in the description of the classroom described? When creating a democratic classroom, how do you develop cohesive curriculum, management, and assessment practices? Is the strategy for group points described a good fit with the curriculum in which the students are engaged?

Discussion

Recently, there has been a notable shift in education toward the use of curriculum practices that rely on the self-motivation and independent thinking of students. Educators who strive to initiate democratic practices within their classrooms find that these innovative curriculum practices provide a strong measure of support for their efforts. Cooperative learning, authentic assessment, math as problem solving, writers' workshops, and integrated curriculum are just some of the practices that bring a democratic sense of student involvement to classrooms at every grade level. These strategies are as practical for addressing a variety of educational needs and interests as they are engaging and fun. Teachers continually seek ways to meet a variety of individual needs while at the same time working to manage classrooms with more students who represent the increasingly diverse nature of our country's population.

Many excellent democratic curriculum models on which teachers can build exciting and motivating learning opportunities are available. This chapter is not intended to provide an overview of the choices from which educators can pick and choose; instead, this chapter is devoted to addressing some issues that pertain to cultural and educational needs and how innovative curriculum practices can address these needs.

The important focus of this chapter is how democratic curriculum strategies employed at every grade level can be interwoven with democratic management practices. This integration, along with equitable assessment strategies, is critical for an overall democratic school climate. The particular models by which the integration is actually achieved can be selected and implemented in ways that best meet the needs of individual educators and their students.

DEVELOPING CONSISTENCY BETWEEN CURRICULUM AND MANAGEMENT

Many teachers have embraced independent learning strategies or at least have been willing to experiment with them. However, some teachers are still attempting to manage all of these student-directed learning configurations through teacher-directed discipline strategies. Consequently, students experience a mismatch between the expectations for the intrinsic ways in which they are expected to gather and process subject matter content and the extrinsic ways in which the behaviors they exhibit during these activities are judged.

At some level, this mismatch of discipline and curriculum can be understood through the nature of how some educators and students view each other and the beliefs they hold toward each other. The creation of a seamless integration of democratic management and curriculum relies on educators and students who have worked to build a level of trust toward one another. The ability to genuinely trust one another is an essential component of the process, yet it is a rare commodity in most schools. Students who genuinely engage in democratic learning opportunities have to trust that their opportunities for learning will be equitable, just as they need to be secure in the knowledge that the assessment criteria for any activity will focus on their academic understanding of subject matter and not reflect who they are.

TRUST: THE CRITICAL ELEMENT

Teachers who facilitate their students' learning through democratic practices, as opposed to depending on direct instruction, have to believe that their students want to learn and are willing to seek out the information that will help them accomplish their educational goals. Such practices rely on the idea that students will exhibit a level of personal responsibility for their own learning. In fact, the driving force behind designing curriculum in this fashion is that the motivation of students to master the content is higher when they have some measure of control over the topics they explore, how the content is presented, and how their work will be assessed. In short, teachers must rely on students to elect to exhibit appropriate levels of personal responsibility to achieve their own learning goals.

Yet trusting students to accomplish what needs to be accomplished can be a very difficult thing for teachers. Much of what occurs in schools mitigates against this sense of trust. The structure of many schools and classrooms almost ensures that deceit will be the order of the day. The power differential that exists between educators and their students often convinces young people that lying about why homework is late, what is actually in their desks, or where they really need to go when they ask to use the restroom may be easier than telling the truth. Teachers who discover students engaging in a lie feel justified in believing that most students will deceive them and that they should view with skepticism much of what students say.

Educators reflect this sense of wariness when they express disbelief that students who are left to their own devices and given the necessary information will actually want to manage their own learning opportunities in ways that are conducive to achieving their educational goals. In addition, many teachers opt not to entrust students with control over their behaviors or learning. More typically, teachers help students learn self-directed strategies for investigating aspects of subject matter content that spark their interests. At the same time, these educators retain tight control over student behaviors.

This is not a minor contradiction but rather a primary indicator of whether the classroom climate is truly reflective of a democratic foundation for self-determination in regard to thoughts and actions. It is highly unlikely that students will ever feel a genuine sense of personal responsibility for their own learning when they know that the ultimate judgment regarding their value in the classroom community is being made by the teacher. Teachers simply cannot have it both ways; the mix of student-directed learning with teacher-directed management leaves students feeling confused about the true nature of their teachers' expectations for what is valued in the classroom.

"YES, BUT IT WOULDN'T WORK WITH MY STUDENTS."

Some teachers say that their students have to receive stickers or other rewards for what they have achieved during an activity. These educators explain that perhaps other students might be able to handle the responsibility for managing their own behaviors, but their own students just are not capable of such things.

However, experience indicates that those who say their students would not act responsibly if there were no token rewards for good behaviors have never genuinely instituted alternative approaches. Such teachers have come to rely on behavioral strategies they have practiced for years. Often, these are the only strategies teachers have ever tried, and their use came about in a desperate search for something that would keep their classrooms quiet. They have difficulty envisioning the potential for success that other management approaches might have to offer; as a result, they tend to dismiss the value of these ideas out of hand. Other educators justify their use of extrinsic rewards by saying that in life people work for money to buy material goods. Given that social reality, they feel the tokens distributed in their classrooms help to prepare students for their adult lives.

Our society certainly views the evidence of achievement through the homes, cars, clothing, and other property a person obtains in life. What is missing from that argument is the quality of the relationships a person forms during a lifetime. Adults go to work to earn money to maintain a certain lifestyle. However, when they go to work, when they interact with their coworkers, and when they go home to those with whom they share their private lives, it is important to consider the quality of those personal relationships. This has little to do with monetary earnings or any other tangible goods.

Relationships are sustained and enriched through a personal sense of social responsibility and empathy. These qualities cannot be reinforced through the use of stickers or candy. They are, though, the qualities individuals must nurture to lead a fully engaged existence.

CLASSROOM CHATTER AND THE LEARNING PROCESS

There is a sound rationale for being skeptical about the ability of one individual to adequately serve the educational needs of a widely diverse group of students. It is impossible to imagine that every student in a classroom can achieve subject matter competency as a result of the direct instruction given by any one person. Learning styles, special needs, primary languages, and cultural perceptions all come into play in the acquisition of information, and no single teacher can address every aspect of students' diverse learning needs.

Management issues are accentuated when one person attempts to be the sole source of all content information in the classroom One basic concern frequently expressed in connection with this form of content delivery is trying to quiet everyone enough to hear the instructions being given. There are many reasons why it can be difficult to quiet a group of individuals, some of which are associated with learning styles, some with learning disabilities, and some with developmental levels of socialization. Adults sometimes recall that they were good students in elementary school but got into trouble in middle school for talking. This is a fairly typical example of how a naturally occurring developmental process of socialization can interfere with the styles of teachers who rely on direct instruction to deliver information.

Some students process the excitement they feel when they hear new ideas by sharing their thoughts with others. Adults often share a comment or even a brief conversation with people sitting next to them at lectures, plays, movies, or other events at which the audience is expected to be quiet. These same behaviors are seen among teachers during workshops, presentations, or classes to upgrade skills. New ideas trigger the need to share a thought with another participant. Teachers whisper, write a quick note to a friend, or engage in a quick side conversation. This behavior is more characteristic of how some individuals process new information than of a malicious intent to disrupt a learning environment.

Rather than assuming students are engaged in side conversations because they intend to be disruptive, teachers might try to view the behavior as a student's attempt to comprehend an idea that challenges a prior belief and causes a sense of disequilibrium. As suggested in an earlier chapter, teachers could respond to such behaviors by asking all students (as opposed to singling out one student) how they are doing. The teacher can then wait to hear students' thoughts and ideas.

The question can be asked in a tone of inquiry rather than a tone that challenges the behaviors. New information being presented might require further clarification, and students may be checking with each other because they fear that asking for more details will be considered a dumb question. Asking students how they are doing allows them to think aloud with their teachers and formulate their questions as they speak.

A variety of cultural issues mitigate against students quietly attending to every word uttered by their teachers. Students who come from cultures that encourage community interactions often feel it is a natural part of the learning process to discuss a new idea with a classmate. Students who speak a primary language other than English may be struggling to follow the information being presented from a single, often auditory, source at the front of the room and they may need to seek help from another person nearby. Some students with learning disabilities find they have difficulty following direct instruction and are not able to acquire the subject matter content as it is being presented. Some students simply do not process auditory information effectively.

LOOKING AT THE MAIN IDEA

Why Students Talk during Class

- They are able to process information more effectively when they can talk about it.
- They did not follow the information being presented and are seeking clarification from a peer.
- Their cultural background embraces communal interactions.

Waiting for students to be quiet and listen can absorb a good deal of precious instructional time. However, if the instruction is coming from only one source, then waiting until everyone is listening becomes an integral part of the learning climate. The problem is that there always seems to be a buzz that will not go away. When teachers want to begin a lesson or share some critical directions for an activity, they can quickly become frustrated by the desire to start conflicting with the need to extinguish the continuing buzz of talking. If teachers wait and wait for absolute quiet, chances are that more and more students will begin to engage in side conversations because it seems that nothing is happening.

ALTERNATIVES TO DIRECT INSTRUCTION CAN ELIMINATE CONCERNS ABOUT CHATTER

If curriculum is designed so that every piece of information garnered by the students comes from the teacher, the teacher is likely to either spend time waiting for every child to be quiet or to use some form of extrinsic control to achieve the silent attention of their learners. On the other hand, if educators facilitate learning with strategies that include cooperative learning, self-assessment, individually developed projects, and other approaches that help students become self-directed learners, the entire issue of maintaining a constantly quiet classroom goes away.

Rather than constantly quieting students, teachers can direct their energies toward instituting curriculum practices built on self-exploration and peer support. The focus in such classrooms is no longer on implied power differentials between students and teachers but rather on helping students make decisions about their academic goals and how they can support and work with their peers.

Additional support for becoming a facilitator of learning as opposed to being in charge of delivering a constant flow of direct instruction has been provided by various modern technologies. Young people have available to them a wide variety of information through the World Wide Web, CD-ROMs, and other technological resources with which they are both familiar and comfortable. In the face of this incredible and rapidly increasing world of information, it is improbable that one person can satisfactorily account for all the content pertinent to all individuals on any given subject. Teachers can no longer imagine that they are the gatekeepers to the universe of knowledge. Information on anything one could imagine is readily available to young people anywhere who have access to a computer with a modem.

When students are working in groups, pursuing their own learning, documenting their own achievements in self-generated portfolios, and assessing their achievement with the use of scoring guides, they are more likely to gain the skills to support the continual pursuit of their individual interests. The potential for fostering the spirit of lifelong learning is enormous. Teachers who interweave strategies for the individual pursuit of learning into their classrooms' curriculum find that they have altered their own roles from being the source of all knowledge to guiding students in the directions that will best yield the information being sought. The whole issue of maintaining quiet classrooms becomes secondary to the exciting atmosphere generated when students learn to access and process information in ways that are personally meaningful.

THE MIX OF TIME, MANAGEMENT, AND CURRICULUM

Many teachers look for quick solutions to difficult problems. As discussed in an earlier chapter, there is no quick path to a well-managed democratic classroom. There must always be an investment of time. The critical word, though, is *investment* because the returns, or the effect of the time spent in community building, enhance every interaction for the rest of the academic year.

Teachers can devote time at the beginning of the year to developing mutual expectations as they apply not only to management issues but also to learning goals and outcomes. Management issues and learning goals and outcomes cannot be seen as separate; accordingly, each needs to be carefully discussed. Practice sessions that include role-playing and other creative expressions help students further understand the part each plays within the learning community.

It is not enough to tell students they will be investigating areas of study that appeal to them; they need to know what resources are available, how to access them, and what to do if one student is using a resource another student needs. If the teacher wants students to work together in groups, then time needs to be spent discussing and practicing group processes. How are tasks identified, assigned, and completed? What happens when students disagree about which task needs to be done before another? How are leadership and supporting roles established? These important community concepts cannot be left to chance.

One comprehensive approach to teaching a unified approach to curriculum and management can be accomplished by spending time learning the skills of problem solving. The time spent teaching problem-solving skills is not an additional subject matter topic but rather a thread that may be carried through and applied to all aspects of the learning community. Mathematics, spelling, group consensus, peer conflict, assessment, art projects, and any other aspect of curriculum or management may be approached as a problem-solving opportunity. Therefore, the teaching of skills for effective problem solving can help educators to facilitate a broad range of learning opportunities and to assist with behavioral issues.

UNDERSTANDING WHO STUDENTS ARE
BY UNDERSTANDING HOW THEY LEARN

When teachers seek to know more about the students with whom they will be working and how they might approach problem solving, it is not enough to understand the individual representations of culture, learning disabilities, power differentials, and family values. Teachers also need to have some sense of what strategies their students innately use to access and retain information. Young people access all sorts of information in all sorts of settings, and only some of that learning occurs in the classroom. No matter what the topic or issue of interest, young people devise ways to learn what they are motivated to learn. A typical example might be a child who cannot seem to retain any information about basic arithmetic computations such as times tables and yet is able to identify the make, year, and model of any car. Parents and educators experience this dichotomy all the time. The challenge for educators is to identify individual interests and abilities and tap into them to foster greater learning gains within the classroom.

There are many ways to identify students' interests. For instance, educators may choose personal interest, learning style, or personality inventories available commercially or develop their own. Regardless of the specific tool being used, these inventories can yield valuable insight into how students access information and what is important to them. Teachers cannot tailor every learning experience to each student's interests and learning styles. Armed with the knowledge of how their individual students learn best, however, teachers can design curriculum that addresses different strengths at different times.

> Increasingly, educators are understanding the complexity of learning styles that students bring to the classroom. Schools have traditionally rewarded only those students who can fit into a fairly rigid mold of achievement. When there is only one "right" way to learn, those who have other strengths, skills, and talents are denied access to academic success. Teachers must constantly challenge themselves to find the strengths of each student and to provide a multiplicity of opportunities for each child to succeed. All children can learn. It is up to us to discover the most effective ways to teach them. (Greely & Mizell, 1993, p. 229)

In other words, a truly democratic curriculum provides students equal opportunity to experience lessons designed to meet their learning style needs and strengthen areas with which they are not as comfortable or compatible.

LOOKING AT THE MAIN IDEAS

Curriculum Can Be Tailored for a Variety of Learning Needs through Inventories That Assess

- Learning styles
- Attitudes toward school

- Skills and abilities
- Personal interests

Some learning styles can also be reflections of the cultural diversity represented among students. Howard Gardner's (1993) work in the area of multiple intelligences is one approach to helping teachers understand the variety of strengths represented in a classroom and some of the cultural influences reflected in those strengths. For instance, Gardner identifies one of the intelligences as linguistic, which incorporates a range of language skills including the ability to tell stories, a skill with cultural associations. It is difficult to separate the learning style from the culture and equally inappropriate to make assumptions about the storytelling skills of students based solely on their cultural heritage:

> The learning styles research has significant possibilities for enhancing the achievement of culturally diverse students. This body of research reminds teachers to be attentive not only to individual students' learning styles but to their own actions, instructional goals, methods, and materials in reference to their students' cultural experiences and preferred learning environments. (Irvine & York, 1995, p. 484)

Teachers at every level have available a wide variety of resources to help them assess their students' interests and learning styles. In terms of the connection between management and curriculum, a curriculum designed to address a diverse range of learning abilities and styles invites students to be part of a welcoming learning community rather than making them feel out of step in an environment where the cards seem forever stacked against them.

Taking the time to assess the various learning styles that might be represented among students can help teachers to more effectively address a broad range of educational needs and maintain a classroom that is calm, safe, and inviting.

Another appropriate use of learning style inventories is to assess how teachers themselves access and retain information. If the teacher's learning style does not match those of the students, miscommunication and misunderstanding are possible. Accordingly, learning style inventories should not just be used to design student learning opportunities but should also pervade the decisions educators make in terms of how information is delivered.

Teachers who use learning style inventories can compare the data gathered from the students in terms of preferred learning modalities with the results of their own learning style assessment. If the inventories of students reveal strengths in music, art, and visual learning and the teacher's strengths are in logical thinking and auditory learning, some conciliatory adjustments may have to occur to make the classroom a productive environment for everyone. For instance, if most students have strengths in the area of musical ability, a teacher need not sing a lesson; however, playing a tape of music while students work on a task or as students enter the room is a way of addressing that strength.

Teachers who are willing to explore strategies that address a wide variety of learning styles and needs often find additional benefits because their lessons become more accessible to those with learning disabilities. For instance, if teachers have several visual learners in their classrooms, they might be more conscious of using prepared overhead transparencies to emphasize key points in a lesson. Transparencies are appropriate at any grade level and usually are much easier to read than writing on a chalkboard. Prepared overheads can be duplicated so that students can follow the information being presented and write clarifying notes on their own copies. Although visual learners may find this practice comfortable, students who have a visual disability or who have difficulty processing auditory information may also find this use of overhead transparencies to be effective. In other words, changing a few basic practices can be helpful in addressing several different kinds of learning needs and abilities.

COOPERATIVE LEARNING

Cooperative learning is one of the most easily implemented strategies available to help students become responsible for their own behaviors and to function effectively in groups without the constant oversight of a teacher. In addition, research seems to support the role cooperative learning can play in establishing an equitable climate for learning. Banks (1997, p. 63) believes that

> Concepts should be taught when possible with different strategies so that students who are relational in their learning styles as well as those who are analytic will have an equal opportunity to learn. Researchers such as Slavin (1983) and E. G. Cohen (1986) have documented that cooperative learning strategies appeal to ethnic-group students and foster positive intergroup attitudes and feelings. . . . Educational equity will exist for all students when teachers become sensitive to the cultural diversity in their classrooms, vary their teaching styles so as to appeal to a diverse student population, and modify their curricula to include ethnic content.

Including cooperative learning activities within other constructivist curriculum practices can also be a part of effective time management. Teachers cannot be everywhere in a classroom to constantly address all students' needs. However, teachers can work carefully with students to establish expectations and outcomes for learning activities, create cooperative groups either randomly or selectively (depending on the activity), and then monitor the progress of the groups through either observations or direct questions. Establishing a climate in which students learn to rely on their own abilities and the support of their peers does not relieve teachers of any professional responsibilities but allows them to focus their professional energies on resolving problems with students privately. Issues concerning the learning or behaviors of students can be addressed in a quiet, one-on-one conference while the rest of the class stays on task and moves forward with the curriculum.

There are some practical guidelines to implementing cooperative learning, and a number of models are available. Notable researchers in this field David Johnson and Roger Johnson (1991, p. 207) recommend the following rules to guide cooperative learning groups. They advise teachers that some useful rules might include having students

1. Stay with their group and not wander around the room.
2. Use quiet voices.
3. Make sure every group member shares ideas.
4. Listen with real care to what other group members are saying.

These separate rules can be introduced, discussed, and practiced in role-playing scenarios. If time is spent on explaining and understanding these four basic rules, students will be able to get to work quickly and stay focused on their assignments and the teacher's time can be used for one-on-one interactions, observations, assessment, or any other appropriate professional activity.

In addition, practicing these basic rules allows students to transfer their cooperative skills to a variety of situations. In one school, a small group of upper elementary students was working collaboratively on a class activity. One member of the group, however, seemed unfocused and left the table frequently to visit other tables and talk with his peers. The behavior of this one student was upsetting to the rest of the group members, who felt frustrated that the activity would suffer as a result of one person's actions.

They resolved the problem by applying what they knew about cooperative learning skills and problem solving. The members of the group decided that they would address the problem directly and not seek out the help of their teacher to resolve the situation. While the student was gone from their group, the other students came to the consensus that if he left again, they would say something to him. They decided that one of the group members would invite the student into the hall for a brief conference. The student returned briefly, but when he got up to leave again, he was asked to step out in the hall. The two students were out of the room less than two minutes. When they returned, they were both smiling and seemed at ease. The wandering student sat down, got to work, and did not leave the team again.

It must be emphasized that this resolution did not just occur. The students had discussed and practiced rules for appropriate group behaviors. They had been involved in establishing the rules and reviewing the expectations for this activity. As a result of the information they had and the practice sessions in which they had engaged, these students developed the confidence to advocate for themselves. The fruits of all the efforts made by the teacher were evident in this scenario. At no time did this group of young people need the help of an adult to resolve the problem. They knew what it meant to be productive group members, and they also knew how to help one person get back on track.

These students were engaged in the significant life skill of cooperative problem solving, one that is worth the time spent in teaching and practicing it. If students gather in groups but rely on an adult to solve their problems or are allowed to arbitrarily eliminate group members who are not helping, they miss out on the opportunity to discover how satisfying it can be to resolve these problems on their own.

EFFECTIVE CURRICULUM PRACTICES
FOR STUDENTS WITH SPECIAL NEEDS

Although educators must make every attempt to ensure equal educational opportunities for all their students, there are particular and accentuated concerns when their efforts are directed toward ensuring the equitable experiences of students with special needs. The law tips the scales in favor of these students because their needs are so great and the playing field on which they stand is so uneven.

One potential barrier to adequately serving these students is correct identification of their needs. Some students' special needs will already have been identified when they enter the classroom, and they may bring with them individualized educational plans.

Some students enter their classrooms with clear evidence that they are having trouble fulfilling the expectations of the learning activities or exhibiting negative behaviors when given a task. These students may or may not have some form of disability; teachers are part of the referral process to get at the heart of students' problems.

One complicating factor in all of this is the misperception that the disabilities presenting themselves in the classroom are congenital or genetic. Therefore, this line of thinking goes, whatever learning difficulties students might have will be identified and perhaps even diagnosed by the time they have entered school.

Students may or may not be born with the disabilities that limit their opportunities to succeed in school. The body is dynamic and can change dramatically at any point in a person's development. Eyesight can deteriorate, eardrums can become infected or even rupture because of a sudden illness, and students can become anemic and thus tire easily. These are but a few examples of human physical dynamics. Teachers harbor serious misperceptions if they believe that students who are functioning "normally" one year will continue with that same pattern during every other year of their school experience.

Some students' disabilities may have been incorrectly diagnosed. Teachers need to track the progress of students with diagnosed disabilities to ensure that their corrective educational plans are appropriate. At times cultural bias becomes a barrier to an accurate diagnosis of why students are not able to learn at the same rate as their peers. Nonnative English speakers are often mislabeled as learning disabled when they do not quickly adapt to the academic expectations of their teacher while in transition from their primary language to English. Conversely, some students with learning disabilities are enrolled in English as a second language programs when their native language is English but their names and physical aspects make them appear to have been born elsewhere.

One fifth-grade teacher in Oregon had a student with a severe disability that kept him from being able to process information auditorily. As a result of this disability, or perhaps because of some additional complications as yet unidentified, the student could barely read or write. The student also had a Hispanic last name. The teacher was continually frustrated because her school wanted to place this student in an English for speakers of other languages program. In fact, this student was a native English speaker and had never spoken Spanish.

ATTENTION DEFICIT DISORDER OR ATTENTION DEFICIT–HYPERACTIVITY DISORDER

Some students with disabilities fall outside the realm of the special education programs available in public schools. They are disabled, but their disabilities are not recognized by the laws that govern the education of students with special needs. Some students do not qualify for special services under the Individuals with Disabilities Education Act (IDEA) but qualify under the original umbrella act known as Public Law 504. This legislation, which preceded IDEA by a number of years, is typically the one used to serve the needs of some students with learning disabilities and those identified as having attention deficit disorder (ADD) or attention deficit–hyperactivity disorder (ADHD). This portion of the chapter is not meant to be a review of the symptoms or conditions related to ADD or ADHD or a discussion of the diagnostic process. However, it is important to devote some time to a discussion of students who have or are suspected of having ADD or ADHD because some consistent problems seem to occur when educators attempt to address these particular needs within a mainstream classroom.

To be sure, addressing the needs of students with ADD or ADHD can include coming to terms with a confusing mix of issues. Essentially, every student has a right to the opportunity to be successful in school—not the right to succeed, but the right to an opportunity to succeed. That right is protected not only through an educator's management practices but also in how curriculum is designed and delivered. Educators cannot take any steps that will limit or exclude students from any curricular activity on the basis of a physical, mental, emotional, or learning disability.

Many educators are careful to protect the rights of their students by following their individualized educational plans and exploring creative ways to include all students in the learning process. Nevertheless, some discriminatory practices still occur, both unintentionally and, unfortunately, intentionally. Many discriminatory practices are related to issues of confidentiality. Some disabilities are highly visible. A students with severe cerebral palsy, ADD, ADHD, or any other form of disability inevitably becomes highly visible within the mainstream classroom. Educators need not exacerbate this situation by creating circumstances that further contribute to students' high visibility, as discussed in chapter 7.

Curriculum, Management, and Issues Concerning Students with ADD and ADHD

The volume of information available to educators about many of the special needs with which students might be afflicted is increasing. Teachers often receive sound guidance from specialists, who can help with curriculum strategies and in developing management plans. More problematic, however, are issues associated with students who have been identified as having ADD or ADHD. With any disability, curriculum is inseparable from management issues; this is particularly so when the disability is ADD or ADHD.

Problems that occur are primarily related to issues of confidentiality and curriculum. The balance of this section is devoted to how educators might balance individual needs, issues of confidentiality, and curriculum design.

Working to maintain a productive and on-task classroom populated with some highly active students, regardless of whether they are or are not actually afflicted with ADD or ADHD, is a challenge for teachers at all grade levels. Educators commonly share similar areas of concern when they discuss their work and interactions with highly active children. They typically express frustration at trying to deliver curriculum content while at the same time attempting to control behaviors that seem unmanageable and for which there seem to be few solutions. Too often, attempts to manage behaviors consist of using highly visible punitive measures rather than corrective techniques that would be more appropriate for students with these particular special needs.

A number of misperceptions are associated with students with ADD and ADHD, the most common of which seems to be that they can be "cured" if their disabilities are treated as behavioral problems rather than brain disorders. Many good resources are available to parents and teachers to provide insight and understanding into the symptoms of these conditions and strategies for working with students who are so afflicted. Some of these resources can be accessed on the World Wide Web.

Students who exhibit classroom behaviors such as being off task for more time than they are on task, having bursts of high energy, and displaying an inability to focus on topics for any significant time are often suspected to have some form of ADD or ADHD, which may or may not be the case. Adults sometimes can be too quick to apply this label to students regardless of whether they have been diagnosed as having ADD or ADHD or actually have this condition at all.

Only medical doctors and psychologists can determine whether students have ADD or ADHD. A student who appears to have ADD or ADHD may be suffering from that condition or instead may be bored, frustrated, tired, suffering from some allergic condition, or having a bad day. Mislabels that result from guesses are not helpful to the success of any student.

LOOKING AT THE MAIN IDEAS

Addressing the Needs of Students with ADD or ADHD

- Help them learn strategies for managing their behaviors when their medication has worn off.

- Provide them with information about appropriate ways to move around and stretch when they need to.

- Provide them with a varied curriculum that includes movement and peer interactions.

Certainly behaviors associated with ADD and ADHD can be very taxing to teachers who are trying to move through the curriculum and address the learning needs of a number of students. What makes these disabilities unique in terms of classroom management is that by their very nature they are disruptive to quiet learning environments. Symptoms can appear to be the attributes of a problem student who just will not sit still. Too often these students are isolated from their peers and punished for behaviors they have not yet learned to manage.

Teachers must remember that these behaviors are not an inconvenience or temporary disruption. ADD or ADHD is a condition with which these young people will contend their whole lives. They need to learn how to cope with the distractions they experience so that as adults they can manage their disabilities responsibly and appropriately.

Students who are diagnosed with ADD or ADHD often take medications designed to balance their body chemistry and assist them in being able to focus on learning tasks. However, a number of issues are associated with taking those medications. One is some educators' assumption that when a student takes medication, the problems have all been solved.

> In a perfect world we would be able to zero in on a specific chemical in a particular synapse and make the change that's needed, but the drugs available to us aren't advanced enough to this point to treat a specific disorder. The brain is complex, and very few medications are "clean"; that is, when a patient takes a drug, it is rare that the level of only one brain chemical is affected in only one part of the brain. (Koplewicz, 1996, p. 54)

Sometimes educators use their own observations to determine that students have ADD or ADHD and on that basis encourage parents to seek prescription medication from their doctors to relieve the symptoms. Although medications may help students who actually have ADD or ADHD, no medicine should be recommended without a formal diagnosis by a medical doctor, nor should the assumption be made that to medicate is to cure.

Any medication recommended for ADD or ADHD is likely to have side effects of varying degrees for students. Teachers must be cautious and prudent about recommending that parents ask their physicians to prescribe medicine that will impact not only students' school behavior but can often affect their appetites and sleep patterns. Prescriptions are the purview of the medical profession, not educators.

Prescribed dosages for medications that can control the symptoms of ADD or ADHD vary depending on the age and size of the student. Teachers frequently comment that the prescribed dosages wear off by the afternoon, at which point they are left with students who are off task and difficult to handle for the rest of the day. However, students' misbehaviors cannot be excused just because the medicine wore off.

Dosages may need to be adjusted several times before the right level is found. This is a matter for teachers, parents, students, and medical professionals to solve as a team. During this process, however, teachers can still expect students to be on task. That may mean that much of the content work must be accomplished in the morning while the medication levels are at their most effective. In a high school, this adaptation may prove to be more challenging than in a self-contained classroom. However, approaching the situation from a team perspective rather than only the view of teachers assigning work for each period of the day is beneficial for students.

Medications sometimes wear off, but that is not an excuse for students with ADD or ADHD to become disruptive. William Glasser (1969), in *Schools without Failure,* speaks of not accepting excuses for inappropriate behavior. That principle is particularly applicable to this discussion. Glasser encourages educators to be compassionate problem solvers, which is especially important for students who have ADD or ADHD. Teachers should work with these students to help them develop strategies for making appropriate decisions about how to manage their behaviors and to develop their ability to stay on task. Because this is a long-term disability and not just an inconvenience for one school year, teachers must help students work out long-term solutions.

The symptoms of ADD or ADHD do not usually disappear as the student grows into adulthood. Although medication may alleviate the symptoms in childhood, it does not cure the disability. Students need to develop life skills to help them cope with their conditions in ways that are socially acceptable. They can be helped to understand their disability and to manage it, but they must be given some trust and flexibility to do so.

Curriculum and management are an inseparable blend when considering the best ways to address the special needs of any student. When teachers find themselves responsible for a continuum of student needs, they must adjust their classroom curriculum to help all their students learn and be successful. Given the range of special considerations to be met in today's classroom, there is no one way to accomplish this goal. Most important is that teachers address each student's needs while at the same time protecting the learning opportunities for everyone.

Aspects of some curriculum practices mitigate against the abilities of students with ADD or ADHD. When students are expected to sit still for long periods of time and attend to one task after another without an opportunity to take a break or move around, students with ADD or ADHD experience much difficulty. To create a level playing field for educational opportunities, teachers need to challenge students but avoid creating circumstances in which students have no chance of succeeding. Students who have ADD or ADHD cannot attend to tasks for long periods of time and cannot sit still endlessly. Creating curriculum expectations for something they cannot do only accentuates their problems rather than relieving them.

Some teachers, on the other hand, have developed productive ways of working with students who have been diagnosed with ADD and ADHD; their efforts begin with a recognition of what these young people can do as opposed to what they cannot do. Teachers who work well with ADD and ADHD students understand that certain accommodations must be made. For instance, students who must move around can identify for themselves a special and out-of-the-way place in a classroom to do so. It might be a corner of the room, a space underneath a designated table, or some other place where students can go to pull themselves together. Having students identify the spot will make it a place they want to go, not a place of condemnation.

Students with ADD or ADHD can also be taught how and where to move when even their special places are not working for them. They might be able to stand at the sides of the classroom when they need to do so. Their teachers can help them to understand other students' needs not to be disturbed and ask that they respect those needs by standing quietly at the side or back of the room when they get restless. Teachers do not have to fear that all of their students will stand up and move around, although students understand they can do so if they feel the need. Classrooms will continue to function smoothly, learning will go on, and a variety of student needs will be served.

In addition, teachers should use an overhead projector for most of the information they are presenting. When the overhead projector is on, the rest of the classroom lights are off. This provides students with ADD or ADHD one clear visual focus in the room and clear visual representations of whatever information is being presented. Using the overhead projector also allows teachers to constantly monitor the students without having to turn their backs for any length of time.

A curriculum design that allows for periodic movement, group activities, and other opportunities to do something other than just sit at a desk for an extended period of time is helpful not only to students with ADD or ADHD but also students who are kinesthetic learners. Whether teachers are working with students diagnosed as having ADD or ADHD, with students who have high energy levels, with learners who are kinesthetically gifted, with students who have strengths in the areas of leadership or interpersonal skills, or with students gifted in the performing arts, incorporating a variety of hands-on and cooperative curriculum strategies can provide everyone with opportunities to learn in ways that best suit their needs and abilities. Developing lessons that permit students to engage in social interactions with peers, work with manipulatives, and set their own learning goals significantly enhances the learning experiences of active young people who need the chance to burn off some of their energy and to be productive at the same time.

Although some of the needs of active students can be met through an interactive approach to curriculum, students should also acquire the skills that will assist them in developing the ability to stay on task for increasingly longer periods of time. However, the key word in this discussion is *develop*. If students with ADD or ADHD are forced to sit by themselves all the time to accomplish assigned tasks, their interests are not being served and they are not receiving treatment appropriate to their special needs. It may be appropriate for them to work by themselves at times; however, continually isolating students with ADD or ADHD from their peers on the basis of their disabilities is discriminatory. No matter how challenging these students might be, they deserve opportunities to learn appropriate behaviors within a structured and supportive environment. The skills they develop in the classroom will serve them well in their future workplaces and in every other aspect of their adult existence.

Students with suspected or diagnosed ADD or ADHD need patient guidance to learn appropriate behaviors to be successful in school. Creative lesson plan designs, conflict resolution strategies, and a welcoming classroom environment are all important methods of coping with these challenging disabilities. Affected students cannot be fixed by the interventions of their teachers, but they can gain crucial information about how to manage being active and on task rather than restless and lacking focus. In adulthood, that knowledge will make a vast difference in their abilities to successfully attain their personal goals.

TEACHING A CURRICULUM OF RIGHTS AND RESPONSIBILITIES

The curriculum strategies discussed to this point are useful for facilitating learning for a broad range of students. In addition to incorporating cooperative learning practices or designing curriculum that addresses diverse learning styles and special needs, democratic classroom environments can also be sustained by means of curriculum content that is particularly focused on the principles of democracy.

The most common and convenient vehicle for teaching democratic ideals is social studies. Because social studies can serve as an umbrella heading for integrating all other content areas, it makes sense to begin a discussion of democratic curriculum practices by examining the possibilities available through the rich and varied world represented by the title *social studies*. Social studies units can be designed to investigate any place in the world at any time in history or some imagined place that is representative of some of the real issues and problems faced by humanity. In other words, social studies can allow a class to investigate the realities of an early 1900s farm family in Kansas or the problem-solving abilities called into play while exploring the land of Oz. That level of flexibility allows educators to create an integrated curriculum that incorporates a mix of math, science, literature, writing skills, and lessons about social responsibility.

For instance, a middle school unit on weather might begin with recording raw data about temperatures. Students might be asked to track the high and low temperatures recorded in different cities across the United States, or anywhere in the world, for one week. These raw data could be organized and compared through graphs that would reinforce math concepts, and students could calculate temperature averages. Then this sampling of temperature ranges could be discussed in terms of the effects on society. How is society affected when the range of temperatures is greater than 20 degrees on any given day? How is society affected when the temperatures are moderate in one area and very cold in another? How does extreme cold affect people who are struggling economically? What responsibilities does the larger society have toward homeless people during times of extreme cold?

Students can investigate the resources and responses available within their own community for dealing with the effects of extreme weather conditions. If communities experience temperate climates rather than a wide range of temperatures, students could investigate how the favorable weather affects the community. Do people move to that community for the weather? Is the community more likely to attract businesses because of the weather? Do people who are economically deprived come to the community because they are seeking warm weather? Does their presence in the community require a social response to their needs? Students can evaluate these issues and engage in informed debates about how the weather affects their own communities.

LOOKING AT THE MAIN IDEAS

Curriculum Can Promote a Sense of Social Responsibility by

- Encouraging students to work together and share ideas to promote common learning goals
- Creating opportunities for all students to appreciate the range of learning styles and needs represented within any given classroom
- Looking beyond baseline data to understand how society is impacted by the common elements around us, such as weather

Educators often describe public education as an opportunity to prepare informed citizens who will make reasoned decisions in the voting booth. In the example of weather, students have the opportunity to engage in an in-depth exploration of their own communities and how the social resources available are allocated. Students can make their own decisions about whether this is the most appropriate use of private and public funds. The point is that they will learn how to inform themselves rather than depending on others to tell them how to think about any social issue.

Teaching students the process of seeking and evaluating information on social issues is not the same as teachers selecting such topics to sway students toward some personally held set of values. Teachers can help students identify sources of information, teach them how to organize and analyze data, and encourage them to make their own decisions about what they discover.

However, teachers more often develop curriculum units on weather that include activities such as making barometers, learning the names of cloud formations, and measuring rainfall amounts. Less common are examples of teaching the topic of weather beyond this limited perspective. In reality, weather affects much of what happens in any society and even dictates the times of year people have social contact with each other. Weather affects purchasing decisions, architectural design, and a sense of social consciousness about the welfare of neighbors, particularly during times of extreme hot or cold weather. Dramatic and devastating storms can suddenly force people into community shelters, where they need to rely on communication, conflict resolution, and peer mediation to make their difficult circumstances tolerable.

The effects of weather can also be documented historically through primary source materials. Original journal entries that include accounts of weather and its impact on the writer can be found from almost any historical period. The subject of weather is only one example, but it serves as a good illustration of how curriculum can be integrated to move beyond the obvious and into topics that will encourage students to explore the ways that something as seemingly innocuous as weather can impact their communities' resources and moral values.

The dynamics of a student population that is both culturally and economically diverse are reflected in the perspectives each student brings to such topics. Teachers should not be afraid of touching on these subjects. This is an opportunity for students to learn how their communities function, what decisions need to be made by the citizenry when facing difficult times, and that there are avenues available in a free society to effect change when change is needed.

MAINTAINING THE HOLISTIC CLASSROOM WHEN THE PLAYERS CHANGE

Substitute teaching has a culture and set of mythical constructs all its own. In the minds of many people, substitute teaching is characterized by a teacher who spends each school day screaming at a new group of students in someone else's classroom. The remainder of this chapter investigates strategies for using a substitute teacher or being a substitute teacher.

Some substitute teachers experience long and difficult days when they are called to work in schools. Some have even been driven out of the classrooms by students. Some substitute teachers are called to work once or twice but never called again; other substitute teachers are repeatedly called and quickly earn a reputation as the adults teachers would most like to have in their classrooms when they cannot be there themselves.

Many teachers work as substitute teachers at some point during their careers. Substitute teaching can often serve as an entry into a full-time classroom assignment. Some teachers serve as substitute teachers when they are raising young children and want some flexibility in their daily schedules.

Some licensed teachers never seek full-time positions, preferring instead to remain substitute teachers because they enjoy the daily variety of teaching experiences and appreciate being able to take a day off now and then when they choose. Although their salaries and benefits will never equal those of full-time classroom teachers, they view the endless challenge and excitement associated with new environments and students as more than compensating for the financial shortcomings associated with a career as a substitute teacher.

Some individuals become substitute teachers because there is a teacher shortage or a need for a replacement teacher in a small, isolated community. These individuals may or may not have any professional training or classroom experience. Teaching licenses are not required for substitute work in all states and even in states that do require substitute teachers to have licenses, circumstances and need can sometimes cause school personnel to look the other way when hiring an adult to assume a teacher's professional responsibilities for a period of time.

Substitute teachers represent every level of professional training and experience. They are in the classroom for a number of reasons and bring with them a number of interests. They are called in to face sanguine young people who will cheerfully work with them through the school day or students who are angry and hostile about education and who view the substitute teacher's presence in the classroom as a reason to express their rebellion. In short, the temporary status of the substitute teacher can be an intriguing element on which to build an interesting time at school or it can be the spark that leads to an exercise in anarchy. Many factors impact which of those two options will best characterize the experiences of substitute teachers, some of which can be more easily controlled than others. Although full-time classroom teachers must orchestrate management and curriculum, the primary focus of substitute teachers is management, with curriculum as a secondary concern. It is important that a substitute teacher maintain the productive learning environment that has been established in the classroom. Good substitute teaching is not characterized by threatening, yelling, or removing students from class. Substitute teachers who employ such strategies typically face resistance from the students and spend their time struggling for order rather than accomplishing any educational purpose. Such substitute teachers will not likely receive invitations to return to a school or classroom, because neither principals nor teachers will want a repeat of the disruptions that have occurred.

THE WORLD OF THE SUBSTITUTE TEACHER

In the beginning, substitute teachers should be willing to try working in any classrooms, with any age group, and teaching most subjects, and they should be ready to step in at any moment. Although substitute teachers may prefer a particular age level or subject matter, they should try their hand at most of the assignments that come their way and for which they are licensed. This flexibility is not impossible, but it requires thought, organization, and preparation.

The experience gained from attempting to work in a range of classrooms and with a variety of subjects is invaluable and may lead substitute teachers to develop an entirely different focus for their careers. It is not uncommon for teachers to be licensed in one area, substitute teach in another area, and then return to school to qualify for an additional license that will allow them to work in that second field on a permanent basis.

Preservice teachers who are in professional preparation programs know that they may have to do some substitute teaching before they are hired for full-time positions. This reality provides another good reason for expanding the range of substitute teaching positions people are willing to try. Working in a variety of classrooms exposes new teachers to a wide range of ideas and activities. New teachers can collect from their substitute teaching assignments inspiration and practical strategies for lessons, management practices, and even bulletin board decorations.

Substitute teachers, especially those just starting out, should carry a notebook and note in it the interesting procedures and routines they encounter. It is also advisable to add a note or two about how the new practices and ideas can be adapted to other age groups and how they can be transported from one site to another. Every classroom a substitute teacher visits or works in contains strategies and ideas that they might want to appropriate. Substitute teachers need to remember a basic tenet of teaching: everyone borrows ideas from everyone else. The number of ideas available to substitute teachers increases as they work in different classrooms.

Responsibilities of the Classroom Teacher

To ensure that the transition for students from regular teacher to substitute teacher is a relatively smooth experience, it is important to address some common elements that unite the two professionals. The responsibility for a satisfying substitute teaching experience is initially shared by both the classroom teacher and the substitute teacher. One basic preventive practice is essential for setting in motion an effective transfer of responsibility from the full-time classroom teacher to a substitute teacher. The more information concerning rules and expectations of the classroom and school a teacher can collect and make available to a substitute teacher, the easier the substitute teacher's day will be.

When the school year begins, teachers are typically inundated with color-coded memorandums that cover school schedules, fire drill regulations, expectations for emergency procedures, and other information that reflects how administrators anticipate the school will function. The classroom teacher should photocopy each of these papers and place them in a file labeled "Substitute." Teachers can add to this file any information about classroom rules, seating charts, homework deadlines, study hall supervision rotations, and other pertinent data that will help a substitute teacher get up to speed quickly in the classroom. The file should be continually updated and left in a location that is easily accessible. Because some of the information contained in the file may be confidential, it should not be left on a desk but may be kept face up in a center desk drawer so that it can be quickly located by a substitute teacher. If a classroom teacher teaches in several rooms, one easily accessible location, perhaps the teacher's mailbox, may be appropriate.

At the elementary level, additional information may be included in the file. Lunch count procedures, playground or lunch room supervision responsibilities, which students report to which special pullout programs at what time, and any other pertinent schedules and expectations that govern the school day should be readily available for whomever might have to take the classroom teacher's place for an hour, a day, a week, or longer. At any grade level, absences can occur suddenly and unexpectedly. Teachers may not have a chance to adequately plan lessons, leave instructions, or provide any other materials to assist the substitute teachers who will replace them. However, if all of the information that guides the daily routine of a classroom is assembled and easily available to substitute teachers, everyone will be more comfortable when a sudden absence occurs.

LOOKING AT THE MAIN IDEAS

Teachers Can Support Their Substitutes by Creating a File That Contains the Following:

- Daily schedules and duties
- Seating charts, classroom rules, and any other information that pertains to how the classroom typically functions
- Information on a need-to-know basis about students who have identified special needs or require special services during the day

In addition to the file containing basic school and classroom information, teachers should maintain a separate file with confidential information to be shared with their substitutes on a need-to-know basis. If some students have histories of being prone to seizures, have been diagnosed with emotional disorders that can result in outbursts of violence, have individualized educational plans and require special attention on a daily basis, or require the teacher to wear a microphone during certain parts of the day, that information should be objectively documented and made easily accessible to substitute teachers.

Again, this information is shared on a need-to-know basis, and the criteria for including such information in this second file are whether some students are known to have emergency needs, ongoing health and safety considerations, or legitimate educational needs that might require special attention. Teachers can include information about the schedule for addressing special needs and whether students require weekly, daily, hourly, or continuous monitoring; gossip about students and about behaviors that might occur is not appropriate.

In terms of deciding what to include in either file, teachers will best serve the needs of their substitute teachers and their students if they ask themselves what information would be essential to their own ability to function successfully in the classroom. If teachers are uncertain, they might ask their colleagues about what would help any of them to be effective in a different classroom.

Principals and other building administrators can also provide useful support for substitute teachers. A quick visit to classrooms to greet substitute teachers in front of the students can serve to send a message that the adults are working together, whatever their status in the building. This is also a preventive measure that can help administrators spend their day doing something other than disciplining students who have been evicted from the classroom by substitute teachers.

Preparations for Being a Substitute Teacher

Although classroom teachers and administrators need to do everything possible to support substitute teachers, substitute teachers carry much of the rest of the responsibility for an effective and successful experience. Some substitution work is long term and has a flavor all its own. The role of a long-term substitute teacher is discussed later in this chapter. The preparation for a day or even a week of substitute teaching that will be both productive and pleasant begins long before a teacher even applies to be included on the school district's list of substitute teachers. One essential element for successful substitute teaching is to identify, collect, and adapt a wide variety of resources that can inspire individual lessons, activities, and learning centers for a range of age groups and situations.

Newspapers, magazines, almanacs, and other reference materials are useful as initial resources from which substitute teachers can draw ideas for developing general lessons that can be implemented in many grade levels. Books and magazines that contain word puzzles are resources for sponge activities, although they would not necessarily be appropriate for students with limited English skills or students who are disabled in ways that interfere with successfully attacking word games. For these students and others, visual activities, audio tapes, and picture puzzles also should be included among the items substitute teachers might bring with them into the classroom. A few picture books, a really good chapter book written for juveniles, or a book of short stories appropriate for older students should always be included in the materials substitutes routinely carry to their assignments. Students at every age level enjoy hearing a good story, and reading to them or telling them a story can fill extra time.

Whatever activities and plans substitute teachers bring, they should always try to have more with them than they would ever need for a full day. By over-planning and carrying a number of activities, a substitute can be prepared to walk into any classroom and manage to keep students busy and engaged. One substitute teacher with an excellent reputation often joked that she could live off the contents of her "subbing bag" for a week in the woods. That may be something of an exaggeration, but her bag did contain books, activities, backup lesson plans, and other items such as a flashlight, dried fruit and nuts, extra batteries, a comb, and other toiletry articles for her own use. She kept this bag either by her front door or in the trunk of her car. She could add to it any additional items she might need for a particular assignment, but the essentials were ready to go at a moment's notice.

The key element of good substitute teaching is to keep a classroom filled with students engaged in activities and, for the most part, out of trouble for however long the assignment lasts. If lessons are not available and the planned curriculum is not taught, full-time classroom teachers can always make up for the missing lessons when they return.

If nothing of the standard curriculum is taught, but the students are on task and cooperative, the classroom teacher will be delighted with the substitute teacher's efforts. Teachers dread returning to the classroom to discover that most of their students were disruptive and many spent time talking with the school's discipline officer or principal. Although the curriculum can be put on hold for one or two days, good management cannot be. If the classroom teacher will be absent for more than a few days, a substitute teacher will have time to check in with the classroom teacher or another colleague to get the students back on track in terms of their learning goals.

Because a telephone call summoning a substitute teacher to a day of teaching can come at the last minute, it is wise to try to get ready for a possible assignment at night. In addition to keeping generic materials in a subbing bag that is always ready to go, it is also a good idea to get to the school as early as possible to become familiar with the physical layout of the building, the materials available in the classroom, the expectations for daily routines, and whatever plans might be waiting.

Some substitute teachers even maintain a small designated wardrobe of "subbing clothes." These clothes typically consist of some basic clothing such as shirts or blouses, pants or skirts, ties, scarves, vests, and so forth that are clean, pressed, and ready to go. Whether it is the well-stocked subbing bag or designated clothing, preparation and forethought are essential elements of a satisfying substitute teaching experience.

The Day Begins

Good preparation and organization help substitutes get over the biggest hurdle to a successful day of teaching: their own confidence. The next step is meeting and greeting the students. Students develop a bond with many of their teachers based on personalities, career aspirations, encouragement, shared interests, or sometimes fear. Whatever the basis, the relationship students form with their teachers is a significant one and becomes part of their daily school routine. The presence of a substitute teacher is disruptive to students, and for some the change can be disconcerting.

Some young people experience lives in which many adults come and go. The sudden absence of a respected teacher can fill such students with a sense of dismay and disequilibrium. Substitute teachers need to be sensitive to the fact that their presence in a classroom can set in motion a wide range of conflicting feelings. Therefore, it is essential that substitute teachers make the effort to say hello to each student if at all possible. The relationship they have with students will likely be fleeting, but, nevertheless, but they should attempt to build trust and respect.

If substitute teachers are replacing full-time classroom teachers for a long period of time, it is even more important that they make an initial effort to get to know the students. Although some long-term substitute teaching assignments are not always immediately identified as such, the importance of building a level of trust with students is worthy of a substitute teacher's attention. Sometimes devastating medical conditions remove a full-time teacher from the classroom. Sometimes the full-time classroom teacher dies suddenly and a substitute teacher is brought in to complete the year. These situations heavily impact the emotional sense of security experienced by everyone in the learning community. Time must be spent with students to help them work through the feelings they are experiencing. It is best if a counselor can be brought in to guide the discussion and provide some sense of perspective. If that option is not available, substitute teachers should at least be willing to set aside time for students to write or speak openly about the confusing mix of emotions they are experiencing over the loss of a teacher.

There are few things in the world of education that a teacher should *always* do, but one is to begin every day and every class by setting out expectations. Substitute teachers should review the rules and expectations already in place so that students will understand that everyone knows the classroom's basic tenets of management. Although a classroom may not use a democratic approach to management, substitute teachers can establish some democratic practices for the time they are with the students without undermining the classroom teacher's authority. Rules must still be followed, and expectations must still be established. Although they might differ in terms of implementation and language, the goals for each are ultimately focused on achieving productive and safe classrooms.

One way to set out expectations is to say something like the following: "We have an interesting day ahead of us. I am really looking forward to working with you. We need to have some rules that will help us get our work done and show our respect for each other. What rules do we need to make sure those things happen?" If students seem reluctant to volunteer ideas, the substitute teacher can ask them to work with partners to develop one or two rules and then share their ideas with the rest of the class. The teacher can then write down three or four of their ideas and ask students if any of them came up with something that has not already been mentioned. This strategy will serve to reduce the number of duplicated ideas shared. The process for developing rules need not take long, but it is critical for setting the tone of the day. If the school population has a reputation for being tough, a substitute teacher might want to prepare some activity for students to do when they enter the classroom. An age-appropriate writing prompt written on the chalkboard is one idea.

LOOKING AT THE MAIN IDEAS

A Pleasant Substituting Experience Is More Likely When Substitute Teachers

- Are ready to go at a moment's notice
- Are prepared with activities and lesson plans that are age appropriate, if not subject appropriate
- Greet the students in a warm and friendly manner
- Do not take personally the games that students will want to play

When students enter a classroom and see a substitute teacher, many of them assume that this school period or school day will be disruptive and chaotic. One substitute teacher who worked in an urban environment at the secondary level began each period by saying, "Hello. I am Ms. Jones. I am your substitute teacher for the day and I am here to protect your rights." Students were so surprised by this opening that she had an opportunity to quickly begin establishing expectations for the day.

The Name Game

One game students enjoy is changing names, changing seats, or some other act that might confuse a substitute teacher. If a student wants to be called Thomas Jefferson, Bill Gates, or Captain Picard for a day, so be it. Substitute teachers who understand youthful rebellion for what it is do not see these acts as being those of defiant students. As long as the names students choose are not vulgar, substitute teachers can let them be who they want to be. The names students wish to be called are not worth drawing lines and getting angry over; a little humor can go a long way in such situations.

When substitute teachers understand that students are choosing new names or switching names with someone else, they can simply take it in stride. It is not worth getting angry about this very common sort of practical joke. Substitute teachers can tell students that people often choose to change their names informally and some-times legally. If the students want to try out different names that day, they can let the substitute teacher know what they want to be called and their wishes will happily be accommodated. A calm attitude usually deflates the disruptive nature of what students are doing, and the substitute teacher can move onto getting the class started.

Things Will Be Done Differently

Substitute teachers should acknowledge that things will be done differently that day. All teachers—including substitute teachers—have their own ways of doing things. Substitute teachers can let students know that although some things may be done differently that day, the person in charge will work with them to help them succeed. If students interrupt a lesson or some instructions to inform their substitute teacher about how the "real" teacher does things, the substitute teacher can thank those students for wanting to help and gently remind the class that things will be different that day.

If substitute teachers are uncertain about a procedure, they can ask their students for help. In this way, substitute teachers can help students come to terms with the differences they are experiencing. Most important, as with any good management style, substitute teachers need not take the attempts of students to disrupt as being personal attacks on the teacher. Students are just testing the winds; when they find them to be calm and noncombative, they will likely settle down to work. Some classrooms are tougher than others, and some days are longer than others. Whatever the realities, substitute teachers should at least strive to end each day with their sense of professional dignity in place.

Creative Curriculum Options Can Help to Keep Students on Task and Calm

One basic tenet of successful substitute teaching is keeping students busy. Substitute teachers can draw on the interesting activities they have collected and brought with them. If students finish an assignment the teacher left for them and time remains, a book or backup activity can mean the difference between chaos and order.

Extra time is not a reason for students to leave the classroom or to be disruptive. Substitute teachers can keep students engaged in challenging puzzles, an exciting story, or some other activity. Worksheets that are clearly busy work will not serve this purpose. Substitute teachers must be willing to investigate and employ activity options that can be genuinely challenging to a variety of students.

Substitute teachers may find that these sponge activities are most effective when students can work on them in small groups, which also allows time for some social interaction. A brief review of the rules for monitoring and managing the noise that will inevitably occur is appropriate before any sort of group work takes place. However, allowing students to interact with each other can be a useful strategy to save substitute teachers from trying to keep all students quiet all the time.

Ending the Day

At the end of the day, substitute teachers take a little time to do some housekeeping. As the students leave, it is appropriate to thank them for a good day. After they have left, substitute teachers should remain in the classroom long enough to correct any assignments the students completed that day, make sure any other paperwork is in order, and leave a note for the full-time classroom teacher that reviews the events of the day. The substitute teacher should describe any problems with students as thoroughly as possible and include in the note any follow-up actions taken to resolve the situations. Before substitute teachers leave the school for the day, they should stop at the office to complete any necessary paperwork and to let the support personnel and the administrators know how much their call was appreciated. Regardless of whether substitute teachers wish to be called again to work in a particular school, a thank-you is a good way to end the day.

Long-Term Assignments

As mentioned earlier, a substitute teacher may at some time be asked to replace the regular classroom teacher because of a serious illness or some other personal trauma. Students need to know that their substitute teacher will not feel personally threatened or upset if they carry some feelings of disappointment or even grief over losing their regular teacher. This expression of emotions can help to clear the air and unite the class around the common goal of a successful, if different, school year.

One piece of sound management theory applicable to any setting is that new managers should not move too quickly to change everything when they step into a new role. It is important for substitute teachers to value the worthwhile practices that are already in place and to demonstrate that it is valued by not immediately overhauling the status quo. In this case, changes may need to be implemented, but out of respect for the teacher who is being replaced and the students these changes should be incorporated gradually.

One idea is to ask the students what they like best about the way the classroom has been run and the curriculum they have been experiencing. Teachers may also ask students what activities, topics, or lessons they would like to see included in the future. Once a substitute teacher has some input from the students, it will be easier to determine which of the classroom teacher's ideas should be kept and which should be altered. Students can talk about their ideas in a class meeting, journal entry, or even letters they write to the substitute teacher. Students could be asked to include questions in the text of the letters they write; responding with a personal note to each student and answering the questions can be a powerful way for substitute teachers to demonstrate respect. However time consuming this process might be, it will create a great deal of trust and help to soothe the ill feelings and sorrow students may have in regard to the loss of their teacher. Students should be able to see their ideas being implemented after a week or so. Responding personally to letters may help, but acting on students' suggestions will have great meaning for them.

Long-term substitute teachers should honor the process of learning that has been established in the classroom. Any outstanding assignments, projects, or other activities that were in progress should be completed and graded. Students should have the opportunity to experience closure to the work they were doing with their full-time teacher. The substitute teacher can invite parents to a parents' night open house to meet the new substitute teacher and invite questions about how the new teacher plans to address their children's needs and interests.

Imprinting a new management style   Management practices unique to the person serving in the substitute position should be part of the transition process. Students cannot be expected to shift gears (assuming they need to) and adjust to a whole new management system overnight. Again, the long-term substitute teacher may want to ask students how they feel about the management style of the classroom, what they like about it, and what suggestions they have to make it better. If the teacher being replaced had a very different philosophy from that of the substitute teacher, a gradual transition from one style to another is essential if the classroom is going to run well. If the classroom was out of control for the full-time teacher, a substitute teacher needs to first gain control by clearly letting students know that a competent professional is serving as their educational leader. Rules and expectations can be developed as if it were the first day of school.

A Final Word about Substitute Teaching

Substitute teaching need not be the nightmare some people believe it to be. Some professionals remain substitute teachers for their entire careers. Many say they like the flexibility of the work schedule or the variety of subjects, schools, and students. Others see substitute teaching as an interim solution to unemployment. When they become full-time classroom teachers, though, they take with them a wealth of ideas and a good measure of confidence from the experience. Either way, substitute teaching can be a wonderful opportunity to interact with new environments, students, and communities and to learn a wealth of teaching strategies on which to build or enhance a solid career.

SUMMARY

In well-orchestrated classrooms the educational leaders have paid attention to the cognitive abilities and emotional needs of their students as evidenced by the strategies they employ in their management practices and curriculum design. Educational leaders understand that management and curriculum are not separate issues but intertwined aspects of a holistic approach to creating and sustaining democratic classroom practices. Educators' concerns about classroom management are essentially the same fears they have in regard to curriculum. They worry that they will not be able to teach their subject matter content because they are constantly being interrupted by rowdy and disruptive children. They want quick, easy answers for their concerns and are often disappointed to learn that there are none. However, students are far less likely to be rowdy and disruptive when their minds are actively engaged in solving interesting problems and working with meaningful content. And so management and curriculum design become one seamless topic, each capable of enhancing the other.

APPLYING THE CONCEPTS

Please return now to the opening scenario. Given all the information in this chapter, what are some ideas you might use to monitor student progress when students are engaged in an open-ended activity such as the one described? What management strategies would you employ to mirror the democratic structure of the curriculum? What expectations would you and your students need to develop before engaging in this or similar activities?

Conclusion

> The vision of American education should not be limited to making the
> United States "number one" in the international marketplace or to more
> grandiose dreams of presiding over a "new world order." Quite the
> contrary, the real challenge of leadership is to broaden its definition
> beyond the ethically truncated parameters of these concerns to the more
> vital imperatives of educating students to live in a multicultural world,
> face the challenge of reconciling differences and community, and
> addressing what it means to have a voice in shaping one's future. (Giroux,
> 1993, p. 20)

The issues associated with classroom management are as complex as the times in
which we live and as diverse as the students we teach. *There are no easy answers to anything.* This is a lesson life teaches us early and one that it repeats often, just in case we
did not get it the first time. Teachers have the phrase imprinted on their hearts and
minds because it is obvious from the first moment they enter the classroom and

reinforced every day of their professional lives. There are no easy answers to designing a curriculum that addresses the needs and interests of all the students present in the classroom. There are no easy answers to encouraging, coaxing and otherwise drawing parents into the role of educational partners to work with teachers and administrators for the welfare of their children. And there are certainly no easy solutions to the complex behavioral problems facing teachers, particularly when these problems are so heavily influenced by the many external variables that exist in today's society.

In the past educators received their professional training when cognitive management strategies were scarce, legal issues were largely misunderstood or completely absent from the conversation, and multicultural issues were relegated to discussions about this or that exotic group of faraway people. Many of the teachers and administrators who graduated and began their careers at that time were likely ill served either because they had no training in management practices or were taught a one-size-fits-all approach to curriculum design or management models. The idea that all student learning and motivations might be effectively addressed by one plan and that all student behaviors might be controlled by one set of reward and punishment responses denigrates both the creative spirit of teachers and the complex nature of the students they teach.

Many educators are learning how to leave behind the more traditional, regimented curriculum designs in which they were instructed. Instead, they are adopting more constructivist approaches that include many of the practices discussed in this book. At the same time, these teachers are also seeking out and implementing management strategies that are at once democratic, inclusive, eclectic, and legal. Knowing that there are no easy answers to anything, educators are increasingly willing to roll up their sleeves and dig into the tough, challenging, and rewarding task of creating a classroom environment that effectively assists all students in achieving to the best of their potential.

RETAINING THE BABY AND THE BATH WATER

In education, when an innovative strategy surfaces, there is a tendency to "throw the baby out with the bath water." That is as true with classroom management as with curriculum. In the case of management, educators adopt or are instructed to adopt one approach and abandon all the ideas that came before. I do not suggest that there are no worthy ideas associated with traditional (i.e., behavioral) management practices or that one single perspective is better than another. Educators have a number of strategies and practices to draw on that promote safe, productive learning environments, and all of these strategies have their place in the democratic classroom.

As educators set about determining which management practices to use when and with what age groups, their first concern is to look beyond immediate whatever-works solutions. Using strategies that work may seem to be a reasonable approach to management; however, missing from "whatever works" is the understanding that students have varied and special needs. It is critical that flexible practices capable of addressing a broad range of student interests be the primary consideration that leads an educator to adopt any management structure.

Educators should critique their management practices against a set of standards that include teaching students how to make prudent and appropriate decisions about their own behaviors. Management practices that teach personal decision making versus those that teach students to obey the commands of others without question are far more closely aligned with the framework of our social system. At times, the whatever-works approach can appear to be desirable because it often leads to a quick resolution. Problem solving and decision making take more time.

In some cases, the faster approach holds the kernel of a democratic idea but has been streamlined to the point of defeating its original purpose. Schools will implement step-by-step problem-solving activities, but the steps are so proscribed that there can be no genuine engagement on the part of students. One school developed just such a program. In that school, when a problem occurs, students are asked to: (1) apologize, (2) determine some form of restitution, and (3) assign themselves a punishment. In one instance a teacher reported trying to resolve a problem with three students who had damaged something in her classroom. The teacher reported the problem to the school counselor, who ordered the three students to report to the problem-solving room and to complete the three steps for problem solving required by the school. When the teacher who had experienced the problem with the students met for the problem-solving session, the students quickly apologized, said they would repair the damage they had done, and said their punishment would be that they would not use the class computers for a week.

At that point the students considered the session to be over. The teacher was dismayed that, as these students moved through this process, they did not appear to be engaged in moral reasoning or any critical reflections concerning their actions. The teacher rightfully believed that reasoning and reflection should have been evident for students of that age level. The school had developed the three proscribed steps for problem solving with good intentions, but the process allowed students to move through the steps without seriously considering the implications of their actions or engaging in any reflection that would keep similar problems from happening in the future.

For democratic management practices to be effective, students must at least be expected to be involved in some level of authentic reflection, no matter what the age level or circumstances. As discussed earlier, this process may require more time, but it allows students to seriously consider how their actions and decisions have the ability to positively or negatively impact those around them. Although it is impossible to have 29 different management approaches for 29 different students, it is possible to have guidelines rather than rules and to use negotiation rather than proscribed solutions.

SOME FINAL THOUGHTS

Democratic classroom management is evidenced in the equitable rules, educational consequences, and respectful interactions that comprise the daily give and take within an educational setting. Patience may wear thin, time may be a scarce commodity, and positive changes in student behaviors may not always happen as quickly as educators would like; however, teachers and administrators who are able to persevere and stay focused on the expected outcomes of cognitive interventions usually experience the satisfaction of knowing their consistent professional demeanor has set a positive, safe tone for the classroom and has contributed significantly to the success of their students.

I have discussed a number of common management issues and situations and strategies for peacefully resolving problems. Through it all run the persistent threads of equity, tolerance, and the value of using good communication skills. Finally, giving students and their problems the time needed to resolve issues is critically important. Once all the elements needed for democratic classroom management are in place, teachers have only begun the journey. They must understand that mixing the parts together is not the same as blending ingredients in a cake that can be baked and considered done. Democratic education is a process of continual professional growth. Just when we think we get it, we realize there is more to discover.

Some educators believe that a workshop or series of in-service training sessions they attended 5 or 10 years ago contained sufficient information to make them into effective managers of classrooms for the rest of their careers. However, educational practices are continually being informed by brain research, cognitive psychology, a growing understanding of issues associated with an increasingly diverse student population, and a heightened sensitivity to family values as they are represented in classrooms.

Management practices, like curriculum, must continually be expanded and enhanced to embrace the new information available to educators. It is not possible to obtain perfection in teaching, but moving toward a personal definition of perfection should be ongoing. The effort itself can be viewed as pleasurable, stimulating, and continually challenging.

The intent of this book is to spark ideas, encourage conversation, help to build community in our schools, and perhaps raise an eyebrow or two. If we can agree to equate the raised eyebrow with Piaget's theories concerning the importance of disequilibrium to the learning process, then the disequilibrium readers may have experienced when encountering some of the ideas presented in these pages can be a part of educators' professional growth. Not every idea will be accepted—nor should it be—and not every strategy will be useful to every reader. These are only ideas and are designed to serve as springboards for the good ideas readers will develop as a result of this and other management resources.

Some basic practices serve all students and teachers well. It is important that educators always state their expectations clearly, revisit them often, and count to

10 while framing I messages. Most importantly, educators all need to remember that patience and respect cannot be overemphasized.

Finally, be assured that each of you has the creative spirit and the intelligence to be an effective manager of a classroom. We all have taught lessons that fell apart and had days that were better than others. We have also experienced those soaring moments of synergy in our teaching that we wish we could relive over and over again. Focus on the latter, learn from the former, and good luck to all of you.

References

Ackerman, R. (1983). *Children of alco-holics: A guidebook for educators, thera-pists, and parents* (2nd ed.). Holmes Beach, FL: Learning Publications.

Alexander, A. & Kempe, R. S. (1984). The role of the lay therapist in long-term treatment. *Child Abuse and Neglect, 6* (30), 329–334.

Ayers, W. (1993). *To teach: The journey of a teacher.* New York: Teachers College Press.

Banks, J. (1994). *An introduction to multi-cultural education.* Needham Heights, MA: Allyn & Bacon.

Banks, J. (1995). Multicultural education: Historical development, dimen-sions, and practice. In J. Banks & C. Banks (Eds.), *Handbook of research on multicultural education.* New York: Macmillan.

Banks, J. (1997). *Educating citizens in a multicultural society.* New York: Teachers College Press.

Blaufaus, D. (1995). Judicious discipline and grading practices. In B. McEwan (Ed.), *Practicing judicious discipline: An educator's guide to a democratic classroom.* San Francisco: Caddo Gap Press.

Borus, M., & Carpenter, S. (1983). A note on the return of dropouts to high school. *Youth & Society, 14,* 501–507.

Bowditch, C. (1993). Getting rid of troublemakers: High school discipli-nary procedures and the production of dropouts. *Social Problems, 40* (4), 493–509.

Brantlinger, E. (1991, November). Social class distinctions in adolescents' reports of problems and punish-ment in school. *Behavioral Disorders, 17* (1), 36–46.

Canter, L., & Canter, M. (1979). *Assertive discipline.* Los Angeles: Canter and Associates.

Canter, L., & Canter, M. (1992). *Assertive discipline.* Los Angeles: Canter and Associates.

Charney, R. S. (1991). *Teaching children to care: Management in the responsive classroom.* Greenfield, MA: Northeast Foundation for Children.

Clark, W. W., Jr. (1976). Violence in urban public education in the United States. In C. J. Calhoun & F. A. J. Ianni, (Eds.), *The anthropolog-ical study of education,* 257–265. Paris: Mouton.

Cohen, E. G. (1986). *Designing groupwork: Strategies for the heteroge-neous classroom.* New York: Teachers College Press.

Cohen, J. (1983). Commentary: The relationship between friendship selection and peer influence. In J. L. Epstein & N. Kurweit (Eds.), *Friends in school.* Orlando, FL: Academic Press.

D'Amato, J. (1993). Resistance and compliance in minority classrooms. In E. Jacob & C. Jordan (Eds.), *Minority education: Anthropological perspectives.* Norwood, NJ: Ablex Publishing.

Dacey, J. & Kenny, M. (1994). *Adolescent development.* Madison, WI: Brown & Benchmark.

Davern, L. (1996, April). Listening to parents of children with disabilities. *Educational Leadership, 53,* (7), 61–63.

Dreikurs, R., Grunwald, B., & Pepper, F. (1971). *Maintaining sanity in the classroom: Illustrated teaching tech-niques.* New York: Harper & Row.

Dunn, R. (1983). Learning style and its relation to exceptionality at both ends of the spectrum. *Exceptional Children, 49,* 496–506.

Eisenhart, M., & Graue, M. E., (1993). Constructing cultural difference and education achievement in schools. In E. Jacob & C. Jordan (Eds.), *Minority education: Anthropological perspectives.* Norwood, NJ: Ablex Publishing.

Ekstrom, R. B., Goertz, M. E., Pollack, J. M., & Rock, D. A. (1987). Who drops out of high school and why? Findings from a national study. In G. Natriello (Ed.), *School dropouts: Patterns and policies* (pp. 52–69). New York: Teachers College Press.

Erickson, F. (1993). Transformation and school success: The politics and culture of educational achievement. In E. Jacob & C. Jordan (Eds.), *Minority education: Anthropological perspectives* (p. 9). Norwood, NJ: Ablex Publishing.

Examining gender issues in public schools, *The American Teacher 1997.* (1997). New York: Metlife.

Family Educational Rights and Privacy Act of 1974 (FERPA)

Fischer, L., Schimmel, P., Kelly, C. (1995). *Teachers and the Law* (4th ed.). White Plains, N.Y.: Longman Press.

Froyen, L. (1993). *Classroom management: The reflective teacher leader* (2nd ed.). New York: Macmillan.

Gage, N., & Berliner, D. (1988). *Educational psychology* (4th ed.). Boston: Houghton Mifflin.

Gallimore, R., Boggs, J. W., & Jordon, C. (1974). *Culture, behavior and education: A study of Hawaiian-Americans,* Beverly Hill, CA: Sage.

Gardner, H. (1993). *Multiple intelligences: The theory in practice.* New York: Basic Books.

Gathercoal, F. (1994). *Judicious discipline* (3rd ed.). San Francisco: Caddo Gap Press.

Gathercoal, F. (1998). *Judicious discipline* (4th ed.). San Francisco: Caddo Gap Press.

Gathercoal, P. (1995). Judicious discipline from a neurological perspective: Providing context for living and learning in our democratic society. In B. McEwan (Ed.), *Practicing judicious discipline.* San Francisco: Caddo Gap Press.

Gay, Lesbian, and Straight Teachers Network (GLSTN). (1997). *What you can do: Ten action points and resources for educators dealing with gay and lesbian issues* [On-line]. Available at http://www.glstn.org/respect/

Giroux, H. A. (1993). *Living dangerously: Multiculturalism and the politics of difference.* New York: Peter Lang.

Glasser, W. (1969). *Schools without failure.* New York: Harper & Row.

Greely, K., & Mizell, L. (1993). One step among many: Affirming identity in anti-racist schools. In T. Perry, & J. Frasier (Eds.), *Freedom's plow: Teaching in the multicultural classrooms.* New York: Routledge.

Greene, M. (1993). The passions of pluralism: Multiculturalism and the expanding community. In T. Perry & J. Frasier (Eds.), *Freedom's plow: Teaching in the multicultural classroom.* New York: Routledge.

Halford, J. (1996, April). How parent liasons connect families to school. *Educational Leadership, 53,* (7), 34–36.

Hentoff, N. (1980). *The first freedom.* New York: Delacorte Press.

Hidalgo, N., Bright, J., Sau-Fong, S., Swap, S., & Epstein, J. (1995). Research on families, schools, and communities: A multicultural perspective. In J. Banks & C. Banks (Eds.), *Handbook of research on multicultural education.* New York: Macmillan.

Higgins, K. (1995). The case for alternative assessments. In B. McEwan (Ed.), *Practicing judicious discipline: An educator's guide to a democratic classroom.* San Francisco: Caddo Gap Press.

Hoover, R., & Kindsvatter, R. (1997). *Democratic discipline: Foundation and practice.* Columbus, OH: Merrill/Prentice Hall.

Hunter, M. (1981). *Increasing your teaching effectiveness.* Palo Alto, CA: Learning Institute.

Igoa, C. (1995). *The inner world of the immigrant child.* New York: St. Martin's Press.

Individuals with Disabilities Act (1997) (IDEA)

Irvine, J., & York, D. (1995). Learning styles and culturally diverse students: A literature review. In J. Banks & C. Banks (Eds.), *Handbook of research on multicultural education.* New York: Macmillan.

Johns, K., & Espanoza, C. (1996). *Management strategies for culturally diverse classrooms.* Bloomington, IN: Phi Delta Kappa Educational Foundation.

Johnson, D., & Johnson, R. (1991). *Learning together and alone: Cooperative, competitive, and individualistic learning* (3rd ed.). Englewood Cliffs, NJ: Prentice Hall.

Johnson, D. W., & Johnson, R. (1995). *Teaching students to be peacemakers.* Edina, MN: Interaction Book Company.

Jones, V., & Jones, L. S. (1998). *Comprehensive classroom management: Creating positive learning environments for all students* (4th ed.). Needham Heights, MA: Allyn & Bacon.

Kauggman, J., Mostert, M., Trent, S., & Hallahan, D. (1998). *Managing classroom behavior: A reflective case-based approach* (2nd ed.). Boston: Allyn & Bacon.

Kohn, A. (1996). *Beyond discipline: From compliance to community.* Alexandria, VA: Association for Supervision and Curriculum Development.

Koplewicz, H. (1996). *It's nobody's fault.* New York: Times Books.

Kozol, J. (1990). *The night is dark and I am far from home.* New York: Touchstone.

LaMorte, M. W. (1996). *School law: Cases and concepts.* (5th ed.). Boston: Allyn & Bacon.

Lee v. Weisman, 505 U.S. 577 (1992).

Levine D. (1972). Cultural diffraction in the social system of the low-income school. In W. Brickman & S. Lehrer (Eds.), *Education and the many faces of the disadvantaged.* New York: John Wiley & Sons.

Lickona, T. (1991). *Educating for character: How our schools can teach respect and responsibility.* New York: Bantam.

McEwan, B. (1994). Behavior form. In B. McEwan (Ed.), *Practicing judicious discipline: An educator's guide to a democratic classroom.* San Francisco: Caddo Gap Press.

McEwan, B. (1995). *Practicing judicious discipline.* San Francisco: Caddo Gap Press.

McEwan, B., Gathercoal, P., & Nimmo, V. (1997, March). *An examination of the applications of constitutional concepts as an approach to classroom management: Four studies of judicious discipline in various classroom settings.* Paper presented at the American Educational Research Association Conference, San Francisco.

Morgan-D'Atrio, C., Northup, J., LaFleur, L., & Spera, S. (1996). Toward prescriptive alternatives to suspensions: A preliminary evaluation. *Behavioral Disorders, 21* (2), 190–200.

Nieto, S. (1992). *Affirming diversity: The sociopolitical context of multicultural education.* New York: Longman.

Nieto, S. (1995). A history of the education of Puerto Rican students in U.S. mainland schools: "Losers," "Outsiders," or "Leaders"? In J. Banks & C. Banks (Eds.) *Handbook of research on multicultural education.* New York: Macmillan.

Nolte, M. C. (1980). *How to survive in teaching: The legal dimension.* Chicago: Teach 'em.

Ogbu, J. (1993). Variability in minority school performance: A problem in search of an explanation. In E. Jacob & C. Jordan (Eds.), *Minority education: Anthropological perspectives.* Norwood, NJ: Ablex Publishing.

Olneck, M. (1995). Immigrants and education. In J. Banks & C. Banks (Eds.), *Handbook of research on multicultural education.* New York: Macmillan.

Peng, S. (1983). High school dropouts: Descriptive information from high school and beyond. *National Center for Education Statistics Bulletin.*

Purkey, W., & Novak, J. (1984). *Inviting school success: A self-concept approach to teaching and learning* (2nd ed.). Belmont, CA: Wadsworth.

Queen, J., Blackwelder, B., & Mallen, L. (1997). *Responsible classroom management for teachers and students.* Upper Saddle River, NJ: Merrill.

Quint, S. (1994). *Schooling homeless children: A working model for America's public schools.* New York: Teachers College Press.

Raaum, C. (1971). *The contemplative revolution.* Sandy, OR: Empyrios.

Redding, S. (Ed.). (1995). *Families and schools: A handbook for practitioners based on research sponsored by International Academy of Education.* Special Issue of the *School Community Journal* by the Academic Development Institute.

Repp, B. J. (1997). A study of the climate for gay, lesbian, and bi-sexual issues in higher education. Unpublished doctoral dissertation, Oregon State University, Corvallis, OR.

Research for Action, Inc. (1996). *Girls in the middle: Working to succeed in school.* Washington, DC: American Association of University Women Educational Foundation.

Rinne, C. (1997). *Excellent classroom management,* Redmond, CA: Wadsworth.

Roessel, R., Jr. (1969). The Indian child and his culture. In J. Stone & D. DeNevi (Eds.), *Teaching multi-cultural populations: Five heritages.* New York: Van Nostrand.

Rumberger, R. (1983). Dropping out of high school: The influence of race, sex, and family background, *American Educational Research Journal, 20,* 199–220.

Saravia-Shore, M. (1992). An ethnographic study of home/school role conflicts of second generation Puerto Rican adolescents. In M. Saravia-Shore & S. F. Arviza (Eds.), *Cross-cultural literacy: Ethnographies of communication in multi-ethnic classrooms* (pp. 227–251). New York: Garland.

Schimmel, D. & Williams, R. (1985). Does due process interfere with school discipline? *High School Journal, 68,* 42.

Silin, J. (1995). *Sex, death, and the education of children: Our passion for ignorance in the age of AIDS.* New York: Teachers College Press.

Slavin, R. E. (1983). *Cooperative learning.* New York: Longman.

Smith, D., Gilmore, P., Goldman S., & McDermott, R. (1993). Failure's failure. In E. Jacob & C. Jordan (Eds.), *Minority education: Anthropological perspectives.* Norwood, NJ: Ablex Publishing.

Teacher Standards and Practices Commission. (1996). Discrimination and the Oregon educator. Salem, OR: Author.

Terman, D., Larner, M., Stevenson, C., & Behrman, R. (1996, Spring). Special education for students with disabilities: Analysis and recommendations. *The Future of Children: Special Education for Students with Disabilities, 6*(1).

Tinker v. Des Moines Independent School District, 393 U.S. 503 (1969).

Tripp, P. H. (1986). Greenfield: A case study of schooling, alienation and employment. In P. Fenshaw, (Ed.), *Alienation from school* (pp. 27–159). London: Routledge & Kagan Paul.

U.S. Department of Education. (1989). *Report to Congress on final reports submitted by states in accordance with section 724 (b) (3) of the Stewart B. McKinney Homeless Assistance Act.* Washington, DC: Author.

Valente, W. (1998). *Law in the schools.* (4th ed.). Upper Saddle River, NJ: Merrill.

Valente, W. (1998). *Law in the schools.* Columbus, OH: Merrill/Prentice Hall.

Wagenaar, T. (1987). What do we know about dropping out of high school? In R. G. Corwin (Ed.), *Research in sociology of education and socialization* (pp. 161–190). Greenwich, CT: JAI Press.

Williams, M. D. (1981). Observations in Pittsburgh ghetto schools. *Anthropology and education quarterly 12*(3), 211–220.

Zanger, V. V. (1993). Academic costs of social marginalization: An analysis of Latino students' perceptions at a Boston high school, In R. Rivera & S. Nieto (Eds.), *The education of Latino students in Massachusetts: Research and policy considerations* (pp. 170–190). Boston: Gastón Institute for Latino Public Policy and Development.

Index

Ackerman, R., 149
American teacher, The, 153
Appeal, 11
Ayers, W., 5, 8, 123

Banks, J., 5, 8, 15, 16, 200
Blaufaus, D., 87
Borus, M., & Carpenter, S., 102
Bowditch, C., 100, 101–102
Bratlinger, E., 149

Canter, L., & Canter, M., 155
Catch them being good, 152
CD-ROM, 196
Charney, R., 19
Clark, W. W., 130
Class meetings, 64
   and flexibility, 67
   and structure, 68
Classroom expectations, 18
Cohen, E. G., 200
Cohen, J. (with Dacey, J., &
      Kenny, M.), 151
Compelling state interests, 41
Compulsory education, 7

Dacey, J., & Kenny, M., 150
D'Amato, J., 19, 30
Davern, L., 185, 186
Diversity activity, 6
Dreikurs, R., 39
Dreikurs, R., Grunwald, B., & Pepper,
      F., 105, 128, 129, 134
Due process, 10
Dunn, R., 13
Duty of care, 52

Eisenhart, M., & Graue, M.E., 78
Ekstrom, R., Goertz, S., Pollack, J., &
      Rock, D., 102
Equal educational opportunity, 12
Equal protection, 146
Erickson, F., 125
Examining gender issues, 153

Fair hearing, 11
Fairness conference, 111–112
Family Education Rights and Privacy
      Act (FERPA), 148
First Amendment, 10
Fischer, L., Schimmel, D., & Kelly, C.,
      77
Fortas, Justice A., 10
Fourteenth Amendment, 76
Froyen, L., 78, 170–171

Gage, H., & Berliner, D., 126, 131, 139
Gallimore, C., Boggs, J. W., & Jordon,
      C., 130
Gardner, H., 13
Gathercoal, F., 14, 32, 51, 80, 88, 107,
      108, 134
Gathercoal, P., 103–104
Gay, Lesbian, Straight Teachers
      Network, 161
Gender equity, 152–153
Giroux, H., 14, 221
Glasser, W., 206
Goss v. Lopez, 101
Greely, K., & Mizell, L., 198
Greene, M., 15

Halford, J., 181
Hentoff, N., 29

Higgins, K., 93
Hildago, N., Bright, J., Sau-Fong, S., Swap, S., & Epstein, J., 172, 186–187
HIV/AIDS, 159
Hunter, M., 43

Individuals with Disabilities Education Act (IDEA), 185, 203
International Academy of Education, 171
Ioga, C., 17, 32, 157
Irvine, J., & York, D., 199

Johns, K., & Espanoza, C., 152
Johnson, D., & Johnson, R., 20, 21, 117, 200–201
Jones, V., & Jones, L., 41, 65, 67, 85, 137
Judicious discipline, 41

Kauggman, J., Mostert, M., Trent, S., & Hallahan, D., 172
King, M. L., 127
Kohn, A., 27, 34, 65, 103, 140, 150
Koplewicz, H., 205
Kozol, J., 126–127, 127

LaMorte, M., 10, 11, 50, 52, 146
Lee v. Weisman, 178, 179
Lemon v. Kurtzman, 180
Levine, D., 80
Liberty, 76
Lickona, T., 40, 111

McEwan, B., 29
McEwan, B., Gathercoal, P., Nimmo, V., 44–45, 66
Minority sexual identity, 161
Moral climate, 62
    supported by rules, 62
Morgan-D'Atrio, C., Northup, J., LaFleur, L., & Spera, S., 103

Nieto, S., 4, 157
Nolte, M. C., 78
Notice, 11, 30

Ogbu, J., 156

Olnek, M., 181–182
Oregon Teacher Standards and Practices Commission, 129–130

Peng, S., 102
Permanent value, 39, 131
Procedural due process, 10–11
Property, 76
Public Law 504, 203
Purkey, W., & Novak, J., 142

Queen, J., Blackwelder, B., & Mallen, L., 128
Quint, S., 34, 81

Raaum, C. F., 121
Redding, S., 171
Repp, B. J., 161
Research for action, 160
Rinne, C., 160
Rowe, M., 160
Rumberger, R., 102

Saravie-Shore, M., 157
Schools without failure, 206
Seven protected classes, 147
Silin, J., 159, 161
Skills of independence, 43
Skinnerian practices, 152
Slavin, R., 200
Smith, D., Gilmore, P., Goldman, S., & McDermott, R., 75
Standard of care, 52
Substantive due process, 11, 35, 38

Terman, D., Larner, M., Stevenson, C., & Behrman, R., 183, 184
Time, place, and manner, 43
Tinker v. Des Moines, 9, 10, 29
Tort liability, 50
    and making plans, 53
    and sharing plans, 54
    and sticking to plans, 56
Tripp, D. H., 130

U.S. Department of Education, 81

Valente, W., 101, 148, 169–170

Wagenaar, T., 102
Wait time, 160
Williams, M. D., 130

Woods, T., 14
World Wide Web, 196, 204

Zanger, V. V., 157